38/50

18∝

Folger Monographs on Tudor and Stuart Civilization

ENGLAND AND THE FRONDE

*The Impact of the English Civil War
and Revolution on France*

FOLGER LIBRARY MONOGRAPHS

FROM time to time the Folger Library plans to publish monographs on significant problems concerning British civilization of the sixteenth and seventeenth centuries. Since the source materials collected by the Folger Library provide one of the greatest repositories in the Western Hemisphere for such studies, the Library hopes to make available a sequence of essays on various aspects of British civilization. The collections of the Folger Library also include material that illuminates the interrelations between Britain and Europe. This second volume of the series deals with the influence on France of the English political upheaval in the seventeenth century. Dr. Philip A. Knachel, Assistant Director of the Folger, has made extensive use of the Library's large collection of Mazarinades in completing this study.

ENGLAND AND THE FRONDE

The Impact of the English Civil War
and Revolution on France

PHILIP A. KNACHEL

PUBLISHED FOR

The Folger Shakespeare Library

BY

CORNELL UNIVERSITY PRESS

Ithaca, New York

Preface

SEVERAL years ago the Folger Shakespeare Library in Washington, D.C., acquired a large collection of Mazarinade pamphlets, to which it has subsequently made many additions. Dr. Louis B. Wright, Director of the Library, suggested to me that a study of these pamphlets might help explain more fully what impact if any the English Civil War had on the Fronde. Some work on this theme had already been done, but the quantity of Mazarinade literature is so large that it appeared a more intensive study might be rewarding. On this basis the investigation began.

It soon became evident that the Mazarinades told only a part of the story. Anglo-French economic and maritime conflicts, fears of subversion and of invasion, and diplomatic maneuvers were also important. But to obtain information about such matters often required documentation of a different kind. What began as a study of the Mazarinades therefore broadened to include other relevant materials as well.

When the study was virtually completed, I learned that a distinguished Russian historian, Boris Porshnev, had written several articles which treated some phases of this subject. Because of Porshnev's differences of interpretation and of emphasis, I found myself repeatedly challenged to re-examine and reconsider my own conclusions. Though little has been altered as a result, the exercise was a stimulating one. It is unfortunate that Mr. Porshnev's contributions on this subject have not been translated from the Russian, and so have reached only a limited audience in the West.

One of the many practical problems encountered in writing a study of this sort involves the amount of general French and English history to provide as background. The English Civil War and Revolution and the Fronde are probably not equally familiar to most students of seventeenth-century history. An introductory chapter is intended to give some background, particularly regarding conditions in France. But obviously it has not been possible to furnish anything like a history of the Fronde and of the English Civil War and Revolution. A chronological table showing the dates of some of the more important occurrences of the period on both sides of the Channel may therefore be useful for reference and has been appended.

The different systems of dating used in France and England may also be a source of confusion to the reader. English history is usually written to conform to the Old Style Julian calendar which was then employed in England. French history naturally follows the New Style Gregorian calendar adopted on the Continent in 1582. Although some readers may be annoyed to see the date of Charles I's execution given as February 9, 1649, instead of January 30, 1648/1649, it seemed best to use the New Style system of dating throughout the text. Sources dated according to the Old Style calendar will be so noted in the citations. In some instances it is unclear which system of dating Englishmen on the Continent were following. In such cases, the uncertainty will be remarked in the citation.

The resources of the Folger Library in the field of seventeenth-century French and English history have proved invaluable in the preparation of this work. However I have also drawn heavily on the Library of Congress in Washington, D.C., on the Bibliothèque Mazarine, the Bibliothèque Nationale, the Ar-

Preface

chives Nationales, and the Archives du Ministère des Affaires Etrangères in Paris, the Musée Condé at Chantilly, and the Public Record Office and the British Museum in London. To all these institutions and to their helpful staffs, I am much indebted.

I am particularly grateful to Professor Francis Haber of the University of Florida, to Professor William Haller, Fellow of the Folger Library, to Professor Edward Sokol of the University of South Carolina, and to Professor Henry Young of Dickinson College for the time they gave to read the manuscript and for the many valuable suggestions and criticisms they offered for its improvement. Thanks are also due Miss Virginia LaMar of the Folger Library for her expert editorial assistance and to Mrs. Gail Rasmussen, Mrs. Mona Sorelius, and to Misses Mary Cook, Brenda Groves, and Anne Moss, also of the Folger staff, for typing the manuscript.

Above all I wish to acknowledge the very great debt I owe to Dr. Louis B. Wright, Director of the Folger Library, for his constant encouragement and for the assistance of every kind furnished during the course of this investigation. Without that help, this book would most certainly never have been attempted, let alone completed.

PHILIP A. KNACHEL

The Folger Shakespeare Library
May, 1966

Contents

Abbreviations

A.E. Angleterre	Archives du Ministère des Affaires Etrangères, correspondance politique, Angleterre
B.M.	British Museum
B.N.	Bibliothèque Nationale
MS. f.fr.	Manuscrit fonds français
P.R.O.	Public Record Office

ENGLAND AND THE FRONDE

*The Impact of the English Civil War
and Revolution on France*

I

Introduction

THE "Puritan Revolution" which racked Great Britain in the mid-seventeenth century differed markedly from the revolution of 1789 which swept away the *ancien régime* in France and from the revolution of 1917 which toppled the czars in Russia; but revolution it assuredly was, and men of the seventeenth century never doubted that England had made a violent and shattering break with the past. England was not alone in her troubles, however. A number of European states were encountering serious turbulence in their own passage through the middle years of that century. The Spanish crown grappled with rebellion in Portugal, in Catalonia, in Sicily, and in Naples. In Holland, the death of Prince William II provided an opportunity for his enemies to impose a government of their own choosing; while, in France, discontent flared into civil war and burned on for almost five years. Internal crises were recorded in such scattered parts of Europe as Poland, Russia, Sweden, and Switzerland, and in some cases resulted in insurrections.

Was it sheer coincidence that unrest found violent expression in so many different places in this period? And did the revolt of one area occur without reference or relation to those in other areas? Or was there, after all, some common pattern of causation; or at least a link, of whatever kind, among them? A small but growing band of historians in recent years has sought to answer these questions. One phase of the investigation involves a careful comparison of the revolts themselves, their origins, and their subsequent development. Another line of inquiry, and the one of interest here, is concerned with the impact which rebellion in one corner of Europe may have had elsewhere.[1]

One might choose to look for evidence of outside reverberation from any of the revolts, but, quite understandably, prime consideration has gone to the shock waves radiated from England, where years of bitter contest finally led to the temporary establishment of a republic in 1649. Most studies of English influence on the Continent have been the product of Marxist historians who, following the lead of Marx himself, stress the "English Bourgeois Revolution" as the opening act in the drama of modern history and who emphasize the international aspects of the unrest of these mid-century decades.[2] Non-Marxists have been somewhat less inclined to view these revolts against an

[1] The two questions, though related, are separate. To establish that rebellion in one area had impact on rebellion elsewhere does not necessarily mean the two shared common origins or pursued the same objectives.

[2] An essay by Christopher Hill, "The English Revolution and the Brotherhood of Man," included in his *Puritanism and Revolution* (London, 1958), pp. 123–152, is the best example in English of this point of view. See also the essay by Gerhard Schilfert, "Zur Geschichte der Auswirkungen der englischen bürgerlichen Revolution auf Nordwestdeutschland," in *Beiträge zum neuen Geschichtsbild, zum 60 Geburtstag von Alfred Meusel,* ed. Fritz Klein and Joachim Streisand (Berlin, 1956), for English influence in Germany. Boris F. Porshnev has written several studies on English impact on France including a chapter, "Angliiskaia revoliutsiia i sovremennaia ei frantsiia," in *Angliiskaia burzhauznaia revoliutsiia XVII veka,* ed. E. A. Kosminskii and IA. A. Levitskii (Moscow, 1954), II, 71–89, and several articles, including "Angliiskaia respublika, frantsuzskaia fronda i vestfalskii mir," *Srednie veka,* III (1951), 180–216, and "Otkliki frantsuzskogo obshchestvennogo mneniia na angliiskuiu burzhuaznuiu revoliutsiiu," *Srednie veka,* VIII (1956), 319–347. Porshnev also has written an article, unavailable to the author, on the second Fronde and the English Republic, according to a reference of Olivier Lutaud, "Le parti politique 'Niveleur' et la première Révolution anglaise (Essai d'historiographie)," *Revue historique,* CCXXVII (1962), 405. Porshnev indicates other studies of English

Introduction

international backdrop.[3] Within the last few years, however, several challenging articles which have appeared in the English journal *Past and Present,* and a conference of historians arranged by the same journal, have stimulated more general interest in the international implications of these uprisings.[4]

As one might easily suppose, the news of revolution in England did not strike every area of the Continent with equal force or in the same manner. One of the states most sharply affected, it would seem, was England's closest neighbor, France.

This relationship receives no emphasis in the many histories of the Fronde written in the last century and a half. Occasional allusions to English influence in France occur in some of the older histories (the most notable examples, perhaps, are to be found in the works of Sainte-Aulaire [5] and Chéruel); [6] but, when the subject was broached, authors generalized from only a tiny sampling of the evidence. Nor have later historians of the

influence on the Continent in his "Otkliki frantsuzskogo obshchestvennogo mneniia na angliiskuiu burzhuaznuiu revoliutsiiu," *Srednie veka,* VIII (1956), 323, 329. An article by A. V. Artsikliovsky and D. I. Nadtocheev, "Teaching of the Social Sciences in the Higher Educational Establishments of the USSR," *International Social Science Journal,* UNESCO, XI (1959), 193, also refers to a *kandidat* thesis defended at Moscow State University on the "English Bourgeois Revolution as Reflected in the Press of the (French) Fronde."

[3] See Roger Bigelow Merriman, *Six Contemporaneous Revolutions* (Oxford, 1938) as an example of non-Marxist interest in the problem.

[4] E. J. Hobsbawm, "The General Crisis of the European Economy in the 17th Century," *Past and Present,* No. 5 (1954), 33–53, and No. 6 (1954), 44–65. The discussion held in London was reported briefly under the title "Seventeenth-Century Revolutions," *ibid.,* No. 13 (1958), 63–72. Of particular interest is the article of H. R. Trevor-Roper, "The General Crisis of the 17th Century," *ibid.,* No. 16 (1959), 32–64. These and other articles published in *Past and Present* have been gathered together in *Crisis in Europe, 1560–1660,* ed. Trevor Aston (London, 1965).

[5] Louis-Clair de Beaupoil de Sainte-Aulaire, *Histoire de la Fronde* (3 vols.; Paris, 1827).

[6] Pierre-Adolphe Chéruel, *Histoire de France pendant la minorité de Louis XIV* (4 vols.; Paris, 1879–1880), and his *Histoire de France sous le ministère de Mazarin* (3 vols.; Paris, 1882).

Fronde taken more than a perfunctory notice of England. To go back no further than the last thirty-five years in the historical literature on the Fronde, Louis Madelin [7] in 1931 and Pierre-Georges Lorris [8] in 1961 considered England's impact of so little consequence as to require virtually no mention. Ernst Kossmann in 1954 included brief reference to the fear of revolution which Mazarin and the French court experienced in the later months of 1648, but Kossmann did not develop the point.[9]

It is not from histories of the Fronde, but from studies of other kinds that we presently sense England's importance to France in this period.[10] Georges Ascoli's remarkable survey of England's place in French public opinion during the sixteenth and seventeenth centuries has revealed in passing some of the many echoes of the English Civil War and Revolution resounding in France at the time of the Fronde; [11] and Roger Merriman has provided a description of some of the political and diplomatic "cross currents" then running between France and England.[12]

---

[7] Louis Madelin, *La Fronde* (Paris, 1931).

[8] Pierre-Georges Lorris, *La Fronde* (Paris, 1961).

[9] Ernst H. Kossmann, *La Fronde* (Leiden, 1954), pp. 77–78.

[10] François P. G. Guizot, *History of the English Revolution of 1640,* trans. William Hazlitt (London, 1846), also his *History of Oliver Cromwell and the English Commonwealth,* trans. Andreas R. Scoble (2 vols.; London, 1854); Jules de Cosnac, *Souvenirs du règne de Louis XIV* (8 vols.; Paris, 1866–1882); Samuel R. Gardiner, *History of the Great Civil War, 1642–1649* (4 vols.; London, 1898–1901), and his *History of the Commonwealth and Protectorate, 1649–1656* (4 vols.; London, 1903). Articles by J. B. Rathery, "Des relations sociales et intellectuelles entre la France et l'Angleterre," *Revue contemporaine,* XXII (1855), 159–178, and by Louis Battifol, "Les idées de la révolution sous Louis XIV," *Revue de Paris* (March, 1928), pp. 97–120, reveal interest in the Anglo-French relationship as it affected public opinion. Another aspect of the Anglo-French relationship is treated, rather disappointingly, by David R. Serpell, *The Condition of Protestantism in France and Its Influence on the Relations of France and England, 1650–1654* (Toulouse, 1934).

[11] Georges Ascoli, *La Grande-Bretagne devant l'opinion française au XVIIᵉ siècle* (2 vols.; Paris, 1930).

[12] Merriman, *Six Contemporaneous Revolutions,* pp. 170–189.

4

Introduction

But the latest and most concentrated study has been undertaken by the Russian historian, Boris Porshnev. In several articles and in a chapter for a collective history of the "English Bourgeois Revolution," he has explored some facets of the English revolutionary impact on France and has reached a number of thought-provoking conclusions about it.[13]

The research of Porshnev and his predecessors has important bearing on our understanding of the mid-seventeenth-century revolts in general and on the Fronde in particular. Quite evidently, we must inform ourselves better about the Anglo-French relationship in these critical years. For in spite of all that has been written about that relationship, many dark corners need illumination. Moreover, certain conclusions reached by Porshnev and others call for re-examination. But most of all, perhaps, there is need to expose more fully the manifold ways in which the revolutionary struggle in England left its mark on France. So many studies in the past have touched upon only a particular aspect of this English impact that it is hard to maintain perspective. The following chapters are hopefully intended to provide a broader and more balanced account of the problem as a whole. Before addressing ourselves to this task, however, it may be useful, first, to situate rapidly England and France in their mid-seventeenth-century settings.

Naturally the chronology of happenings in England and France is highly relevant. In the early morning of January 6, 1649, the Queen Regent of France and her advisers stealthily slipped out of Paris, provoking the quarrelsome city to break out in revolt and to begin in earnest the French civil war called the Fronde; less than seven years had elapsed since Charles I of England had battled for the first time against the army of the English Parliament. In the final weeks of January, 1649, while the Frondeurs of Paris feverishly sought to pull the whole of France into their rebellion, the Civil War in England was mov-

[13] See note 2 for studies by Mr. Porshnev.

ing swiftly and inexorably to a spectacular climax with the unprecedented trial and public execution of Charles I. The entire four-and-a-half years of the Fronde unfolded while memory of the English Civil War was fresh and while radical innovations of all kinds were being introduced in England as part of the continuing revolutionary settlement. In addition, those four-and-a-half years of French rebellion were to coincide with the emergence of the English republic as an aggressive, yet uncertain, force in European power politics. These things were to occur at a time when princes well knew embarrassment abroad could spell political weakness—perhaps disaster—at home.

Precisely how and why England had embarked upon revolution, and what it all might mean to France, did in fact generate keen interest—and dispute—as we shall try to demonstrate later. Without rehearsing the familiar events of the English Civil War and Revolution, it will be useful to remind ourselves how confused the path to revolution in England might appear to men of the time whose thoughts were pre-empted by the distracting uncertainties of the here and now and whose judgments were warped by the blinding passions of that struggle. The distance traveled in England from Elizabeth's last Parliament to Charles I's Long Parliament was enormous; enormous, too, the span separating James I's Hampton Court Conference from the arrest and finally the execution of Archbishop Laud in 1645. On the eve of the Civil War, a poll of the members of the Long Parliament would have uncovered precious few who either conceived a republic to be likely in England or were willing to stand up then and demand one. Yet, in less than a decade, the Commonwealth displaced a monarchy of centuries and brought with it profound religious changes as well as social and economic adjustments. Not everything accomplished in the revolution had permanent significance. But, especially in terms of political liberalization, the imprint was enduring.

Introduction

It is not a simple task today to fit all the pieces of the English Civil War together meaningfully. The more obvious causes can be searched in the long constitutional struggle over prerogative between Parliament and crown, in the grievances of Puritans against the Anglican establishment, in the hostility toward the King's many revenue-raising schemes, and in the opposition to his foreign policy, which collided for religious and economic reasons with the desires of many of his subjects. Or one may consider the King's entrapment in an economic cul-de-sac because of the decline in real value of his customary revenues, discuss the limitations imposed upon him by the creaking administrative machinery he had to work with, and analyze the role played in the war by the gentry and the various other classes and groupings of English society. The list is almost endless. However, to understand the coming of the Puritan Revolution to England involves more than a simple compilation of causes and forces. It requires some perception of the weight to be assigned each, an appreciation of how they were linked together, and some consideration of their place in the English historical setting. If a balanced picture of the English Civil War and Revolution comes hard today, how much more difficult must it have been for contemporaries! [14]

The French observer of England naturally labored under some added handicaps. He transposed into his own frame of reference the problems and controversies of a society whose traditions and whose institutions were relatively unfamiliar. Distortion was inevitable. He followed at a distance the course of the English Civil War and Revolution, dependent for his opinions on the amount and kinds of information which reached him in France. Furthermore, he remembered certain internal

[14] An interesting commentary on interpretative problems is given by Christopher Hill, "Recent Interpretations of the Civil War," *History*, new ser., XLI (1956), 67–87.

frictions in France which preceded the actual explosion of the Fronde, and such recollection certainly colored his notion of English events.

But if the French found England's problems hard to comprehend, the crisis at home presented an equal challenge to interpretation. In the case of England, Frenchmen knew in 1649 that civil war there had culminated in revolution; but where would civil war lead in France? Only a few years before, the transition from the régime of Louis XIII to that of Louis XIV had appeared smooth and popular. On May 18, 1643, the Monday following Louis XIII's death, approving shouts had greeted his widow, Anne of Austria, and her four-year-old son, Louis XIV, as they emerged from the chamber of the Parlement of Paris. The chancellor of the realm had just finished reading aloud a declaration conferring upon Anne full power to govern as regent during the minority of her son; and the testament of Louis XIII which required her to share authority with a governing council was thrust aside and forgotten. The great aristocratic families, the Parlement, and the general populace had, to all appearance, united behind their queen. How quickly that illusory unity vanished!

Some of Anne's ensuing troubles stemmed from the very fact that hers was a regency government, traditionally a "time of troubles." For many, a regent was by definition a caretaker, unable to initiate new legislative acts or to launch out boldly in new directions, intended rather to preside benignly over the routine of administration until the king came of age. At first, nobody had anticipated any great difficulty from Anne. Everyone knew how much she had suffered under the previous régime because of what Louis XIII and Cardinal Richelieu had adjudged to be her compromising activities at court. Those who had cause to dislike the repressive features of that previous government, and they were many, confidently expected a general relaxation under Queen Anne. The basic weakness of her position as a regent and the fact that she had personally shared in their discomfiture under Richelieu supported this belief.

Cardinal Mazarin, who replaced Richelieu on the King's Council in the last months of Louis XIII's reign, was not at the outset thought especially dangerous. It had occasioned some surprise, to be sure, that Queen Anne would retain in her Council a protégé of Cardinal Richelieu; but Mazarin's obliging manner contrasted agreeably with the haughty forcefulness of his predecessor. Experienced persons at court expected Mazarin to be outmaneuvered and dropped from the government before many months of intrigue should pass. Discovery came quickly, however, that Mazarin's deference was a tactic to befuddle the unwary, that he was a clever man, remarkably adroit at the infighting of the court and fully determined to strengthen royal authority. Worse yet, the esteem which Anne accorded her minister, and the bond of personal affection which grew stronger between them, promised the Cardinal a long tenure in his post of command.

Reduced to simplest terms, the policy which Mazarin urged upon the Queen Regent was twofold: to make the French monarchs the real masters of France, and to substitute France for Spain as the most influential and honored state in Europe. The two objectives were complementary and so entwined in Mazarin's thinking that it was pointless to work toward one without also working for the other. After some initial hesitation, Anne had thrown her support to Mazarin's program, doubtless from a conviction that she was acting in the best interests of her young son, Louis XIV. By one of those odd twists of history, Anne of Austria, whom Louis XIII and Richelieu had so much distrusted and so often humiliated, became the ardent defender of their policy.

Louis XIII, as King, had found it difficult to move the state in accordance with the authoritarian philosophy of Richelieu; Anne, as Queen Regent, found it much harder still. The resentment, long pent up against the restrictions of Louis XIII and Richelieu, was too strong, too widespread throughout French society, and the providential arrival of a regency government in France too tempting an opportunity for breaking loose. The war against Spain and the Empire (the Thirty Years' War), which Anne and the Cardinal felt obliged to continue, had already emptied the treasury. Conventional revenue could not meet the frightful cost of paying for the troops, the ships, the supplies, and the subsidies for allies. On the other hand, no amount of financial legerdemain, no amount of borrowing against the tax receipts of years yet to come, could postpone indefinitely the day of reckoning. As if this were not enough, a deflationary movement of prices gripped the country and caused particular suffering to peasants and artisans, who were paid less and less for the product of their labor.

The economic demands of fighting the Thirty Years' War, and the effects of deflation, simply accentuated, however, the inadequacy and the inequity of the tax structure in France. Privilege allowed many in France to escape financial obligation to the state. Nobles of the sword, jurists, holders of office, clergy —in short, virtually everyone of position and means, eluded the heavier demands of the tax collector; and so it was that the un-privileged, the peasants and the urban lower classes, staggered under a disproportionate share of the load. Well before the Fronde, well before the engagement of France in the Thirty Years' War, patience had worn thin. For more than twenty years prior to the Fronde, peasants had revolted in one region after another. Theirs were not isolated protests but full-blown rebellions in which whole regions, indeed whole provinces, went on the march. Some of the uprisings became so virulent and so widespread that they rivaled the *jacqueries* of ages past. Often, to make matters worse, the local nobility, unhappy themselves with the penetration of royal authority into their estates and with the drain of peasant taxes into the royal treasury instead

Introduction

of their own, aided and even led the peasants against the officers of the King. The disobedience of the peasants had its parallel in the towns and cities. Each year from 1623 until 1648 from one to a half-dozen towns reported serious uprisings: their people professed inability to meet the demands of the royal tax collectors. Paris had its riots before the Fronde, and so did virtually every other town of importance in France.

In the highest reaches of French society, conspiratorial meetings of those restless, ambitious spirits who surrounded the Queen Regent at court posed a constant threat. Only a few months after Louis XIII's death, a palace plot against the government (the Cabale des Importants) had been uncovered. Though they smashed it quickly, Anne of Austria and Cardinal Mazarin had every reason to anticipate more plots from the band of malcontents at court—those fascinating ladies who thrived on the excitement of intrigue and delighted in the importance it gave them, and those proud, unscrupulous courtiers who yearned to increase their pensions and their influence by the most convenient means at hand.

The Huguenots were another dubious element. They had suffered crushing defeat at La Rochelle in 1628 and over the years had lost to Catholicism most of the important noble families which had furnished them military and political leadership in the sixteenth-century wars of religion. But the memory of their role in previous disputes with the government was strong and the very weakness of their present position could precipitate a panic and cause them to embark upon some desperate political adventure in league with the other enemies of the Queen Regent. Although Huguenot leaders proclaimed a staunch loyalty to the crown, the French Protestants constituted a volatile, chronically unhappy group within the state. They could not be taken for granted.

One of the gravest causes for concern, especially in the early days of the Fronde, was the belligerent attitude of the Parlement of Paris and of the other sovereign courts of Paris. Richelieu had forbidden the jurists a policy-making role in the state, but the sovereign courts intended to reassert their claim to power, at least for the duration of the regency. The opportunity came soon enough when the crown presented new legislation to the sovereign courts for registration. As far as the Queen Regent and Cardinal Mazarin were concerned, registration was a mere formality, a public acknowledgement by the jurists of an addition to the general body of royal legislation. To the jurists, however, the act of registration implied their concurrence in its legality. It further implied that, if they believed the act illegal, they could refuse to register it, and deny it enforcement in the courts.

In effect, the jurists were asserting a right of veto over the legislative acts of the crown. This attitude placed the crown in an understandably awkward predicament. The government needed new revenue legislation urgently, but, if it were to be enforceable, it would have to be registered. The Queen Regent could bring the boy King to Parlement and override the objections of the jurists in a *lit de justice*. This was done. But many questioned the propriety of doing so, particularly during a regency, and a storm of controversy was almost certain to result.

The jurists felt all the more inclined to resist registration of some of the new revenue acts because their own financial interests were often at issue. Their positions represented a very considerable financial investment under the prevailing system of venality of office. To have additional taxes imposed upon the office, or to have its value lessened in any way, meant an economic loss for themselves and their heirs, as well as a loss of prestige. As might be expected, the stubborn resistance of the courts of Paris gained the rapt attention of other Parlements in France, including those at Rouen, Bordeaux, Aix, and Toulouse. The jurists were watched by the rest of that vast and pervasive bureaucracy in France. They, like the jurists, worried about increased charges, sale of new offices, and appointment of officials who usurped powers they had traditionally exercised.

Thus the sovereign courts of Paris could pose as the protectors of the many in their battles with the crown by remonstrating, not only against acts which directly affected themselves, but also against those which affected other groups in the society. For a time at least, the Parlement of Paris appeared to champion almost all those in the state who wished to avoid greater contribution to the fisc. A noteworthy exception were the tax farmers, the *traitants* or *partisans,* who lent money to the government at great profit and then collected their due from the taxpayers. For obvious reasons these individuals were universally envied and detested, and the Parlement was happy to increase its own popularity by calling on them for heavier contributions. But to attack the tax farmers was to attack the only ready source of funds available to the government and to add to its embarrassment.

Several times the Queen Regent resolved to teach the Paris jurists a proper respect. A few prominent members of Parlement were arrested in 1645 as a salutary warning, and the same device was tried again in August, 1648. The arrests of 1645 did not discourage the Parlement for long, however, and the repetition of those tactics in 1648 simply crystallized resistance to the crown. The latter crackdown had been spurred by the union of the sovereign courts of Paris in May of 1648, in defiance of the Queen Regent, and by their action in preparing and presenting a program of administrative and fiscal reforms to the government that summer. In seizing several of the leaders in retaliation, the Queen Regent and her Council seriously miscalculated the effect of this action on the general populace and on the allies of the jurists. In the frenzied riots which followed, the government almost immediately lost control. It was forced to release those who had been seized and to abandon the quest for others. Grudgingly, in October, 1648, the Queen Regent accepted the reforms demanded by the courts in order to stave off disaster. But though calm returned to Paris, the humiliation of the crown had escaped no one, and the Parlement was riding at the crest of its popularity. Since the government of the Queen Regent had no intention of abiding by these concessions, a more serious clash was inevitable. When Anne of Austria and her government departed Paris, January 6, 1649, to be free of intimidation by Parlement and its allies in the city, and so to be able to marshal military force against the city, the time for a showdown had arrived.

In synopses of the Fronde, it has long been customary to divide the revolts into two broad stages: the first, lasting only a few months, was dominated by the Parlement of Paris; the second, which with interruptions continued until 1653, was dominated by the Princes and in particular by the Prince de Condé. In the first phase, the Parlement of Paris, assisted by certain aristocrats lay and clerical, like the Duc de Beaufort and the Coadjutor of Paris, sought with the help of the populace of the city to break the siege imposed by the troops of the Queen Regent under the command of the Prince de Condé. Several months of fighting brought no conclusive results. Neither side could score a decisive victory, nor could either side afford to endure prolonged hostilities. Attempts by the Parisian Frondeurs to enlarge the revolt had met with some success in the provinces but not enough to plunge the whole country into rebellion. At the same time, the threat of invasion by Spanish forces was giving the French government anxious moments. Under the circumstances, both camps were ready for a cease-fire in April of 1649; but the agreement, though termed a "peace," left the future as uncertain as before.

In the ensuing months of 1649, the Prince de Condé, whose military leadership had initially been so valuable to the government, betrayed signs of ambition to displace Cardinal Mazarin at the helm of state. To forestall that, Queen Anne and the

14

Introduction

Cardinal suddenly clapped the Prince under arrest in early 1650, along with his brother, the Prince de Conti, and their brother-in-law, the Duc de Longueville. The imprisonment of the Princes did not prevent their family and friends from scurrying off to the provinces, where they soon helped kindle new revolts. These struggles marked the beginning of the second phase of the Fronde, i.e., the Fronde of the Princes. Although the movement in the provinces failed to open the prison gates immediately to the Princes, a coalition formed among their friends with certain individuals who had played leading roles in the Parlementary Fronde did bring about the liberation of the Princes in early 1651, as well as the exile of Cardinal Mazarin.

Within months, the coalition began to collapse under the stress of mutual jealousies, and the Prince de Condé, fearing the Queen Regent would take advantage of the breakup to procure his arrest once again, launched a new revolt in the fall of 1651. Backed by a number of important aristocrats and encouraged by a treaty of assistance with Spain, the Prince did his best to exploit the general discontent in France and mounted a formidable challenge to the government. During this new outbreak of civil war, Anne of Austria welcomed Cardinal Mazarin back to France and installed him in his former position at the head of the government. Though the Cardinal later retired for another brief period of exile in the summer of 1652, the government succeeded during his absence in defeating the Fronde in the Paris region that fall. Another year of fighting passed, however, before the Fronde could be similarly extinguished in the Bordeaux area of France.

Writers of the "Three Musketeers" school of history like to dwell on the colorful activities of a few of the leading aristocratic Frondeurs and to picture the Fronde as comic-opera intrigue. However, it is important to remember that, before the Fronde collapsed, most of the French state was at one time or another drawn into the revolts. Paris and provinces as scattered as Normandy and Provence, Guyenne and Burgundy, had been scenes of conflict, though a conflict co-ordinated loosely if at all. Each region adopted a rhythm of its own under the stimulus of grievances of differing character. Segments of almost every important class or grouping of French society resisted the authority of the Queen Regent and Louis XIV. At least some portion of the courtiers, the provincial aristocracy, the Parlement, the bureaucracy, the Church, the Huguenots, the middle class, the urban lower classes, and the peasantry fought against the government.[15]

The Frondeurs had been divided throughout the rebellion, however, by the contradictory goals they pursued. Men of property drew back with alarm as soon as riotous mobs went shouting through the streets. Catholic Frondeurs feared Huguenot Frondeurs in Bordeaux. Many jurists distrusted the Frondeur aristocrats and were in any case far from united among themselves. But if the Fronde was something more than a charade of court intrigue, it was also something less than a mighty collision of class against class or of class against the monarchy. In the outpouring of grievances there was a notable lack of focus. The Frondeurs disagreed among themselves upon changes in the French constitution capable of checking the trend toward centralized royal power. None of those who entered the Fronde ever managed to produce a formula or program sufficiently broad and meaningful to capture lasting support from any large group. The Frondeurs were doomed instead to watch their rickety alliances come unstuck almost as soon as they had been patched together.[16]

Precisely because the Frondeurs could not agree among them-

[15] Discussion of interpretations can be found in Kossmann's *La Fronde*, pp. vii–x, and in Boris F. Porshnev, *Les soulèvements populaires en France de 1623 à 1648*, ed. Robert Mandrou. Ecole Pratique des Hautes Etudes, VI⁰ Section, Centre de Recherches Historiques, Oeuvres Etrangères, IV (Paris, 1963), pp. 505–537.

[16] A good bibliography of the literature on the Fronde is contained in

Introduction

selves, the government had trouble gauging how far the revolts might be carried. It was possible to believe almost anything that rumor or imagination might suggest. One may argue that contemporaries should have been accustomed to malaise in the state, for it was more or less endemic under the *ancien régime*. The record of the hundred years before the Fronde was filled with a dreary assortment of civil wars, assassinations, and acts of disobedience. Memory of these events lingered. But there was also something about the Fronde which seemed to set it apart from past disturbances—a special climate of its own which many thought unusually dangerous.

That England may have contributed something to this sense of danger is a reasonable hypothesis. Given the ringing echoes from the English Civil War and the presence of a dynamic, revolutionary England flexing its muscles across the Channel, some persons in France were going to examine the tensions of French society in the light of English experience; some were going to weigh the possibility of English interference in the Fronde. Here was an important new element for the Queen Regent and her friends, as well as the Frondeurs, to ponder.

Kossmann's *La Fronde,* pp. 262–272. A number of excellent articles on the Fronde have appeared in the journal *Dix-septième siècle.* Very important is the article of Roland Mousnier, "Recherches sur les soulèvements populaires en France avant la Fronde," *Revue d'histoire moderne et contemporaine,* V (1958), 81–113. See also his "Quelques raisons de la Fronde: les causes des journées révolutionnaires parisiennes de 1648," *Dix-septième siècle,* Nos. 2–3 (1949), 33–78, and his reply to Trevor-Roper reprinted in *Crisis in Europe, 1560–1660,* pp. 97–104. Also useful are recent articles by Pierre Deyon, "A propos des rapports entre la noblesse française et la monarchie absolue pendant la première moitié du XVIIᵉ siècle," *Revue historique,* CCXXXI (1964), 341–356; Robert Mandrou, "Les soulèvements populaires et la société française du XVIIᵉ siècle," *Annales: économies, sociétés, civilisations,* XIV (1959), 756–765; A. Lloyd Moote, "The Parlementary Fronde and the Seventeenth Century Robe Solidarity," *French Historical Studies,* II (1962), 330–355, and "The French Crown Versus Its Judicial and Financial Officials, 1615–1683," *Journal of Modern History,* XXXIV (1962), 146–160. For an introduction to the political theory of the Fronde see Paul Doolin, *The Fronde* (Cambridge, Mass., 1935).

II

Court Opinion of the
English Revolution

PROBABLY few persons in France were more anxious to learn
what was happening in England than Cardinal Mazarin. In the
early days of the English Civil War, it was his concern with the
shaping of French foreign policy which drew him to study the
revolt in progress across the Channel. To be sure, the Comte de
Brienne, not Mazarin, actually administered French diplomacy,
but the Cardinal maintained his own close watch.

Diplomacy had always cast a bewitching spell for the Cardinal. He owed his position of leadership in the French state
primarily to his diplomatic talents, for it was his dazzling
agility as representative of the papacy which had first brought
him to the notice of Richelieu and Louis XIII. As a young man
in his late twenties, he had with uncommon skill helped settle
conflicting interests in Northern Italy in a manner which delighted the French. Later, when the Pope sent Mazarin to be
his nuncio at Paris, Mazarin seized on the opportunity to ingra-
tiate himself further with the French and in due course received
an invitation to enter the service of the French government—an
invitation which he readily accepted. At Cardinal Richelieu's
death in December, 1642, the King selected Mazarin, by now a

cardinal, to fill the vacancy in the Council. The range of Mazarin's duties in the state greatly extended, but neither then, nor later, could he resist the lure of foreign affairs.

Seen in context, England's civil war was only one of a number of foreign problems competing for the attention of Cardinal Mazarin and (at Louis XIII's death in May, 1643) the Queen Regent; but the English problem, though not the most serious, was peculiarly vexing. Despite a preoccupation with fighting the combined forces of Spain and the Empire—perhaps one ought better say *because* of it—the French government dared not sit back comfortably indifferent to the internal agonies of one of the great commercial and naval powers of Europe. Though England had avoided participation in the Thirty Years' War, who could say what course she might steer in the future? Who could say how the convulsive struggle in England might affect the whole complex of relationships by which England governed her conduct toward France and toward all her other European neighbors?

For many reasons the victory of a party of religious and political radicals in England suited French interests less than a royalist victory. But though they might hope for a royalist success, Mazarin and the Queen Regent were not prepared to sponsor an expedition to save Charles; and certainly not while battle with the armies of Spain and the Empire claimed all available French troops and resources. Yet if Charles received no substantial help, could he subdue the rebels? This was the tormenting question which had no certain answer. Therefore the French government had to weigh the possibility of a Parliamentary victory in England and all of its consequences.

This dilemma made it difficult to draft a policy toward England. If the French committed themselves fully and openly to Charles I and to the English royalists, and Charles went down to defeat, probably the new government of England would seek revenge. And since the war of France against Spain and the

19

Empire had reached a precarious balance, an angry English Parliament might tip the scales decisively by some unfriendly act, perhaps even an alliance with the enemies of France. All the gains for which France had bled herself white might be wiped out.

The safe and prudent course for the French government to follow, it seemed (and the one actually chosen), was to preserve the appearance of French neutrality in the English Civil War while working covertly for a royalist victory. This choice limited the French chiefly to indirect diplomacy and intrigue, but this could still be of value to Charles. Perhaps the French could help work out an agreement which would bring peace to England and yet leave Charles with some measure of authority. If the French succeeded, presumably Charles would be duly grateful. If on the other hand the royalist cause should fail, the French could remind the world of their professed neutrality, and then establish friendly relations with the Parliamentary party.[1]

Obviously the policy toward England had to be flexible and devious, and so it was a plan which kept the French government walking a diplomatic tightrope. Those whose responsibility it was to keep French strategy closely attuned to changing events in England—persons like Cardinal Mazarin, the Comte de Brienne, and others highly placed in the government—required a familiarity with conditions in England and the most detailed, up-to-date information obtainable.

The chief suppliers of vital intelligence were French diplomats positioned in the British Isles. The proliferation of parties and factions in the Civil War and the geographic scattering of the warring groups over England, Scotland, and Ireland complicated their task. Because a single person could not hope to keep abreast of the confusing swirl of events, the French government normally had several agents, with varying titles and missions,

[1] For discussion of the diplomatic background, see pp. 112–117.

operating simultaneously in the principal trouble spots.[2] The more conscientious of these diplomats dispatched to Paris reports of their activities every three or four days and supplemented them with more detailed accounts for verbal delivery by special messengers. Ordinarily, within a week or two at the most, Paris officials knew what Charles I had had to say at Oxford, Newcastle, or wherever the French agents could track him down; of what their discussions with leaders of Parliament in London had brought to light; and of what they had learned in conversations with Scots Presbyterians and Irish Catholics. The French agents, as would-be mediators of the Civil War, extracted at first hand from all factions data denied the idly curious. An extraordinary amount of confidential information found its way to France by this route.

Mazarin liked to cast an eye over as much government business each day as he could. He naturally valued his time. Politely but firmly he discouraged those in the government who tried to correspond directly with him about matters he judged to be of lesser importance.[3] For all his interest in foreign policy, the Cardinal manifestly could not wade through all the diplomatic correspondence which streamed into the office of the Comte de Brienne from all parts of Europe. In many instances, the Cardinal preferred to have French diplomats address themselves solely to Brienne, on the assumption that the Count would cull through their reports and send on the more important ones for his own perusal. It is significant, therefore, that the more the Cardinal learned about the alarming trend of the English Civil War, the more he wanted to receive direct reports about it

[2] Charles H. Firth and S. C. Lomas provide lists of the diplomatic agents sent from France into the British Isles in their *Notes on the Diplomatic Relations of England and France 1603–1688* (Oxford, 1906), pp. 36–41.

[3] See for example the letter of Mazarin to d'Aiguebonne, March 27, 1643, *Lettres du cardinal Mazarin pendant son ministère*, ed. Pierre-Adolphe Chéruel, I (Paris, 1872), 130–131.

21

from the agents in the field. In 1644 he notified the Sieur de Sabran, then on a diplomatic mission in England, that while the details could be left for correspondence with the Secretary of State, he wished to be informed directly of the general progress of his negotiations in England and to be consulted as necessary.[4] The Sieur de Sabran's successor enjoyed a similar working arrangement. Then, as the tempo of the struggle in England quickened further, French agents in Britain were authorized to communicate not only the substance but the very details of their activities for the Cardinal's benefit. They sent Mazarin copies of all letters which they addressed to the Comte de Brienne, with deletions or addenda for the Cardinal's eyes. Mazarin encouraged the practice.[5] When Mazarin expressed a wish that the King of England could look into his heart and see with what passion he was constantly thinking of everything related to the King's interests, "without allowing great preoccupations to divert me from them," [6] one may question the purity of the Cardinal's solicitude—not its existence.

The letters from the French diplomats in Britain were so allusive that they could only have been intelligible if their intended readers in Paris possessed a solid grounding in English affairs. The replies composed by Mazarin and Brienne indicate that they were indeed well-briefed. Perhaps part of the credit

---

[4] Mazarin to Sabran, June 12, 1644, *ibid.*, I, 749.

[5] Mazarin to Grignon, September 4, 1648, Public Record Office transcript, 31/3/88, copied from Archives du Ministère des Affaires Etrangères, correspondance politique, Angleterre, LVII, f. 272. The transcript at the Public Record Office in London contains the great mass of correspondence by French diplomats in Great Britain in this period. It was compiled from a variety of manuscript collections in Paris. The transcript greatly facilitates the task of going through this correspondence. Wherever possible, reference to the document copied in the transcript will be given for the convenience of those who may wish to consult the sources of the transcript.

[6] Mazarin to Bellièvre, November 12, 1646, *Lettres du cardinal Mazarin*, ed. Chéruel, II, 336.

for their grasp of the subject matter should be attributed to the other sources of information about the British Isles upon which the Cardinal and his associates in the government could draw. Mazarin personally corresponded with some of the principals of the conflict, ranging all the way across the political spectrum from Charles I to William Lenthall, Speaker of the House of Commons. Mazarin and others in the government were visited by special emissaries from England and by the English royalist resident in Paris, Sir Richard Browne.[7] In 1644 the English Parliament sent an agent of its own, one René Augier, to establish residence in the French capital and to represent its interests at the court of Anne of Austria. Suspicious French officials kept Augier at arm's length, but they tolerated his presence in hopes of soothing his Parliamentary masters.

Of greater moment was the concentration in France of many leading English royalist exiles, the first of whom had sought asylum there in 1641.[8] The dismal succession of reverses suffered by Charles I soon increased the flow of exiles, until by 1644 Paris had become virtually a second capital for the English royalists. The panicky exodus from England included members of the English royal family. All France heard in 1644 of Queen Henriette-Marie's harrowing escape from Exeter only days after the birth of her daughter Henriette-Anne, of how she had slipped through the lines of the besieging Parliamentary army and then, eluding capture by the Parliamentary navy, had been dragged from her sinking ship to the safety of French soil. How gloriously different it had been nineteen years before when this same Henriette-Marie, sister of Louis XIII, had sailed from France to become Queen of England!

Once lodged in Paris, Queen Henriette and her most trusted

[7] Browne had been appointed by Charles I resident at the court of France in 1641.

[8] Paul H. Hardacre, "The Royalists in Exile during the Puritan Revolution, 1642–1660," *Huntington Library Quarterly*, XVI (1953), 353–370.

adviser, Lord Jermyn, proved unremitting in their quest for French aid. When they were not importuning the Queen Regent and Cardinal Mazarin, they were appealing for financial contributions from zealous French Catholics who were disturbed at the fate of their coreligionists in the British Isles.

The bustling colony of distinguished English royalists in Paris embarrassed the French government because of the affront their presence afforded to the English Parliament—not to mention the annoyance they caused by their wheedling requests for more French help—and the burden Henriette-Marie and her household imposed on the French treasury for their maintenance. Yet to refuse sanctuary to a daughter of Henri IV, aunt of Louis XIV, was unthinkable. On the positive side, Henriette and her entourage provided valuable information about Britain. The Englishman, "good servant of his king and well-informed of his affairs," who poured out to Madame de Motteville the story of his master's woes, was surely only one among many exiles who found a sympathetic ear at court.[9] There was a constant coming and going from Scotland, Ireland, and from England; and not even the eventual establishment of the republic could discourage the more adventurous, like the diarist John Evelyn, from slipping back and forth across the Channel.[10] Correspondence with family and friends remaining in England continued in spite of the penalties imposed by Parliament upon discovery. Some of the French evidently complained about the reliability and the timeliness of the news Henriette and the other English exiles had to offer. Furthermore, they doubted Henriette's persuasive powers over Charles I.[11] But Mazarin obviously thought

[9] *Mémoires de Mme de Motteville,* ed. F. Riaux (Paris, 1869), II, 346.
[10] *The Diary of John Evelyn,* ed. E. S. de Beer (Oxford, 1955), II, 3–4, 9.
[11] Henriette-Marie to Charles I, December 13/23, 1644, Charles de Baillon, *Henriette-Marie de France, reine d'Angleterre* (Paris, 1877), pp. 526–527.

it useful to consult closely with her and with Lord Jermyn.[12]

Not surprisingly, the opinion which the Cardinal formed of the English Civil War agreed substantially with those of his principal informants, particularly the French diplomats in Britain. Repeatedly he praised the soundness of their judgment. "You reason very justly," he would write. "Your conduct could not be more adroit or judicious. . . . I leave to your prudence to act according to the circumstances."[13] This was not a meaningless politesse, for the Cardinal could be sharply critical of diplomats with whom he disagreed.[14] He identified himself less fully with the views of Queen Henriette-Marie and her friends in Paris, especially when French tactics and French aid in support of the English royalists were discussed. This attitude was natural and to be expected. However, the French government allowed Henriette-Marie to draft a memorandum of instruction for Pompone de Bellièvre, newly appointed French ambassador for England in 1646, and permitted Henriette and Lord Jermyn to communicate freely and directly with French agents in Great Britain. Henriette-Marie obviously enjoyed some influence in the French government.[15]

[12] Mazarin could have used his great personal library to advantage in broadening his acquaintance with England. It is tempting to imagine that he did so. Thanks to the enterprise and devotion of his librarian, Gabriel Naudé, his collection contained numerous books on English history along with current publications, some of which treated of England's instability. One must seriously question whether the Cardinal ever found the leisure to use his library for this purpose. Before the Parlement of Paris ordered the library broken up for sale in 1652, the Cardinal had more than 40,000 items of all kinds in the collection. We are told he had time to do little more than glance through the daily additions of books and pamphlets destined for the shelves of his library. See Alfred Franklin, *Histoire de la Bibliothèque Mazarine et du Palais de l'Institut* (Paris, 1901), pp. 50–51, 55, 73.

[13] Mazarin to Grignon, [June 13, 1648], P.R.O. transcript, 31/3/88, copied from A. E. Angleterre, LVII, f. 228.

[14] Mazarin to d'Avaux, May 14, 1644, *Lettres du cardinal Mazarin*, ed. Chéruel, I, 691.

[15] *Recueil des instructions données aux ambassadeurs et ministres de*

The reports arriving in Paris from Britain were full of detail, but were weak in interpretation. They rarely cut below the surface action of the English Civil War. There was little searching for the deeper causes of dissension, no real understanding of the political, religious, social, and economic pressures working against Charles, and no appreciation of the deeply felt grievances against the King. French agents, and Mazarin in turn, saw the rebels engaged in a raw struggle for power. They could not believe that the religious and political principles of which Charles's enemies made such show were other than the pretexts of opportunists. The diplomats frequently complained in their letters to Brienne and to the Cardinal of the "little sincerity," [16] of the "dissimulation," [17] of those opposing the King, described them as "people truly avaricious . . . without faith and extremely interested," and dwelt at length on their lust for power.[18] To this refrain Henriette-Marie joined her voice, suggesting to one of the French agents in England that he inform himself of the rebels' interests and personal ambitions and try to win them over "by the most appropriate means." [19] When those in the English Parliament expressed opposition to Charles and his bishops on religious grounds, the French representatives accused the members of having no religion at all and of behaving as they did because of the rich profits to be had from the alienation of episcopal lands.[20] As for the complaints in England

---

France depuis les traités de Westphalie jusqu'à la révolution française, XXIV, *Angleterre,* ed. J. J. Jusserand (Paris, 1929), I, 41–55.

[16] Bellièvre to Brienne, September 10, 1646, *The Diplomatic Correspondence of Jean de Montereul and the Brothers de Bellièvre, French Ambassadors in England and Scotland, 1645–1648,* ed. J. G. Fotheringham, Publications of the Scottish History Society, XXIX (Edinburgh, 1898), I, 254.

[17] Montereul to Mazarin, March 12, 1647, *ibid.,* II, 38.

[18] Bellièvre to Brienne, August 9, 1646, *ibid.,* I, 243.

[19] *Recueil des instructions données aux ambassadeurs . . . ,* XXIV, *Angleterre,* I, 48.

[20] Grignon to Brienne and Mazarin, October 5, 1648, P.R.O. transcript,

that the King had ruled as a tyrant over his people, the French pointed to the heavy taxes levied by Parliament.[21] They reported that Parliament was forever ready to dupe the people and accused the House of exercising more tyranny over the people of England in one day than the King could have done in a lifetime.[22] All of these observations contained kernels of truth, but the Cardinal's informants, and the Cardinal himself, failed to see the revolt in England in larger terms.

As Mazarin sifted through the mass of detail which reached him from French diplomats in Britain, it seemed clear enough that the English Parliament was the instrument which unscrupulous men were using most successfully against Charles I. Somehow, the dispatches suggested, all organized resistance to the English king originated in the Parliament. Therefore when Mazarin and others in the French government sought to isolate the principal means by which Charles's enemies had succeeded in wresting authority from him, they dwelt on the relationship of the English king to his Parliament.

There was much talk in the French government of restoring Charles to his "original authority" or to his "legitimate authority," but it was recognized that these expressions were not the equivalents of "absolute authority." The government reminded its ambassadors that law and custom in England functioned as a counterweight to royal prerogative, and that under the English constitution the King must share significant powers with his

---

31/3/88, copied from Bibliothèque Nationale, Manuscrit fonds français 15997, f. 549. Sabran had written to the Comte de Brienne on June 8, 1644, that the enemies of the King were desirous of instituting new customs and laws "which tend visibly toward the extinction of the monarchy more than of religion, which is only their pretext" (*ibid.*, 31/3/74, copied from B.N., MS. f.fr. 4138, f. 41).

[21] Grignon to Brienne and Mazarin, June 8, 1648; July 13, 1648; September 7, 1648, *ibid.*, 31/3/88, copied from B.N., MS. f.fr. 15996, f. 273v; B.N., MS. f.fr. 15996, f. 397v; B.N., MS. f.fr. 15997, f. 549.

[22] Grignon to Brienne and Mazarin, February 11, 1649, *ibid.*, 31/3/89, copied from B.N., MS. f.fr. 15997, f. 808v.

Parliament.[23] This, to Mazarin's way of thinking, was a glaring flaw in the English system. He had evidently formed his own appraisal from the ill-tempered outbursts which James I and Charles I had evoked so often from their parliaments and which caused him to believe that the English constitution was inherently defective and unable to sustain effective government.

There was no question in the minds of Cardinal Mazarin and his subordinates that the blame for the bickering in England should be placed on Parliament. Because Parliament enjoyed the right to block the King's wishes in some matters, its members clung overzealously to that right. That seemed clear. Whatever the merit of the King's desire, however much the implementation of his wishes might benefit the kingdom, members of Parliament would interpose the dead weight of their negative when they could, simply to demonstrate what vast and independent powers they wielded in the state. Nowhere, it appeared to those of the Queen Regent's government, was this truth more self-evident than in the financial affairs of England. The ordinary revenue of the English king, revenue which he required no special authorization from his Parliament to raise and to collect, was so small, they noted, that only with the mightiest strain could it be stretched to cover the routine expenses of government. Suppose, however, the King were to incur some extraordinary expense? Then truly he was at the mercy of his Parliament. The English constitution forbade him to make extraordinary levies without approval of Parliament; but if he asked for its assent, he would likely be refused altogether or receive at most only a portion of what he needed so that Parliament might flaunt its power.[24]

At its worst, then, the English constitution appeared to foster a complete breakdown of government, as confirmed by the

---

[23] *Recueil des instructions données aux ambassadeurs,* XXIV, *Angleterre,* I, 35.

[24] *Ibid.,* I, 35–36.

Civil War. But even in better days, it represented to Mazarin a sorry example of flabby rule. A state like England, whose king was subject to constant harassment by an envious Parliament, whose administration was plagued by inadequate revenue, must perforce renounce great ambitions which for their fulfillment required a strictly ordered society at home and involved expensive wars abroad. In short, the English constitution absolutely precluded, it seemed, the development of a state along the grandiose lines which Richelieu, and now Mazarin and the Queen Regent, had marked out for France.

As long as the frailties of the English constitution did not precipitate England into the peril of civil war, the French government rather welcomed the English monarch's weakness. Indeed, the French resident to England, the Sieur de Sabran, was cautioned in 1644 to remember that, although France was supporting Charles I, it had no desire to inflate his authority unduly, or to set aside the laws and customs which restrained his power.[25] Two years later another French ambassador could read in his instructions that France was assisting Charles partly because his weakness made him a less dangerous neighbor than a republic. In a republic, the citizenry were more likely to contribute generously to the public treasury of a government they had created.[26]

In Mazarin's opinion, structural weakness only partially explained England's political breakdown. The Cardinal shared the conviction of his agents in Britain, and to a certain extent confirmed by Queen Henriette-Marie in Paris, that Charles I had exacerbated an already difficult situation by displays of remarkably poor judgment. The French, who were as lavish in their advice to Charles as they were niggardly in their dispatch of material aid, alternated between fits of annoyance and des-

[25] Instructions for Sabran, April 29, 1644, Dorothy A. Bigby, *Anglo-French Relations, 1641 to 1649* (London, 1933), pp. 56–57.

[26] *Recueil des instructions données aux ambassadeurs, XXIV, Angleterre,* I, 35.

pair when Charles elected to follow counsels other than their own. Under the circumstances, then, it was all too easy for them to ascribe a part of the English king's accumulating misfortunes to inept leadership. Often Mazarin was hard put to conceal his exasperation with Charles; and, in one of his bursts of temper, the Cardinal informed the French ambassador in England that he saw "no remedy but to pray to God that He may be pleased to open the eyes of His Majesty and to make him understand his best interests and to make him practice the means of achieving them; for in vain do good doctors hope to restore health to a patient if he rejects all the remedies which can give it to him." [27] It did surely appear, the Cardinal lamented, that the conduct of the King and of those who claimed to be most attached and interested in his service only worsened his position.[28] How unfortunate, the Cardinal exclaimed on another occasion, that Charles's "own best interests have not been able to overcome his stubbornness." [29]

Though never expressed in so many words, French officials nonetheless agreed that many of Charles's errors of judgment arose from his faulty understanding and employment of "compromise" as a tactical weapon against his enemies. In the first place the English king had not understood *what* could be safely compromised. He failed to perceive the vital issues of the Civil War—those upon which the preservation of his authority in the state depended. Why was it, the French wanted to know, that Charles could not comprehend that religious considerations must give way to political exigency—that his obstinate defense of his bishops and of Anglicanism was a senseless handicap?

In this respect Mazarin suffered from the same curious double vision as his informants, who at one moment cynically dis-

---

[27] Mazarin to Bellièvre, November 12, 1646, *Lettres du cardinal Mazarin*, II, 334.

[28] Mazarin to Bellièvre, July 20, 1647, *ibid.*, II, 459–460.

[29] Mazarin to Bellièvre, January 25, 1647, *ibid.*, II, 369.

counted religious motivation in the English Civil War and at the next moment inveighed against Charles and other leading figures for allowing religious principles to stand in the way of political advantage. Presbyterian reluctance to ally with the Anglican Charles because of religious scruple was impatiently brushed aside by the French as an argument of "no great weight." [30] Nor did Mazarin's princely rank in the Roman Catholic Church keep him from venting his annoyance against the Irish Catholics for the embarrassment they were causing Charles. But it was Charles himself who irritated the French most in matter of religion and his obstinacy which they regarded most critically. It apparently did not occur to Queen Anne's government that Charles's past compromises on religion had already led many throughout Britain to distrust him. Nor did the French ever seem to appreciate how many hurdles blocked attainment of the coalitions they believed Charles should head. In their view, simple necessity dictated Charles's union with the Catholics in Ireland and with the Presbyterians in Scotland and England; or, if that failed, his alliance with the Irish Catholics and the English Independents.[31]

French bafflement was compounded when Charles, balking over religious matters "whose concession cannot hurt him in any way," would then turn around, they thought, and yield political advantages to his adversaries, "prejudicial to his service and which will produce no fruit for his re-establishment." After Cardinal Mazarin heard that the English king was willing to hand over the militia to Parliamentary control for ten years, he summed up his stunned reaction for the French ambassador in England by writing that he found it all stranger than he

[30] Montereul to Mazarin, October 26, 1645, *The Diplomatic Correspondence of Jean de Montereul*, I, 27.

[31] *Recueil des instructions données aux ambassadeurs, XXIV, Angleterre*, I, 41–55. These instructions were prepared by Queen Henriette-Marie. French authorities allowed them to be sent to Pompone de Bellièvre.

could say, "and without doubt all those who will learn of this affair will judge it the same." [32]

Charles had committed his most shocking blunder, in Mazarin's opinion, on the eve of the Civil War when he vainly sacrificed his minister, the Earl of Strafford, to appease his critics in Parliament. More than any other single act, this convinced Mazarin of the King of Great Britain's lack of judgment. In the summer of 1648 Mazarin confided to the pages of his private notebook that "when the King of England signed the death warrant of the Chancellor of Ireland, [he] thought he had brought everything to an end; but it was only the beginning of the abolition of the monarchy; for the Parliament considered itself strong enough afterward to obtain everything." [33] The Cardinal warmed to the same theme again in 1649 when he wrote that the English Parliament "insisted to the King that he should surrender the Viceroy of Ireland, his Prime Minister, to Parliament. The King finally did so, and what resulted is that the Viceroy had his neck broken; all that kingdom has been at war against the King, and they have had no rest until the King met the same end, although there has never been an example of a king judged according to law, against the law, by his own subjects. His children have not for that succeeded him, although innocent of what those people there have criminally imputed to their father. . . ." [34]

As the Queen Regent's government blamed Charles for not knowing *what* to compromise, so also did it accuse him of not knowing *when* to compromise. Mazarin, the practiced diplomat, and his associates deemed it axiomatic to negotiate from a position of strength. To wait to compromise until stripped of power was to convince the other side that negotiation was

[32] Mazarin to Bellièvre, November 12, 1646, *Lettres du cardinal Mazarin,* II, 335.

[33] Mazarin's Carnet X, p. 76, quoted in Chéruel, *Histoire de France pendant la minorité de Louis XIV,* III, 135.

[34] Mazarin's Carnet XII, pp. 5–6, quoted in Chéruel, *op. cit.,* III, 190.

pointless. Charles's negotiations with the Scots furnished a perfect example of poor timing, the French believed. There had been a time when Charles could have gone to the Scots army and, with French help, have secured an engagement which the Scots would have observed if only out of respect to Charles's own strength. However, now that Charles was despoiled of everything, it was no wonder that the Scots held him in such small consideration, for they recognized full well that pure necessity had forced him to seek asylum in their army.[35]

Strangest of all, perhaps, Charles and others in his following did not seem to grasp the *purpose* of compromise. According to the conception of the French government, compromise was an expedient to gain time, a means of relieving pressure until a more favorable opportunity presented itself. It did not necessarily impose any fixed and final solution. The French agent Montereul, imbued with this outlook, at one point expressed astonishment that anyone should object to Charles's acceptance of Presbyterianism when there was always the hope of being able to change easily whatever should be resolved touching religion.[36] When Charles was a prisoner of Parliament, the French tried to make it very clear to him that a prisoner could make promises that were not binding, and that "there is greater reason to hope to re-establish authority from the throne, than from prison to be able to climb there." Significantly, this advice had the endorsement of Anne of Austria, Cardinal Mazarin, the Duc d'Orléans, and the Prince de Condé (the Great Condé's father).[37] Here, as so often before, the French criticized Charles for not doing precisely that which his enemies angrily denounced him for doing only too often.

[35] *Recueil des instructions données aux ambassadeurs, XXIV, Angleterre,* I, 30.

[36] Montereul to Mazarin, November 2, 1645, *The Diplomatic Correspondence of Jean de Montereul,* I, 36.

[37] *Recueil des instructions données aux ambassadeurs, XXIV, Angleterre,* I, 60, note 1.

England and the Fronde

How great was the danger which Charles's mistaken tactics and the constitutional defects in English government had thrust upon the English monarchy in the French view? A little over a month before Charles I was beheaded, Cardinal Mazarin had asserted in a letter to the French ambassador at London that he could not understand how subjects could conceive such strange thoughts against their king. And the Cardinal added, "I hope that God will not permit this poor prince to fall in such great misfortune, and I shall never believe that the English will allow themselves to take such dreadful resolutions against him." [38] The fact was, however, that Mazarin saw then, as he and others in the government had seen for a long time, that England suffered from a most dangerous and unpredictable malady. At the very beginning of the Civil War in England, the Cardinal had confessed his inability to penetrate the veil of confusion there; and this was, he said, the opinion of others on the King's Council. [39] In 1644 Sabran advised the Queen Regent from England that affairs there were at an "incredible extremity"; [40] and Brienne, the Secretary of State, after some thoughtful meditation of his own in 1644, gloomily weighed the possibility of an utter collapse of royal authority in England. A republic would inevitably replace it, he assumed, which would mean the downfall of the English nobility. [41] French agents informed Cardinal Mazarin the following year that, should Charles fall under the control of Parliament, he would come into the hands of men "who profess to hate monarchy." [42] The

[38] Mazarin to Grignon, December 16, 1648, *Lettres du cardinal Mazarin*, III, 247.

[39] Victor Cousin, "Des carnets autographes du cardinal Mazarin conservés à la Bibliothèque Imperiale," *Journal des savants* (August, 1854), p. 468.

[40] Sabran to Queen Regent, June 8, 1644, P.R.O. transcript, 31/3/74, copied from B.N., MS. f.fr. 4138, f. 41.

[41] Brienne to Sabran, June 10, 1644, *ibid.*, 31/3/74, copied from B.N., MS. f.fr. 4138, ff. 73–75.

[42] Montereul to Mazarin, December 14, 1645, *The Diplomatic Correspondence of Jean de Montereul*, I, 71.

34

Cardinal reacted to these reports by foreseeing an imminent and complete ruin of the King of England.[43]

Officials exchanged more statements of this sort with each additional setback Charles encountered. Some months after Charles had been held captive by Parliament, Mazarin considered his prospects so bleak he could hardly find words to describe his concern. When he wrote, "God knows how the strangest affair which has occurred in this century will finally terminate, and what will be the last act of this tragedy," [44] it is evident that he already strongly suspected how it would end. Nor was he deceived by stories later in the year that the renewal of violence in England would oblige Parliament to come to terms with Charles. French agents in Britain assured their superiors in Paris that Parliament was using talk of negotiation that summer as a sop to throw to the public; that Parliament was temporizing; that negotiations would lead nowhere.[45]

In October of 1648 the dispatches from England disclosed that the Army contemplated bringing the King to trial, and that a purge of Parliament was in the offing.[46] Ambassador Grignon's letters at the close of the old year and at the beginning of the new simply supplied the detail for the terrifying denouement. On January 11, 1649, he gravely announced that the House of Commons had ordered the King brought to trial; [47] and on February 11, a month later, he wrote the chilling epilogue—the King had been executed on February 9.[48]

[43] Mazarin to Montereul, December 1, 1645, *ibid.*, II, 580.

[44] *Recueil des instructions données aux ambassadeurs, XXIV, Angleterre,* I, 69.

[45] Grignon to Brienne and Mazarin, September 7, 1648, P.R.O. transcript, 31/3/88, copied from B.N., MS. f.fr. 15997, f. 486.

[46] Grignon to Brienne and Mazarin, October 15, 1648, *ibid.*, copied from B.N., MS. f.fr. 15997.

[47] Grignon to Brienne and Mazarin, January 11, 1649, *ibid.*, copied from B.N., MS. f.fr. 15997, f. 754v.

[48] Grignon to Brienne and Mazarin, February 11, 1649, *ibid.*, copied from B.N., MS. f.fr. 15997, f. 808v.

The day-by-day commentary about England composed by those in the service of the French government has interest in itself, but doubly so when set in the context of the churning domestic crisis in France. The same men who anxiously diagnosed Charles's political ills were grappling in France with the Cabale des Importants in 1643, with Paris riots over the tax of the Toisé in 1644. They were ordering the arrest of troublemakers in the Parlement of Paris in 1645 and resorting to a *lit de justice* to secure the registration of new revenue legislation by a surly Parlement. By summer of 1648 they were facing a situation which was fast becoming desperate, with the sovereign courts of Paris demanding reforms, the Paris population in revolt, and the provinces unsteady.

The juxaposition of events in England and France particularly disturbed people like Cardinal Mazarin because the crises on opposite sides of the Channel resembled each other. Mazarin, who heard constantly that the English rebels were an unscrupulous breed of power-hungry men, was convinced he confronted a kindred breed in France. Among the French nobles, Mazarin thought, were those who rejoiced in the troubles of the state because they could use them to promote their personal ambitions.[49] The Cardinal brooded over the presence of "seditious" members of Parlement who he believed were trying to engage their young colleagues in subversion. He estimated the faction could sway a majority.[50] Nor did the Cardinal overlook those who he believed would use the Huguenots for political profit.[51] He was firmly convinced, as he noted on one occasion, that among the Princes, the governors of provinces, the members of Parlement, and the Huguenots, there were those ready to thrust

[49] Mazarin to Servien, August 14, 1648, *Lettres du cardinal Mazarin*, III, 173–174.

[50] Mazarin to Maréchal de l'Hospital, January 10, 1649, *ibid.*, III, 250.

[51] Chéruel, *Histoire de France pendant la minorité de Louis XIV*, I, 133.

a republic upon the country.[52] The analogies which Mazarin and others at court drew between conditions in England and France lent support to that thesis.

In the small, private notebooks which Mazarin maintained, one of the first of his jottings related to England. In a cryptic reference in 1643 to the Parliament of England and to the Parlement of Paris, he wrote, "Consider what the Parliament of England was," which statement he followed immediately with: "The Parlement [of Paris] believes that it is absolutely over the Regent." [53]

Those who had access to the Queen Regent and to Mazarin also showed signs of disquiet. In 1644 a spokesman for the tax farmers elaborated on this theme in a speech at court. Uneasy for the security of their persons and their property, the tax farmers had marched in a body to expose their fears of Parlement to the Queen Regent and to Mazarin. Their leader, La Rallière, warned the government not to abandon them. If it did, they would not advance the funds so essential for the continued functioning of the state. Then, addressing himself to the broader implications of the problem, La Rallière introduced the example of England into his remarks. He likened the Parlement of Paris to the English Parliament and argued that France was already divided into two opposing camps, one royalist, the other containing the friends of Parlement. With England as the point of reference, it was evident what France had to fear.[54]

Madame de Motteville, a confidante of Anne of Austria, acknowledged that in the early summer of 1648 "the Parlement [of Paris] from that time began to claim for itself so exorbitant

[52] Mazarin's Carnet II, pp. 43–44, quoted in *Lettres du cardinal Mazarin*, I, cxix.

[53] Cousin, "Des carnets autographes," *Journal des savants* (September, 1854), p. 546.

[54] *Journal d'Olivier Lefèvre d'Ormesson*, ed. Pierre-Adolphe Chéruel, Collection de documents inédits sur l'histoire de France (Paris, 1860), I, 214–215 and 214n.

a power as gave cause to fear that the bad example the jurists saw in the Parliament of England had made some impression on them." [55] Writing some years after the Fronde and with the benefit of hindsight, Madame de Motteville could heave a great sigh of relief because the Parlement of Paris had been very different, she said, from the other "in its intentions and different, too, in its effects," but she admitted that at the time it had troubled the King and had appeared a dangerous threat. "We could not wonder enough," she wrote, "at that unhappy influence which ruled over the crowned heads who were victims of the two Parliaments of France and England." [56]

The pattern of events which unfolded in the summer of 1648 served to increase anxiety at court and to prompt further reflection upon England's example. The Maréchal d'Estrées, who proved a faithful supporter of the Queen Regent throughout the Fronde, suggested that the decision to arrest Broussel and Blancmesnil of the Paris Parlement in August, 1648, was adopted with an eye turned to the "horrible and frightful tragedy" then taking place in England. The Marshal had no doubt that some in France, in imitation of the English Revolution, were ready to institute a new form of government. [57] A short time after the August riots, the Maréchal de La Meilleraye, newly appointed Superintendent of Finance who had narrowly escaped with his life from a howling mob, rose in the Queen Regent's Council to venture a timorous prediction that rebellious subjects in France might follow the "evil example of the English." [58]

Henriette-Marie was in the company of the Queen Regent and Mazarin during the anxious hours of August 26, 1649, when the Paris riots began. [59] Henriette-Marie was with them later, on

[55] *Mémoires de Mme de Motteville*, II, 97–98.   [56] *Ibid.*, II, 105.

[57] *Mémoires du maréchal d'Estrées*, ed. Paul Bonnefon, Société de l'histoire de France (Paris, 1910), pp. 240, 246–247, 260.

[58] *Mémoires de Mme de Motteville*, II, 240.   [59] *Ibid.*, II, 167.

other tense occasions, warning them that in the early stages of the English Revolution the troubles had been less serious, feeling had been less heated and united than that now animating the furious Parisians.[60] All through the remaining months of 1648, according to one account, Henriette-Marie played the role of Cassandra, prophesying doom for France.[61] Similarly, Sir Richard Browne, the English royalist resident in Paris, wrote in August, 1648, that, as the people had their will upon this occasion, they would proceed to yet higher demands, "so dangerous a thing it is to let that many-headed monster know its own strength." [62]

Associating revolt in England with revolt in France, and the Parlement of Paris with the Parliament of England, Cardinal Mazarin and his colleagues were too well informed to be misled by superficial similarities of nomenclature. They needed no reminder that an English Parliament was a nationally representative body endowed by tradition with important legislative powers, and that it far overshadowed the position of the Parlement of Paris, a judicial body neither national, representative, nor legislative in character. In searching for a French equivalent, the Estates-General came to mind, but even this comparison, the Cardinal admitted, was inadequate to express the more significant role played in the state by the English Parliament.[63]

[60] *Histoire du temps* (Rouen, 1649), p. 199, listed in Célestin Moreau, *Bibliographie des Mazarinades* (3 vols.; Paris, 1850–1851), No. 1644. In future citations of Mazarinade material the Moreau number will be included where possible, to avoid giving the complete title for identification. Spelling of titles will conform to that given in Moreau's bibliography.

[61] *Mémoires de Nicolas Goulas,* ed. Charles Constant, Société de l'histoire de France, II (Paris, 1879), 359.

[62] Original Drafts or Copies of the Dispatches of Sir Richard Browne, British Museum, Additional MS. 12185, I, f. 360v. Spelling and punctuation have been modernized. The same practice will be adopted for subsequent English quotations.

[63] Mazarin's Carnet XII, pp. 5–6, quoted in Chéruel, *Histoire de la France pendant la minorité de Louis XIV*, III, 190–191.

Though the Paris Parlement was a lesser institution, it was still capable, Mazarin believed, of setting off a republican chain reaction throughout the state. As Mazarin reasoned: the other parlements believed that in imitation of the Parlement of Paris they could undertake with impunity anything which appeared advantageous to them. "And the inferior companies dare also ape the others." [64] Admittedly the reforms which Parlement and the other sovereign courts of Paris formulated in the summer of 1648 sounded strange and ominous. They included demands that the crown reduce and cancel back taxes, agree to register all revenue acts in the sovereign courts, halt the creation of new offices for a period of four years, permit freedom of commerce unhampered by special privilege, renounce use of *lettre de cachet* and arbitrary imprisonment of officers of the courts, and so on down a lengthy list. Undoubtedly Parlement and the other sovereign courts were creating for themselves a policy-making role. Perhaps it is true, as one of the most recent historians of the Fronde has argued, that the program of reform was too partial, too superficial in itself to be considered of any momentous constitutional significance.[65] Perhaps Parlement's narrow, parochial outlook would have soon rendered it incapable of assuming leadership. But, in the judgment of a worried Cardinal Mazarin, to accept such reforms as final was to "abolish the best part of the monarchy." [66] With England's recent history at his finger tips, naturally the Cardinal saw signs of a French revolution in the events of 1648.

Nicolas Goulas, prominent in the circle of the Duc d'Orléans and well placed to hear what occurred at court, claimed that the decision to withdraw the court from Paris in January, 1649,

[64] Mazarin to Servien, August 14, 1648, *Lettres du cardinal Mazarin,* ed. Chéruel, III, 173–174.

[65] Kossmann, *La Fronde,* pp. 53–56.

[66] Mazarin's Carnet X, p. 71ff., quoted in Chéruel, *Histoire de la France pendant la minorité de Louis XIV,* III, 91.

was caused by the consternation over the news from England.[67] We cannot know how much Goulas exaggerated, but unquestionably the news from England was anything but reassuring.

The course of the civil war in France confirmed more strongly for Mazarin, for the Queen Regent, and for others at court the validity of an English parallel whose dreadful import was sharpened immeasurably by Charles's death in February. After that, the mere sight of Queen Henriette-Marie was enough to start a train of somber reflection. Madame de Motteville, who had talked with the English queen in Paris shortly after the news of Charles's execution reached there, told how "the state in which I believed her to be, and the state in which France then was, made a very strong impression on me; and I shall never forget the wise words of that queen, who, undeceived and instructed by her own experience, seemed to presage great calamities for us." When Madame de Motteville later managed, with some difficulty, to leave Paris and rejoin the court at St. Germain, she recounted to Anne her distressing interview with Henriette. Queen Anne did not bother to conceal her own shock when she exclaimed that Charles's execution was "a blow to make all kings tremble." [68]

The drumfire of warnings from Henriette-Marie continued. To her sister, the Duchesse Christine de Savoie, she wrote, "For myself, who have seen the beginnings in England to be exactly like these here, you may judge in what pain I may be. I hope that Providence will take care of the little King. I do believe God wants to afflict our family, for if the war continues here, this poor kingdom will be lost. And what will become of this King after that, and of my brother?" [69]

[67] *Mémoires de Nicolas Goulas,* II, 442.

[68] *Mémoires de Mme de Motteville,* II, 354, 356–357.

[69] Cited in Battifol, "Les idées de la révolution sous Louis XIV," *Revue de Paris* (March, 1928), p. 116.

English royalist exiles sounded the same note; they grimly compared the troubles of France and England and, like their queen, concluded that France was in a serious plight. Sir Edward Nicholas wrote in February, 1649, that the French "are here as eager upon rebellion against their governors and government as ever our wretched English were. And the contrivers of the present rebellion in England did not more directly tread in the steps of the League in France, than these here do trace our covenanters in all their acts and proceedings."[70] A year later the English royalist newspaper *Mercurius Pragmaticus* prophesied ominously that Mazarin and Louis XIV could meet untimely deaths in the Fronde because such things "had not looked more improbable in England some eight years before."[71] Sir Edward Hyde continued in the same vein of gloomy prophecy when, referring to the riots in Paris in July, 1652, he wrote that "all the rabble at London when they went highest were not worthy to be named with this people who will burn, kill, and slay all who oppose them." The storm in France must be composed quickly, Hyde added, or the country will suffer irrevocable damage.[72]

French courtiers obviously shared the pessimistic views of the English exiles. The word "republican" came frequently from their pens. Secretary of State Le Tellier reported to Mazarin a

[70] Nicholas to Ormonde, February 1/11, 1648/1649, Thomas Carte, *A Collection of Original Letters and Papers, Concerning the Affairs of England from the Year 1641 to 1660* (London, 1739), I, 198. Sir Ralph Verney wrote from his place of exile in Blois, "I am confident if there is not an accommodation presently the disorders will look like ours in England—irreconcilable" (Verney to Hallelby, February 11/21, 1648/1649, Claydon House MSS.). Hallelby wrote similarly from Paris: "It appears to me to be extraordinarily like the beginning of the troubles in England" (Hallelby to Verney, January 13 [O.S.?], 1649, Claydon House MSS.).

[71] *Mercurius Pragmaticus*, May 25/June 4–June 1/11, [1650], p. 15.

[72] Hyde to Nicholas, July 6, 1652 (O.S.?), *State Papers Collected by Edward Earl of Clarendon* (Oxford, 1786), III, 81.

private conversation Retz, Coadjutor of Paris and one of the most active Frondeurs, had had with him on August 21, 1650. According to Retz, cries of "Republic" had risen during the siege of Paris in 1649. It would have been easy, Retz said, to proclaim a republic then had a few individuals, still wedded to the monarchy, been removed. Colbert agreed with Le Tellier that Retz was a republican. Retz had openly confessed his republicanism, Colbert reported. Colbert believed him capable of ruining the monarchy.[73]

It was not Retz alone who inspired fear. Omer Talon, the royal attorney general in the Paris Parlement, believed in December, 1651, that a party existed which wished to set up a republic in Paris and to blot out royal authority. D'Aligre, later to become Chancellor under Louis XIV, informed Le Tellier on May 12, 1652, that people spoke freely of founding a republic in imitation of the English. More echoes of this fear occur in the writings of others.[74]

Understandably, then, Cardinal Mazarin's anxieties about revolutionary danger in France persisted throughout the Fronde, regardless of periodic lulls in fighting. Shortly after the Peace of Rueil, April, 1649, brought the conflict around Paris to an inconclusive and temporary halt, Mazarin was turning over in his mind the proposition that, once a body like the Parliament of England began to attack the government, it would never stop

[73] Cited in Battifol, "Les idées de la révolution sous Louis XIV," *Revue de Paris* (March, 1928), pp. 113–114.

[74] *Ibid.*, 108–112. One of the agents working for the crown, the Père Berthod, likewise wrote of placards which had appeared in Paris during the summer of 1652 and of their exhortations "to get rid of the King and of the parlement and to establish a republic like that of England." Father François Berthod, "Mémoires," *Nouvelle collection des mémoires pour servir à l'histoire de France,* ed. Joseph F. Michaud and Jean F. Poujoulat (Paris, 1838), XXII, 578. Volume numbers listed for this collection conform to those given by the Library of Congress. Add two for the Bibliothèque Nationale.

until it had gone to the bitter end. "One has only to weigh the recent example which occurred in England to tremble in terror." [75]

As the Fronde progressed, the Cardinal began to identify some of the worst of his enemies with the leaders of the English revolution. In early 1651, as he sensed a new plot forming against the government, the Cardinal privately warned the Queen Regent, the King, the Duc d'Orléans, and a few others that the Parlement of Paris had its Fairfaxes and its Cromwells just like the Parliament of London—a statement which Madame de Motteville judged "very reasonable." [76] The success of the Cardinal's enemies in forcing him into exile a few days later naturally confirmed him in his opinion of the Frondeurs. From his place of exile, he advised the Queen Regent that the Coadjutor of Paris had boasted that he was the Cromwell of the French civil war and that the Duc de Beaufort, another prominent Frondeur, was the Fairfax. Retz, he assured the Queen Regent, had never concealed his aversion for monarchy and constantly praised the conduct of Cromwell. [77] The Cardinal wrote to Secretary of State Lionne in like terms, warning him that Retz was trying to outdo Cromwell. [78] In confirmation that these remarks were sincere, Mazarin scribbled in his private notebook, "It is indeed unfortunate to want to do in France what Cromwell has done in England." [79]

With evidence so abundant that thoughts of England fre-

[75] Mazarin's Carnet XII, pp. 5–6, quoted in Chéruel, *Histoire de la France pendant la minorité de Louis XIV*, III, 190–191.

[76] *Mémoires de Mme de Motteville*, III, 275. For a more complete discussion of the incident see pp. 83–86.

[77] Mazarin to Anne of Austria, April 10, 1651, *Lettres du cardinal Mazarin à la reine, à la princesse palatine . . . écrites pendant sa retraite hors de France, en 1651 et 1652*, ed. J. Ravenel (Paris, 1836), p. 5.

[78] Mazarin to Lionne, March 5, 1651, *Lettres du cardinal Mazarin*, ed. Chéruel, IV, 51.

[79] Cited in *Oeuvres du cardinal de Retz*, ed. Alphonse Feillet, Les grands écrivains de la France (Paris, 1872), II, 653.

quently raced through the Cardinal's mind as he analyzed the Fronde, one is naturally curious to learn whether he adhered to the same strategy in France he had recommended to Charles. In general, it must be conceded, the Cardinal practiced what he had preached. His overriding concern in France, as he thought it should have been for Charles I in England, was political—the maintenance of the authority of the crown. Nothing else—his high position in the Church, the urgings of the *dévots* against the Huguenots—could persuade him to deviate. From the beginning of the regency, it had become a fixed policy to avoid provoking the Huguenots into rebellion. The government constantly reassured Protestant leaders that promises would be scrupulously observed and that the Queen Regent would protect and advance all of her subjects without discrimination, looking only to the fidelity with which they served their king.[80] There will be occasion later to return to the Huguenot problem, but suffice it here to say that all of Cardinal Mazarin's actions, before and during the Fronde, were designed to minimize religion as an issue.

Mazarin has revealed very clearly in his private notebooks the important role he would assign to opportune compromise in fighting the Frondeurs. After the Queen Regent agreed to accept the reforms presented by the sovereign courts in 1648, Mazarin blandly wrote in his notebook that when the time was propitious the government could issue a declaration of noncompliance, explaining it had been forced to accept the demands of Parlement in order to give peace to the kingdom. "We must regain authority at whatever the price," the Cardinal continued, "and raise it higher than ever or else resolve to let our affairs perish and so become more ridiculed and disdained than we have been esteemed and feared until now. The Parlement has

[80] Mazarin to Duc de La Force, October 3, 1643; and to Messieurs de la Religion, September 12, 1644, *Lettres du cardinal Mazarin*, ed. Chéruel, I, 404; II, 62.

performed the functions of the King, and the people have deferred to it entirely. . . . At present we must dissimulate temporarily, evincing a desire to accommodate everything with the Parlement." It would be possible later, he expected, to withdraw troops from Flanders and to punish the Frondeurs. "We must keep this in mind and delay." [81] With a thousand variations to suit the circumstances, this was the strategy the Cardinal used against the Frondeurs until they had finally been subdued five years later. Whether he succeeded because of the strategy or in spite of it is debatable, but it was basically the *modus operandi* he had pressed on Charles I.

In France, as in England, there were some matters so delicate that compromise would not benefit the royal cause, he believed, and might cause it great damage. The King's principal minister, it developed, belonged in this category of the sacrosanct. Cardinal Mazarin had long been vilified after he stepped into Richelieu's place on the Council, but popular hatred of him did not reach truly monumental proportions until the summer of 1648. Previously the Superintendent of Finances had served as a convenient lightning rod to draw off some of the widespread dissatisfaction. But once the Queen Regent dropped Particelli d'Emeri, the finance minister, in July of 1648, the storm centered around Mazarin.

Hatred of Mazarin was the great and sometimes only rallying cry which could hold the quarreling Frondeurs together. Already in September of 1648 members of the Parlement of Paris were calling loudly for the Cardinal's dismissal. Anne of Austria experienced intense pressure from inside and outside the government to rid herself of this minister who, she was told, had become a political liability. As is well known, the Queen Regent had a strong sentimental attachment to the Cardinal—some have claimed the two were secretly married—but it is doubtful

[81] Mazarin's Carnet IX, p. 72ff., quoted in Chéruel, *Histoire de la France pendant la minorité de Louis XIV*, III, 91.

that sentiment alone could have withstood the many determined and vigorous onslaughts against him unless Anne was also convinced of the political wisdom of keeping him at his post.

Mazarin, it will be remembered, had reacted strongly against Charles I's surrender of the Earl of Strafford to the English Parliament and had written about it in his notebook in the fall of 1648. Probably he introduced the topic into his conversations with the Queen Regent and with others. Before the year 1648 was out, Cardinal Mazarin played the Strafford parallel as his trump card in a tense meeting of the Queen Regent's Council when his continuation in the government came under discussion. In an impassioned plea to his listeners, he referred to English experience to show the perils a sovereign risked when he abandoned his minister. The sacrifice of the Earl of Strafford, he told his audience, revealed how the insolence of the people constantly increased. Having spilled the blood of the minister, the people thirsted after the blood of their king. Mazarin's argument presented the analogy with Strafford so persuasively that he won over the Council. His speech later received applause from a number of "very qualified" persons at court.[82]

This was not the end of the matter. When the siege of Paris failed to accomplish the quick defeat of the Parlement and its allies which the Queen Regent and her minister had expected, criticism of Mazarin reappeared at court and the Queen Regent was repeatedly asked why she insisted on retaining so unpopular a figure in her government. Each time, Anne found her answer in the Strafford parallel. After the execution of Charles I, she was wont to add that she refused to dismiss the Cardinal in order that she and her son might escape the fate of the English monarch.[83]

Eventually the combination of enemies proved so formidable that Mazarin had no choice but to go into exile in February,

[82] *Mémoires de Nicolas Goulas*, II, 442.
[83] *Mémoires de Mme de Motteville*, II, 327, 356–357.

1651. However, Anne knew how to bide her time and to wait for the Fronde to fall apart. When in 1652 Mazarin returned to power, the event was justified by harking back to the example of the Earl of Strafford.[84] Mazarin's second exile in the summer of 1652 was simply a tactical maneuver, decided upon by the Cardinal, to expose the fundamental disunity of the Frondeurs; it was understood that he would resume his place in the government at the earliest opportunity. Thus, Mazarin, who by all accounts had become the most vilified and most generally detested public figure in France, somehow managed to ride out the storm. That he did so is a tribute to his own talents. But perhaps some part of the credit should go to the stiffening effect of the Strafford analogy on his own resolve and on that of the Queen Regent, who stood by him.

In spite of the many indications that the English experience had left its mark on Cardinal Mazarin and on the Queen Regent, it would be foolish to give it undue emphasis. English influence was but one of many elements which contributed to their picture of the Fronde and to the decisions they adopted. For all of their attitudes, and for all of their actions against the Frondeurs, there are explanations which can be offered free of connection with England. Mazarin's distrust of the Frondeurs surely owed much to his association with Richelieu, just as his tactics for crushing them probably bear the stamp of his background in diplomacy. One is hard put to assign a precise weight to the impact of the English Civil War and Revolution on the thinking of Mazarin and the Queen Regent when so many other influences were at work. Perhaps the importance of England was not so much to create as to magnify suspicions already present. As one of the Frondeurs remarked, things had reached such a pass that any complaint against the government was interpreted as revolu-

---

[84] "La vérité toute nue, ou avis sincère" (Paris, 1652), printed in Célestin Moreau, *Choix de Mazarinades,* Société de l'histoire de France (Paris, 1853), II, 419–420.

tionary.[85] That Mazarin and those at court exaggerated the dangers of revolution seems clear. Most contemporary assessments of the prevalence of republicanism in France came from persons who regarded it with horror. Occasionally republican utterances, and a few pamphlets, lent a semblance of credibility to the rumors. Actually, republicanism occupied but a tiny place in the calculations of the Fronde, as we shall see in later chapters. Examples from modern history illustrate how fear of subversion can reach almost hysterical proportions with very little substance, save the example of revolution elsewhere. This is exactly what seems to have happened in France under the pressure of events in England.

Fear of revolution tended to produce an undue sense of crisis within the French government and led to defensive reactions which were often excessive. On the other hand, the fate of Charles I was not something to be dismissed lightly by those whose ears rang with the shouts of revolters in their own country. Considering the uncertainty of the times, it is hard to blame Mazarin and Anne of Austria for reading such deeply sinister meaning into the Fronde. But if the English Revolution did no more than intensify the air of crisis hanging over France in the period of the Fronde, this is significant. These were the years when Cardinal Mazarin and the Queen Regent had to meet an opposition of uncertain proportion and uncertain aims. These were the years when Louis XIV absorbed his first lessons in statecraft. The demise of monarchy in England suggested what the penalty of failure might be if the Frondeurs were indeed headed the way of the English Independents.

[85] *La balance d'état* (n.p., n.d.), p. 27, Moreau No. 559.

III

Public Knowledge
of the English Revolution

In the years just preceding the onset of the English Civil War,
the French public had paid scant heed to England; Frenchmen
were far too occupied with their own many domestic concerns
and with fighting the Thirty Years' War. Not since Louis XIII's
sister, Henriette-Marie, married Charles I of England, not since
the Duke of Buckingham headed an ill-fated expedition to aid
the Huguenots besieged in La Rochelle, had England seemed
worthy of much attention.[1] Eruption of civil war in England
abruptly shattered public indifference in France, however, and
aroused an interest which, if anything, grew keener throughout
the war and which remained intense during the republican
revolution which followed.

No one in France, perhaps not even the English exiles, were
able to satisfy their curiosity about England as thoroughly as
Cardinal Mazarin. Nevertheless the educated public could put
together a reasonably detailed picture of the English upheaval,
thanks to the quantity of newspapers, pamphlets, and books
which discussed it. Broadly speaking, the bulk of this literature

---

[1] Ascoli, *La Grande-Bretagne devant l'opinion française au XVII*
siècle, I, 56–58.

touching upon the English Civil War was of two types. One category focused exclusively on England, contained no direct references to the Fronde, and made no overt attempt to compare the two civil wars. Publications of this type supplied the French public with the basic historical raw material for an understanding of the English Civil War. That some authors wrote about England for the veiled purpose of implying comparison with their own country is more than likely. But this was not the avowed object. The other category of this literature introduced the subject of England solely for purpose of comparison or contrast with the Fronde. Authors of this latter material were interested primarily in the issues of the Fronde, and they looked to England for confirmation of their statements about conditions in France. They usually assumed some knowledge of the English Civil War on the part of the reader and simply plucked out isolated incidents from the history of the English Civil War, or briefly alluded to it for purpose of illustration. They were not concerned with expounding English history but with applying it. This chapter will examine the first category of publication, the raw material of English history, and from it try to establish what the French public knew about the English Civil War. The next chapter will consider the manner in which the French press compared and contrasted England and France.

Until 1649, only a handful of pamphlets printed in France on the subject of the English Civil War had appeared, and these principally discussed the fate of the English Catholics. Yet there was no lack of information about the course of the war. The *Gazette de France* saw to that. Beginning in 1639, the year Charles I had taken to the field to lead an army against the Scots Presbyterians, a significantly increasing number of articles about England turned up in the pages of the *Gazette*. Soon the ordinary weekly news bulletins about England no longer sufficed and "extra" editions of the *Gazette* were published, given over exclusively or largely to English news. By 1648 the flood of news from England had reached such proportions that thirty "extra" editions on the English Civil War were printed that year. One of every three special editions in 1648 was reserved for England —a remarkable record, considering the many significant happenings in France and on the Continent generally that year: rioting in Paris, important military operations against Spain, the conclusion of the Peace of Westphalia, and the end of the Thirty Years' War—all major events which one might expect to crowd reports from England well into the background.

The unusual position occupied by the *Gazette de France* deserves some mention, to emphasize the importance of the paper's frequent references to England. The *Gazette* was *the* newspaper in France. Its pioneer editor, Théophraste Renaudot, had acquired a royal monopoly for his enterprise in 1631, and this advantage, as well as the generally high quality of his weekly publication, guaranteed the *Gazette* a wide following throughout the country. In the confusion of the Fronde, competing newspapers sprang up, but none lasted, and none seriously challenged the supremacy of the *Gazette*.[2] Everyone, so contemporaries inform us, read the *Gazette* regardless of his own political opinions; so great was the paper's prestige, affirmed one writer, that those who would deny the truth of a news report had only to scoff, "But it's not in the *Gazette*." [3] It is a fair assumption, then, that the section of the French public which was literate and which could be called "informed" must, through perusal of the *Gazette,* have had some acquaintance with the English Civil War. We may safely assume, too, that the *Gazette*'s editor would not have paid for the publication of "extra" editions devoted to English news unless a ready market of

[2] G. Gilles de la Tourette, *Théophraste Renaudot* (Paris, 1884), pp. 72ff. For a discussion of the origins of the *Gazette de France* see Folke Dahl *et al.,* "Les débuts de la presse française: nouveaux aperçus," *Acta bibliothecae Gotoburgensis,* IV (1951).

[3] Cited in Louis E. Hatin, *Bibliographie historique et critique de la presse périodique française* (Paris, 1866), p. 14.

readers awaited. The heavy concentration of English news carried in the semiofficial *Gazette* is clear proof that in general the French government made no effort to stifle, through rigid censorship, public knowledge of the Civil War in England.[4]

The virtual monopoly which the *Gazette* had enjoyed on news from England came to a sudden end with the execution of Charles I and the abolition of the English monarchy. Almost overnight, public interest in France jumped by several orders of magnitude. "What does the *Gazette* have to say about England?" was the question anxiously framed by many lips;[5] but when the *Gazette* could no longer by itself satisfy the public craving for more detail, pamphlets and books about England soon appeared. The shock of Charles's death was tremendous in France. Allusions to it abound in the pamphlet literature of the Fronde. Memoirists, some of them writing years afterward, had the event so indelibly stamped in their memories that they

---

[4] Porshnev has exaggerated the effect of censorship on news from England. See his chapter "Angliiskaia revoliutsiia i sovremennaia ei frantsiia," in *Angliiskaia burzhuaznaia revoliutsiia XVII .veka,* II, 71, and his "Angliiskaia respublika, frantsuzskaia fronda i vestfal skii mir," *Srednie veka,* III (1951), 184–185. He does not seem to have realized fully the role played by the *Gazette de France* in the transmission of news from England. Porshnev states further that the poem written by Saint-Amant in early 1644, "Albion" (which is a detailed interpretation of the English Civil War on the basis of Saint-Amant's firsthand experiences in England at the time), was suppressed by the censor in France. The poem did remain in manuscript, but it was highly critical of the English rebels and most laudatory of monarchy. There is no reason why it should have been suppressed on purely political grounds. Why it remained unpublished is mere conjecture. The first explanation offered by Paul Durand-Lapie (that perhaps the fate of a previous poem written by Saint-Amant which had run afoul of the censors made the printing houses reluctant to be associated with Saint-Amant so soon after) is probably the correct one. See Paul Durand-Lapie, *Un académicien du XVII° siècle, Saint-Amant, son temps, sa vie, ses poésies, 1594–1661* (Paris, 1898), p. 305. For the text of "Albion" see Marc-Antoine de Saint-Amant, *Oeuvres complètes,* ed. Charles L. Livet (Paris, 1855), II, 437–471.

[5] Hatin, *Bibliographie historique et critique de la presse,* p. 14.

often interrupted their narrations to marvel at the cataclysm in England. Intimate contemporary correspondence revealed the same pattern of intense emotional reaction. It was as if the execution at Whitehall had suddenly jarred Frenchmen into a realization of what perilous times they had entered.

The whole world seemed caught up in strange combustions. French writers pointed to the recent abortive revolt of Naples against the Spanish crown and to the writhings of Catalonia and Portugal to shake off the Spanish yoke. They took note of discontent in the Papal States; and then, enlarging their horizons, they meditated on the murder of the Sultan of Turkey and the reported breakup of the domain of the "King of China." [6] However, England, with its proximity and long historical connection with France, kindled the imagination of Frenchmen. Most people in France agreed that, as one writer expressed it, "among all the revolutions which have taken place in this century, that of Great Britain is the most considerable, the most strange, and the most terrible in all its consequences." [7]

The many accounts of the English Civil War which came before the French public were, with very few exceptions, those which passed through the prism of the French language, either by way of translation or by way of interpretation. The presses in England spewed out a staggering volume of tracts, newspapers, and books representing all shades of political and religious opinion during the Civil War, but most of these polemics were lost upon the French. The Frenchman of the seventeenth century was rare indeed whose command of English allowed him to cope with English publications. When he wished to communicate with his English neighbor, he expected to do it in

[6] For examples of such allusions see *Déclaration du parlement d'Angleterre* (London [Paris], 1649), pp. 25–26, Moreau No. 899; *Gazette de France,* No. 95, July 29, 1651, p. 768; *Mémoires de Mathieu Molé,* ed. Aimé Champollion-Figeac, Societé de l'histoire de France (Paris, 1857), IV, 66.

[7] Robert Mentet de Salmonet, *Histoire des troubles de la Grande-Bretagne* (Paris, 1661), Sig. êiv.

French, or possibly in Latin. More than a decade after the Fronde, the editor of the *Journal des savants* lamented French ignorance of the scientific work of the Royal Society in England because of language difficulty. Happily, he announced, this would soon be corrected because "at last we have found an English interpreter." Some French ambassadors and agents in London in the seventeenth century were no better acquainted with the English tongue than the readers of the *Journal des savants*.[8]

In spite of the language barrier, the French public knew something of both sides of the controversy in England; and, surprising as it may seem, the *Gazette de France* contributed most in bringing them a balanced presentation. Renaudot, the *Gazette's* editor, was a partisan of the regency government in France and a stout defender of monarchy (after all the *Gazette* was a semiofficial publication). He wrote of his bafflement that "there could be found a people so unnatural as to put their king unjustly to death, the best who ever governed England, Scotland, and Ireland." [9] But he was also a newspaper editor in search of news which people would buy. In the case of England, he printed whatever news he could ferret from either side, and he expressed regret that the Parliamentary party in England was less co-operative in keeping him informed than the royalists.[10] Some of Renaudot's readers must have complained of his boldness in printing stories of Parliamentary origin, for he often defended himself. It was pointless, he answered his critics, to ignore matters which were common knowledge and to report only the things people want to read.[11] Furthermore, he wrote,

[8] Charles Bastide, *The Anglo-French Entente in the XVII Century* (London, 1914), pp. 19–38; Camille-Georges Picavet, "Le français et les langues étrangères dans la diplomatie au temps de Louis XIV," *Revue des sciences politiques*, LI (1928), 582–583; J. B. Rathery, "Des relations sociales et intellectuelles entre la France et l'Angleterre," *Revue contemporaine*, XXII (1855), 161–162.

[9] *Gazette de France*, No. 35, April 15, 1649, p. 225.

[10] *Ibid.*, No. 62, May 22, 1643, p. 409.

[11] *Ibid.*, No. 135, November 12, 1649, p. 1033.

sometimes the only news available from England was that supplied by Parliamentary sources.[12]

For his "extra" editions of the *Gazette* devoted to England, Renaudot avidly collected "letters, articles, propositions, and other public acts," a type of material which he adjudged richest in news value.[13] The *Gazette* carried a generous quantity of documents of English royalist inspiration, as for example: "The new manifesto or declaration of the King of Great Britain . . . against the murderers of the late King, his father," and "The declarations . . . of the Prince Palatine Rupert . . . against the procedures of the said Parliament of England." But significantly it also featured such titles as "The act of the Parliament of England to abolish the monarchy," "The manifesto of the Parliament of England sent to the Estates of Scotland to justify its proceedings," "The justification of Sir William Lenthall, Speaker of the House of Commons of the Parliament of England," "The letters of Lt. General Cromwell to the Speaker of the Parliament of England concerning the capture of the town of Drogheda," and a great many others which presented the Parliamentary side of the case. Between a third and a half of all such official and semiofficial pronouncements from the rival groups in England which appeared in the *Gazette* originated with the Puritans. Because of Renaudot's policy of broad coverage, the *Gazette* became the best source in France for extracts in translation of London Puritan newspapers, just as it was the best source for Puritan documents of an official character. Although editorial disclaimers often prefaced these Puritan statements, or rebuttals followed from someone representing the royalist camp, at least purchasers of the *Gazette* had access to the thinking of the English republicans.

The new government of England made some modest effort, for its own part, to provide Frenchmen with a flattering image of the English Revolution. From time to time the Parliamentary

---

[12] *Ibid.*, No. 62, April 29, 1648, p. 533.
[13] *Ibid.*, No. 69, June 22, 1644, p. 449.

Council of State authorized translation into French of important policy statements. Probably the best known is that of March 27, 1649, issued just after the establishment of the Commonwealth.[14] The English republicans doubtless considered this document, like others which came after it,[15] an attractive, irrefutable justification of revolution, and they gave it the widest possible circulation. But it reveals basic difficulties which hampered the republicans from getting their message across to a French audience. As might be expected, the statement was strongly dosed with militant Protestantism, both in its handling of events leading up to the revolution and in its exposition of the goals for the future. In France, however, all the prominent political and military leaders (excepting the Vicomte de Turenne, the Duc de Bouillon, and the Maréchal de La Force) were Catholic. So was the great majority of the French population. Why should French Catholics warm to the defense of an English government which berated the dead Charles I for his failure to relieve the Protestants of La Rochelle twenty years before? Perhaps the Puritans intended their propaganda primarily for the Huguenot audience in France, but as we shall see later, they found Huguenot leaders publicly hostile to republican political doctrine, just as most Catholics were. Naturally, praise of republicanism scandalized the Queen Regent's friends, but most Frondeurs felt embarrassment too. The Frondeurs repeatedly stressed that their own quarrel was not with the King of France but with the King's minister, Cardinal Mazarin. How awkward, then, to have the English explain in this document of March 27 that the Civil War in England, and the ensuing Revolution, had stemmed originally from Parliament's desire to free Charles I from evil advisers.[16]

The English Parliament, which had no lack of skilled literary

[14] *Déclaration du parlement d'Angleterre,* Moreau No. 899.

[15] J. Milton French, *The Life Records of John Milton,* II (New Brunswick, 1950), 302.

[16] For a discussion of Huguenot and Frondeur attitudes to the English Civil War see pp. 83–111.

talent at its disposal for waging propaganda war with the English royalists, selected Mr. John Milton, its Secretary for Foreign Tongues, to answer some of the royalist attacks. Some of Milton's replies found their way sooner or later into France. One of his more important assignments was to compose a rejoinder to the immensely popular *Eikon Basilike*, which Charles I, so the English royalists insisted, had penned during the Civil War. Milton's slashing assault on the "King's Book," which he titled *Eikonoklastes,* was ready for circulation to English readers in 1649. Eventually Parliament paid for a French translation in 1652 and facilitated its export to France by permitting copies of it to leave England in 1653, free of the customary duty.[17]

Milton's *Eikonoklastes* was even less suited for most French eyes than the Parliamentary declaration of March 27, 1649. All of Milton's argumentative skill was wasted, since at the very start he bluntly told his readers he was aiming his blows at the person of the King. "What is properly his own guilt [will] not [be] imputed any more to his evil counselors (a ceremony used longer by the Parliament than he himself desired), [but] shall be laid here without circumlocutions at his own door." Milton extended his remarks to include monarchs generally, proclaiming that "the earth itself hath too long groaned under the burden of their injustice, disorder, and irreligion. Therefore to bind their kings in chains, and their nobles with links of iron, is an honor belonging to His saints." He went on to press the need of overcoming "those European kings, which receive their power, not from God, but from the beast." [18]

By the time a French translation of *Eikonoklastes* was obtainable, much of Queen Henriette-Marie's popularity had eroded. Still there were probably many in France who took exception to Milton's cutting jibes at Henri IV's daughter, whom

[17] French, *Life Records of John Milton,* III, 278–279, 281, 327.
[18] *The Works of John Milton,* ed. William Haller (New York, 1932), V, 66, 306.

he castigated for "papism" and for meddling domination of her husband, Charles I.[19]

Actually the French public knew Milton first from his *Pro Anglicano populo defensio,* a work which, though written after *Eikonoklastes,* appeared in France well ahead of it. He had composed it as a counterblast against the defense of Charles I and monarchy written by Claude de Saumaise. Saumaise had published his *Defensio regia pro Carolo I* in 1649 in Latin.[20] Throughout the following year Milton, at the behest of Parliament, toiled in preparing a reply, also in Latin, which he completed in 1651. Although a French translation of the *Pro Anglicano populo defensio* was rumored to be in progress, it did not appear, and Milton's book had to be read in France in the Latin version.[21]

For the great majority of the French audience, the book was marred by the same kind of political and religious statements present in other examples of Puritan propaganda; and Milton's sneering, personal attacks on Saumaise as a "French mountebank," as a "French vagabond," and as a "crackbrained pursesnatcher of a Frenchman," [22] did not in all probability recommend themselves to French readers. On all sides in France, a mention of Milton's name was enough to trigger vituperation. A partisan of Cardinal Mazarin, sputtering with rage, accused Milton of being, "the most impudent and most wily apologist of the blackest of all parricides, by which the English nation has just been sullied." [23] A Frondeur was equally emphatic in his denunciation of Milton's "pernicious" publication.[24]

[19] *Ibid.,* V, 138–141.

[20] French, *Life Records of John Milton,* II, 248–249.

[21] Francis F. Madan, "Milton, Salmasius and Dugard," *The Library,* 4th ser., IV (1923), 119–120.

[22] *The Works of John Milton,* VII, 487, 529, 531.

[23] *Les sentiments d'un fidèle sujet du roi* (n.p., 1652), p. 40, Moreau No. 3648.

[24] *Lettre d'un marquillier de Paris à son curé* (Paris, 1651), p. 11, Moreau No. 1885.

The book achieved notoriety in France, if not fame. Copies fell into the hands of French authorities by June, 1651, at one of those tense moments of the Fronde when Mazarin brooded in exile and when the factions headed by Retz and by the Prince de Condé contested with the Queen Regent and with each other for control of the government. First official notice of Milton's book came at Toulouse when the Procurator-General brought it to the attention of the Parlement there. The shocked jurists ordered the book burned by the public executioner on June 17, 1651, and warned the citizenry against having it in their possession.

A few days later, Paris officials faced the same problem. The very day the Prince de Condé, fearing new arrest and imprisonment by the Queen Regent, fled Paris, the Civil Lieutenant of the Provost of Paris reached the same decision as had the authorities of Toulouse. He ordered the book burned by the executioner of high justice in the Place de la Grève. The book, he explained, "is filled with various ideas contrary to the doctrine of the Church, [and] to the obedience due to sovereigns, which can only have been put there with the design of exciting the people to sedition." Five days after the public burning, a royal crier, accompanied by three trumpeters, visited the principal intersections of the city and the University of Paris to remind the populace of the order.[25] Later, in August of that summer, the Duc d'Orléans rose in the Parlement of Paris to reassure the members that though there was talk of an evil book which had been written against Saumaise and which defended the English republic against the King, the Civil Lieutenant had burned it.[26]

Some years after, Milton wrote as if his *Pro Anglicano populo*

[25] J. Milton French, "The Burning of Milton's *Defensio* in France," *Modern Language Notes*, LVI (1941), 275–277. See also French, *Life Records of John Milton*, III, 38–40, 48–50.

[26] B.N., MS. f.fr. 18324, f. 139.

defensio had won a sympathetic welcome in France,[27] and some of the contemporary reports published in the English Puritan press seemed to confirm the impression. *Mercurius Politicus*, an English newspaper which hewed to the Puritan line of argument, printed an item purporting to have come from Paris, stating, "all the copies [of Milton's *Defensio*] sent hither out of the Low Countries were long since dispersed." The same newspaper informed its readers in another report of July from Leiden that the doctrines espoused in Milton's book were attracting a growing interest in France and predicted that the burning of the book "will make it a martyr, whose ashes will be scattered far and wide, and the cause and the book be more inquisitively desired." [28] More than four decades later, Pierre Bayle repeated in his *Dictionnaire historique* that efforts to suppress Milton's work in France served only to increase the number of readers. However, Bayle relied on the comments of persons outside France whose knowledge of conditions inside the country was at best questionable.[29]

No positive evidence from inside the country exists to show that Milton's book exercised any considerable influence in France. Sir Edward Hyde, the English royalist, referred approvingly to the "exemplary reproach and judgment it met in France" and only hoped it might encounter a similarly hostile reception in Germany.[30] The error of the *Gazette de France* in ascribing authorship to an Englishman named Hamilton—an easy mistake in view of the similar pronunciation in French of Milton and Hamilton—suggests that Milton's *Defensio* was better known from scandalized references to it in conversation

[27] French, *Life Records of John Milton*, III, 122.
[28] *Ibid.*, III, 46, 60. See also William Riley Parker, *Milton's Contemporary Reputation* (Columbus, 1940), p. 87.
[29] Pierre Bayle, *Dictionnaire historique et critique* (4th ed.; Amsterdam, 1730), III, 395.
[30] Hyde to Taylor, August 23, 1652, *Calendar of the Clarendon State Papers*, ed. W. Dunn Macray (Oxford, 1889), II, 145.

than from any considerable number of copies in clandestine circulation.[31]

In 1650 an English newspaper in the French language called the *Nouvelles ordinaires de Londres* obtained a license to publish from the English Commonwealth and proceeded forthwith to parrot Puritan versions of the news. Its editor, William Dugard, who styled himself "printer to the Council of State" and who may have had help from Milton in launching the paper,[32] intended it for general European distribution rather than for sale in France exclusively. Dugard explained to his readers that he "deemed it not unacceptable to foreign nations to impart in a language that extends and is understood throughout Europe, all the most signal and remarkable happenings in England." [33]

The *Nouvelles ordinaires,* which endured for a decade, must have attained some popularity on the Continent, because Dugard later complained of a counterfeit edition of the paper published at The Hague. Copies of the *Nouvelles ordinaires de Londres* evidently arrived in France each week, but it is difficult to determine how large a circulation Dugard's paper enjoyed.[34] Cardinal Mazarin, it has been said, occasionally read the paper, though evidence for this is not entirely convincing.[35]

[31] *Gazette de France,* No. 95, July 29, 1651, p. 768.

[32] Joseph Frank, *The Beginnings of the English Newspaper, 1620–1660* (Cambridge, Mass., 1961), p. 210; Leona Rostenberg, *Literary, Political, Scientific, Religious and Legal Publishing . . . in England, 1551–1700* (New York, 1965), I, 152–153.

[33] *Nouvelles ordinaires de Londres,* No. 1, July 11/21–July 18/28, 1650, p. 1; No. 44, May 1/11–May 8/18, 1651, p. 176. An earlier pro-parliamentary newspaper, *Le Mercure anglois,* published in London between 1644 and 1648, had provided French readers with Civil War battle information but only superficial political coverage (Frank, *The Beginnings of the English Newspaper,* pp. 70–71, 117, 145–146, 167–168).

[34] *Journal contenant ce qui se passe de plus remarquable* (Paris, 1652), September 20–27, p. 73, Moreau No. 1740; *Le franc bourgeois de Paris* (Paris, 1652), p. 18, Moreau No. 1408.

[35] Bastide, *The Anglo-French Entente,* p. 155. The reference by Mazarin

But in any event, the *Nouvelles ordinaires* had slight impact in France. Dugard refrained from establishing significant relationships between current affairs in England and those in France and from adapting his presentation of the news to French reading taste. The newspaper gave every indication of being, quite simply, an English Puritan newspaper translated almost as an afterthought into French.

Some pro-Parliamentary materials in the English language also entered France by way of the English exiles. Charles II had directed friends in England to supply him at weekly intervals with newspapers and pamphlets, particularly those concerning the activities of the Parliamentary committees. Other exiles did the same because of their hunger for news—any news—from England. Before the royalists passed these reports on to the French public, however, they undoubtedly altered them to suit their fancy.[36]

Virtually all descriptive accounts of the English Civil War and Revolution, friendly to the republicans, were translations in the *Gazette de France* of what the English Puritans themselves had written. French writers rarely presented, on their own, pro-republican histories of the English conflict. Censorship is not the explanation. The many examples of pamphlets printed without permission and in violent opposition to whatever group controlled Paris show how easy it was to elude the censor. Had there existed a burning desire to provide a republican interpretation of the English Civil War, authors could have resorted to clandestine publication.

In contrast, numerous persons in France eagerly translated English royalist propaganda into French and extolled the cause of Charles I in print. Even the Frondeur press presented the

---

to the "nouvelles publiques de Londres" may, but does not necessarily, refer to the *Nouvelles ordinaires de Londres*.

[36] Sir Edward Hyde and Sir Edward Nicholas were among those receiving newsletters from London (*Calendar of the Clarendon State Papers,* II, viii).

English Civil War with pro-royalist coloring. One of the most active printing houses in Paris during the Fronde was that of Guillaume Sassier. More than a tenth of Sassier's output related to England's Civil War with a clear pro-royalist viewpoint. The publishing house of François Prevveray in Paris, also working in behalf of the Frondeurs, surpassed this record and devoted more than a third of its titles to English affairs, all written with sympathy for the royalists. One of the Paris publishers most notoriously hostile to the Queen Regent, Claude Morlot, distributed several pamphlets on England's troubles friendly to the royalists. A great many other printers and publishers, whose normal production supported the Fronde, included one or more pro-royalist accounts of the English Civil War among their pamphlets. Writers of strong Catholic convictions, and such publishers as Pierre Targa who dealt frequently in Catholic literature, helped state the case for Charles I. Not to be outdone, Huguenot translators, authors, and publishers also lent their support to the English royalists. Consequently the reports about England, of pro-royalist hue, originated from widely divergent sections of that French society which was so divided on other issues. It is significant that, while slightly more than 50 per cent of those who printed or published political pamphlets during the Fronde preferred anonymity, they willingly placed their names on brochures concerning England. Only rarely do we find the latter without proper attribution.

Some of this publishing was inspired by the royalist exiles. But probably most of it came spontaneously, independent of English royalist patronage.[37] Indeed, the exiles found it hard at times to hold in check some of their French "friends" who attributed to them opinions they did not actually approve and

[37] W. McNeil, "Milton and Salmasius, 1649," *English Historical Review,* LXXX (1965), 107–108. For other examples see *Prédiction òu se voit comme le Roy Charles II . . . doit estre remis au royaume d'Angleterre* (Rouen, 1650), pp. 6–7; *Manifeste du roi de la Grand' Bretagne* (Paris, 1649), Moreau No. 2394.

which they feared would embarrass them in England or else-where on the Continent. The Sieur de Marsys was such a "friend." Marsys had taken it upon himself to clothe the English royalists in a dress more attractive to French Catholics. Whether he did so because he hoped to improve the standing of the English exiles in France or because he thought his translation would enjoy a greater sale is uncertain. The English royalists believed the latter. He brought out first in 1646 and then again in 1648 a *Histoire de la persécution présente des catholiques d'Angleterre*, peppered with uncomplimentary references to Protestantism in general, and to Charles's Protestant predeces-sors, and to the Church of England in particular. Though he dedicated the book to Henriette-Marie, she took offense at some of Marsys' remarks in the dedicatory epistle and angrily flung the book away.[38]

Marsys daubed the same coloring onto his version of the trial and execution of Charles I [39] and, according to the English royalists, put into Charles's mouth "a false and feigned speech . . . at the time of his being murdered," on grounds that "the speech he [Charles] did make was poor and below a king." But it was what Marsys did to the *Eikon Basilike* that drove the English royalists into paroxysms of rage. Styling himself falsely "Interpreter and Master of French to Charles II and the Duke of York," he made his translation of the *Eikon Basilike* appear to have official sanction. To correct "Huguenot errors" contained in previous French translations, he freely altered the text, sub-stituting expressions more palatable for Catholic taste. He inti-mated in his preface that Charles had pretended to be a Protestant for political reasons, but that he had been a Catholic. Marsys narrowly escaped a beating in the streets of Paris by

[38] See the letter written to Sir Edward Nicholas dated November 6, 1649, in *Eikon Basilike*, ed. Edward J. L. Scott (London, 1880), pp. xiv–xv.

[39] *Le procès . . . du roi d'Angleterre* (Paris, 1649), Moreau No. 2888.

some Scots, furious because his translation of the *Eikon Basilike* allegedly maligned their nation. So great a center of scandal became Marsys, in fact, that Charles II, then on the Isle of Jersey, appointed a committee in Paris to call on him. But Marsys was impervious to the committee's remonstrances. He retorted that he thought it "more advantageous to represent the late King a Roman Catholic than a Puritan . . . that it might be a means to stir up the Romish party to help and assist His Majesty that now is." The committee could do nothing to stop Marsys. As the members freely confessed, it was absurd to expect the French government, directed by a cardinal of the Roman Catholic Church, to suppress a book on the grounds of its "popish" interest. Charles II had to content himself with a public burning of Marsys' books on the Isle of Jersey and with the dispatch of a detailed bill of particulars, reviewing Marsys' errors, for the committee to disseminate in Paris.[40]

For all his shortcomings as a defender of the English monarchy, Marsys' judgment was impeccably correct in one respect: he recognized a best seller when he saw it. In deciding to translate *Eikon Basilike,* the "King's Book," he picked a work whose popularity can only be described as phenomenal. First printed in England at the time of Charles's death, *Eikon Basilike* within a year ran through thirty-five English language editions printed in England and another twenty-five editions in translation, or in English, printed outside England.[41]

In France, *Eikon Basilike* had its first publication in Paris in March or April, 1649, in the original English for the edification of the exile colony. French translations soon followed. The first was published at Rouen in June, 1649, by the Huguenot Jean

[40] Letter to Nicholas, November 6, 1649, *Eikon Basilike,* ed. Scott, pp. xiv–xv; Hatton and others to Nicholas, January 4, 1650, *ibid.,* xviii–xxi. For a more extended discussion see *Eikon Basilike,* ed. Philip A. Knachel (Ithaca, 1966), pp. xviii–xix.

[41] Francis F. Madan, "A New Bibliography of the *Eikon Basilike,*" *Oxford Bibliographical Society Publications,* new ser., III (1949), 2.

Baptiste Porrée, who based his work on a manuscript translation by another Huguenot, Denis Cailloué, probably then residing in England. In July, Porrée's translation was reprinted in Paris; another edition followed at Rouen, probably that September. Marsys' controversial Catholic translation appeared in October, 1649. Still another edition of the *Eikon,* as translated by Porrée, was published in Rouen before the end of the year; and in December, 1649, Denis Cailloué succeeded in putting his original translation into print in London. The following year a reprint of Porrée's translation was printed in Holland.[42]

The number of editions and printings of *Eikon Basilike* in France or in French indicate the demand for the book. Furthermore, Marsys estimated that his rival, Porrée, had sold 4,000 copies of his translation within six months. Marsys' translation was already well dispersed among the public a few months after its printing.[43]

With the exception of Marsys' edition, the French knew the *Eikon Basilike* through Huguenot translators, but this seems not to have bothered French Catholics. Mathieu Molé, First President of the Parlement of Paris, read the *Eikon Basilike* in a Huguenot translation but reacted to it almost exactly as did the Huguenot pastor Samuel Bochart.[44] Molé did not hesitate to recommend the translation and the supplementary prayers to his friends, saying, "it was hard to read it without tears." [45] The English exiles continued to worry about the accuracy of

[42] *Ibid.,* III, 50, 60–68.
[43] Hatton and others to Nicholas, January 4, 1650, *Eikon Basilike,* ed. Scott, pp. xviii–xxi. Some of the English exiles ordered multiple copies of the French translation for distribution among their friends in various parts of France (Verney to Osborne, July 7/17, 1649, Claydon House MSS; Osborne to Verney, July 14, 1649, *ibid.*).
[44] A. Galland, "Les pasteurs français Amyraut, Bochart . . . et le royauté de droit divin de l'édit d'Alais à la Révocation (1629–1685)," *Bulletin—Société de l'histoire du Protestantisme français,* LXXVII (1928), 113.
[45] *Mémoires de Mathieu Molé,* IV, 66, 68.

the French translations and persuaded Charles II of the need for a better one. When the English king learned that a prominent Huguenot minister and theologian at Blois, Paul Testard, had begun a translation, he urged him to finish the task. However, Testard died in 1650 before he could finish, and no other translator replaced him. Charles II was actually reasonably satisfied with Porrée's translation.[46]

Some among the French gave the *Eikon Basilike* a more tempered praise than the exiles. Valentin Conrart, Secretary of the French Academy, recorded that those who had read the English edition told him it was an exquisite work, both for the elegance of its expression and for the depth of its learning, but that matters were not as sincerely represented in it as one might wish.[47] When Conrart had an opportunity to examine a French translation, he described the book as a work of contemplation in which the King appeared very pious but politically naïve.[48] However, there were other authors who advised their readers to consult that "Divine work which his own hand has wrought for us, . . . that noble monument" which "without hyperbole" was equal to the rarest writings.

The extraordinary success of *Eikon Basilike* was due in part to its ability to project in warm, human terms the issues of the English Civil War as seen by Charles I. It was a book composed by the King himself (so the English royalists claimed) and in which he alternately discoursed and prayed about a series of disputes and episodes relating to the Civil War. Unencumbered by heavy-handed appeals to history or with tedious expositions of theory, the "King's Book" pictured the author as a man of

[46] Letter to Nicholas, November 6, 1649, *Eikon Basilike*, ed. Scott, p. xv; Hatton and others to Nicholas, enclosure, January 4, 1650, *ibid.*, pp. xxv, xxxi–xxxii; Charles II to Testard, March 15, 1650, *A Vindication of K. Charles the Martyr* (London, 1711).

[47] Conrart to Rivet, June 4, 1649, René de Kerviler and Ed. de Barthélemy, *Valentin Conrart, sa vie et sa correspondance* (Paris, 1881), p. 518.

[48] Conrart to Rivet, July 30, 1649, *ibid.*, p. 522.

goodwill, reasonable, tolerant, pious, anxious to end the strife which had broken out in his kingdoms, but continually thwarted by quarrelsome, evil men who wished the destruction of monarchy and of religion. Appearing so soon after Charles's death, *Eikon Basilike* was admirably timed to sharpen the sense of personal tragedy which reports of the King's execution had caused in France.

Eikon Basilike set the tone for much of the English royalist propaganda in France. Charles's tragic story fascinated the French. Apologists for the King tortured their imaginations to furnish the public with more details. The trial offered a splendid opportunity for many writers. The English Parliament was itself partly to blame, because it had permitted publication of a full reporting of the trial. This proved a blunder; the account of the trial tended to arouse more sympathy for Charles than for his opponents and made the judges appear, by their own words, rude and spiteful men. Within a few weeks, the Parliament in London had forbidden further publication of this document, but too late to prevent damage.[49] A copy was obtained in France, translated, and soon made available to the public there,[50] with the approbation of the exiles. Various authors adapted the original to give a stronger dramatic impact to the King's martyrdom.[51] When in 1650 the English Parliament finally relented and sent over to France an official French translation of the account of the King's trial and execution, authorities at Rouen confiscated 1,900 copies landed there, and doubtless the copies got no further.[52] The nervousness at Rouen was

[49] C. V. Wedgwood, *The Trial of Charles I* (London, 1964), pp. 210–211.

[50] *Récit véritable de tout ce qui s'est fait au procès du roi* (n.p., 1649), Moreau No. 3016.

[51] For examples see: *Les dernières paroles du roi d'Angleterre* (Paris, 1649), Moreau No. 1037; *Le procès . . . du roi d'Angleterre*, Moreau No. 2888; *Relation véritable de la mort barbare* (Paris, 1649), Moreau No. 3241.

[52] Conrart to Rivet, July 22, 1650, *Valentin Conrart*, p. 548.

probably due to the origin of the pamphlets rather than to their content.

Some pamphleteers concentrated on the aftermath of the trial, including the King's tender leave-taking from his children after he had received the death verdict; or they shifted the scene to the Continent, where they could depict the tearful figure of Henriette-Marie or could reconstruct in imagination the correspondence exchanged after the execution between Charles II in Holland and his mother in Paris.[53]

From this literature there emerges a composite picture of the English king which will convey some sense of the prevailing mood. The propagandists made it plain that Charles had been a "great king", "the greatest king in the world," indeed, "the best king in the world." He was what one expected of a king, they said: tall, handsome, a picture of health, possessed of vast talent, and the most accomplished prince to have worn the English crown in many years. His grasp of history and of law, his gift of literary expression, his oratorical skill, matched his courage in battle, his horsemanship, his possession of all the qualities of the perfect cavalier. His natural piety and hatred of vice rendered all pleasures of the senses repugnant to him. Only those innocent joys provided by music, painting, and sculpture pleased him. And yet, for all his austere moral and religious fervor, he was a kindly person, a man who "loved his wife more than himself," a gentle father to his children and to his subjects. Authors pointedly mentioned his "marked inclination for the French nation" and his choice of a French

---

[53] *Consolations tirées du tableau de la passion de Nostre Sauveur* (Paris, 1649), Moreau No. 776; *Les larmes et complaintes de la reine d'Angleterre* (Paris, 1649), Moreau No. 1805; *Lettre de consolation à la reine d'Angleterre* (Paris, 1649), Moreau No. 1916; *Lettre du prince de Galles* (Paris, 1649), Moreau No. 2129; *Lettre véritable du Prince de Galles* (Paris, 1649), Moreau No. 2258; *Réponse de la reine d'Angleterre* (Paris, 1649), Moreau No. 3395; *Les sanglots pitoyables* (Paris, 1649), Moreau No. 3585.

wife. The calculated effect of this heroic imagery was to increase the sense of tragedy surrounding a king cut down in the prime of life.[54]

In drawing these flattering portraits of the King, writers confronted an obvious paradox. How was it that this paragon of kings had come to lose first his realms and then his life? Some writers, particularly those who simply commented on an episode of the Civil War, chose to ignore what was really the crux of the problem, or touched upon it lightly. But a number of authors actually came to grips with the "causes" of the English Civil War. There was less agreement in this area than with the assessment of Charles I himself, for here authors consciously or unconsciously implied comparisons with France. Huguenots tended to emphasize the role of the Independents in causing the Revolution, to relieve the Presbyterians of guilt. Authors with a Catholic bias indicted Protestantism in general for creating the conditions in which all established institutions might come under attack. Those speaking for the English royalists or the court party of the Queen Regent blamed Charles I for his leniency. All writers, even those published by the Frondeur printing houses, generally agreed that it was the malevolence of ambitious, treacherous men like Fairfax and Cromwell which had doomed the monarchy in England. This theme was woven through all the pro-royalist propaganda regardless of source.

Publications referred to thus far were of a fairly popular nature. However, the English royalists had circulating in France propaganda designed to capture the sympathy of the intellectual elite. Thomas Hobbes was one of those whose writing reinforced the cause of monarchy for a time with an audience of more discriminating readers in France. Hobbes had come to France

[54] Mentet de Salmonet, *Histoire des troubles de la Grande Bretagne*, p. 329; *Les justes soupirs* (Paris, 1649), pp. 8, 10, 12, Moreau No. 1790; *Les nations barbares* (Paris, 1649), pp. 2–3, Moreau No. 2526; *Sommaire de tout ce qui s'est passé* (Paris, 1650), p. 3, Moreau No. 3684.

in 1641 at the first rumblings of civil war in his homeland and did not return to England until the close of 1651. Throughout that period he moved among the English exiles living in the French capital. Scientific-intellectual groups in Paris welcomed him, and his fellow exiles esteemed him highly enough to effect his appointment in 1646 as mathematics tutor to Charles II, then Prince of Wales.

Hobbes had published a political tract in Paris in 1642 (*Elementorum philosophiae sectio tertia de cive*), but in such small quantity that only a few knew of it. Word-of-mouth praise encouraged Samuel Sorbière to translate it into French. It was published in Holland in 1649 in two editions, and then the same translation was reprinted in Paris in 1651.[55] Without mentioning the English Civil War, the book stoutly upheld the English royalists. Hobbes made clear his preference for monarchy and outlined his belief that absolute power was essential to maintain peace within the state regardless of what form the government took. In a chapter on the causes of civil dissension, Hobbes rejected the validity of claims by those who held the possessors of sovereign power subject to civil law. He denied the argument that sovereign power could be shared with others in the state. He could not condone killing a tyrant. In his judgment, "legitimate kings render a thing just in commanding it, or unjust when they forbid it." [56] When his discussion turned to religion, French Catholics could not abide his unorthodoxy. Even Gassendi tempered his praise of *Elementorum philoso-*

[55] Hugh MacDonald and Mary Hargreaves, *Thomas Hobbes—A Bibliography* (London, 1952), pp. 16–22; André Morize, "Thomas Hobbes et Samuel Sorbière," *Revue germanique*, IV (1908), 203–204. Sorbière also translated the pro-royalist account of George Bates, *Les vraies causes des derniers troubles d'Angleterre* (Orange, 1653). See André Morize, "Samuel Sorbière principal à Orange: sa conversion (1650–1653)," *Bulletin—Société de l'histoire du Protestantisme français*, LVI (1907), 503–525.

[56] Thomas Hobbes, *Elémens philosophiques du citoyen, traicté politique* (Amsterdam, 1649), pp. 183, 185, 186, 188.

phiae by excluding the sections on religion, where "we are not of the same sentiment." [57]

The English royalists had an unreliable champion in Hobbes, however. By 1651 he had put the finishing touches on his monumental *Leviathan* but, significantly, had thought best to entrust it for publication to a publisher in London. Later in the year Hobbes presented a copy of his book to Charles II, but he obviously had misgivings about its reception. He admitted to Sir Edward Hyde that the book might not please him, and his premonition was more than justified. Hyde was thoroughly outraged by the book. So strong was Hyde's displeasure, in fact, that after the Restoration he composed for publication a point-by-point refutation of Hobbes's arguments. The major difficulty arose from Hobbes's defense of royalists in England who had compounded and made their peace with the Commonwealth. As Hyde and many of his fellow royalists read the argument, Hobbes was defending the notion that a successful revolt absolved a subject of ties to his traditional sovereign, and, indeed, required him to tender allegiance to the new custodian of absolute sovereign power. Hobbes seemed thereby to legitimize governments produced by rebellion.[58] *Leviathan* had no chance to become influential in France. It was not translated into French before the conclusion of the Fronde, and the French Catholic *dévots* saw to it that Hobbes himself left France before the end of 1651 because of unacceptable religious views.

In any case Saumaise, not Hobbes, was the chief reliance of the English royalists to present their case to the intellectuals of the Continent. Claude de Saumaise was a well-known professor at Leiden, a Protestant *émigré* from France. Charles II formally invited him in March, 1649, to rally the intelligentsia by writing

[57] Gassendi to Sorbière, April 28, 1646, *ibid.*, sig.***8v.

[58] Edward Hyde, *A Brief View and Survey of the Dangerous and Pernicious Errors to Church and State, in Mr. Hobbes's Book, Entitled "Leviathan"* (Oxford, 1676), pp. 8–9, 61.

a solid defense of the English monarchy.[59] Saumaise complied by completing his *Defensio regia pro Carolo I* that same year.[60] Saumaise's treatise attracted wide attention. It was translated from the original Latin into French and published at Paris in 1650, with additions and corrections of the author. A year later the same Paris publishing house which had printed the translation then reissued the Latin text, indicating, perhaps, the rarefied atmosphere in which Saumaise's audience dwelt.[61]

Contemporaries in France adjudged the *Defensio regia* a competent and satisfactory work. Disparaging remarks uttered about Saumaise elsewhere on the Continent must not be taken as typical of French reaction. Conrart reported that the Latin text was highly regarded and expressed his impatience to read the French edition.[62] Claude Sarrau, Huguenot intellectual and councilor to the Parlement of Paris, wrote Saumaise that he had seen his great work and urged him to make all speed to have it translated into French.[63] The Huguenot theologian Moïse Amyraut praised Saumaise for the excellent manner in which he had exposed "the atrocity of the crime" committed by the Independents in England against their king.[64] Samuel Bochart, another distinguished pastor, wrote to Saumaise that he had read through the *Defensio regia* with greatest pleasure.[65] Huguenots felt that Saumaise had dealt too harshly with the Pres-

---

[59] W. McNeil, "Milton and Salmasius, 1649," *English Historical Review,* LXXX (1965), 107–108.

[60] Claude de Saumaise, *Defensio regia pro Carolo I* (n.p., 1649).

[61] Madan, "Milton, Salmasius and Dugard," *The Library,* 4th ser., IV (1923), 119–120.

[62] Conrart to Rivet, June 10, 1650, *Valentin Conrart,* p. 547.

[63] Sarrau to Saumaise, November 16, 1649, *Marquardi Gudii et doctorum virorum ad eum epistolae . . . et Claudii Sarravii senatoris Parisiensis epistolae* (Utrecht, 1697), pp. 216–217; Sarrau to Saumaise, January 29, 1650, *ibid.,* pp. 222–223.

[64] Moïse Amyraut, *Discours de la souveraineté des roys* (n.p., 1650), p. 5.

[65] Bochart to Saumaise, May 17, 1650, Samuel Bochart, *Omnia opera* (Leiden, 1712), I, 1161.

byterians, but otherwise they received the book well. However, the Huguenot community in France was not alone in its appreciation of Saumaise.[66] Gilles Ménage, a prominent writer, had words of high praise for him in 1652.[67] Apparently Saumaise's writings enjoyed great demand from the French public. Sir Edward Hyde wrote from Paris to his friend Sir Edward Nicholas in Holland asking him to send a catalogue of all that Saumaise had written. He inquired whether Saumaise's books were easily obtainable there. For, said Hyde, "though many of them were printed here, they are not to be got in Paris." [68]

Saumaise had undertaken in ponderous scholarly fashion to persuade readers of his *Defensio regia* that all the weight of authority favored the English monarchists. Seeking to rally both Dutch republicans and French monarchists, as well as Englishmen, he attempted a thesis acceptable to all. The real significance of the revolution in England, he wrote, was not to be explained as a collision of monarchical and republican principles but rather as a demonstration of the Independents' voracious appetite for power. The Puritans had not wished to substitute popular government for royal government but to replace the King by forty tyrants. Although it chanced that they had overturned a monarchy in England, they were men who would just as certainly have attacked a republican government had that been the political framework within which they lived. What they wanted was power. They would spare nothing to obtain it.[69]

This latter theme was not the brain child of Saumaise, for it was implicit in much of the English royalist propaganda, and

[66] Galland, "Les pasteurs français," *Bulletin—Société de l'histoire du Protestantisme français*, LXXVII (1928), 115–116. See also Peter du Moulin, *Regii sanguinis clamor ad coelum adversus parricidas Anglicanos* (The Hague, 1652), pp. 5, 106.

[67] French, *Life Records of John Milton*, III, 128.   [68] *Ibid.*, III, 344.

[69] Claude de Saumaise, *Apologie royale pour Charles I* (Paris, 1650), pp. 5–9, 25, 751–752.

it recurred in the correspondence addressed to Mazarin by French diplomats in England. However, Saumaise gave it sharper public expression than most. He also shrewdly adapted parts of *Eikon Basilike* to his treatise in order to create more sympathy for Charles I, just as one of his French correspondents suggested.[70] Admittedly, the *Defensio regia* reveals a certain haste of composition, contains some errors of fact regarding English institutions, and manifests difficulty in contriving arguments which might please everyone—failings which Milton pounced upon in his reply. But for all his biting comments, Milton did not destroy the usefulness of the *Defensio regia* as a propaganda piece for the English royalists in France.

After the shock of Charles's death began to subside, the quantity of pro-royalist literature in book and pamphlet form, centered uniquely on England, decreased. Yet news about the English Revolution still reached the French public in abundance. The *Gazette de France* continued to print regular bulletins about the British Isles with unflagging zeal. Furthermore, during the period of the Fronde, from 1649 to 1653, the *Gazette* maintained its practice of bringing out special editions featuring England. Renaudot published approximately thirty or more such special editions in each of these years. Gradually, he gave more space to naval battles in which the English participated and to diplomatic negotiations in which the English government was a party, but reports about the internal reorganization in England never lacked. The transition of England from monarchy, to commonwealth, and then to protectorate left the editor of the *Gazette* firm in his hostility to the revolutionary régime in England; but, as before, he continued to fill the pages of his special editions with documentary material emanating from all sides.

Clearly, then, Frenchmen had easy access to informative and

[70] Sarrau to Saumaise, July 11, 1649, *Marquardi Gudii et doctorum virorum*, p. 210.

interpretive accounts of the English Civil War and of the Revolution from both the republican and the royalist point of view. Yet the English royalists were much more successful in getting a favorable press in France and in evoking the sympathy of French writers. The variety of publications in France which favored the English royalists and the number of titles which pleaded their cause far outnumbered anything in support of the Puritans. The French press had made Charles I the tragic hero of the English Civil War.

IV

Propaganda Use
of the English Revolution

How pertinent to their own controversies did polemicists during the Fronde consider English experience? All sides valued public opinion. With a political balance so unstable, they had to— and all sides grasped at any weapons useful for their propaganda battles. The Frondeur Guy Joly attributed the general animosity against the Queen Regent in January, 1649, to the effective work of the pamphleteers.[1] From the opposing camp, Cardinal Mazarin bemoaned the "plague of libels" which beset the government. He confirmed their sting by hiring writers to counteract them.[2]

The propaganda war was waged primarily with pamphlets (the so-called Mazarinades), so often slighted in older studies of the Fronde. Admittedly, the Mazarinades usually lacked originality of thought and literary polish, but the reading public eagerly purchased them all the same. When emotions ran high, five or six new pamphlet titles a day were offered for sale. Well over 4,000 different pamphlets—perhaps as many as 11,000—

[1] "Mémoires de Guy Joly," *Nouvelle collection des mémoires,* XXIV, 19.
[2] Mazarin to Bishop of Dol, January 10, 1649, *Lettres du cardinal Mazarin,* ed. Chéruel, III, 255; Mazarin to Ondedei, August 18, 1651, *Oeuvres du cardinal de Retz,* V, 156.

competed for public attention. "Like a wave of grasshoppers," so one contemporary unflatteringly described them, the controversial publications swept over the country. The most popular appeared in quantities of five or six thousand; those of more moderate success were held to a tenth of that; others never reached the printer at all but passed from hand to hand in manuscript. Books, of course, supplemented the pamphlet literature.[3]

An almost complete lack of inhibition characterized this literature. There was no restraining the abusive invective which writers leveled against their opponents. Nor were writers timid in advancing ideas which did not accord with those of the prevailing authority. Only the writer's own ideas and his propaganda objectives imposed a limit. Amid the wild-swinging, often scurrilous, attacks, authors in more sober, reflective moods liked to appeal to history and to precedent to buttress their arguments. The Old Testament and the annals of Roman and French history were crammed with lessons and parallels upon which the erudite could draw, seemingly to any purpose. More recent history and contemporary events provided a similar fund of illustrative material; and perhaps for the general public, whose recollections of ancient and medieval lore had clouded since school days, the references to the immediate past projected a more vivid imagery for purposes of comparison.

Cardinal Mazarin's obsession with English parallels and a like concern by others close to the Queen Regent might lead one to suppose that the government made propaganda capital of the English Civil War. Strangely enough, this was not the case. Those persons in the Queen Regent's confidence deliberately skirted comparison, in public, of France and England, in striking contrast to their private habits.

---

[3] For a study of the Mazarinades and of the propaganda literature of the Fronde see Rolf Anger, *Die Flugschriftenpublizistik zur Zeit der Pariser Fronde, 1648–1652,* Dissertation (Münster, 1957), pp. 3–4, 218, 272.

One pamphleteer writing in support of the regency in 1649 did introduce the example of the Earl of Strafford when he considered the case for Cardinal Mazarin. In words seemingly taken almost verbatim from Mazarin's own notebook the author remarked that "by signing the death warrant of his favorite, [Charles I] did not foresee that he was composing thereby the warrant for his own death. Fortunately for us," the writer continued, "our great princess has demonstrated greater resolution. . . . The threats which intimidated Charles Stuart have utterly failed to shake the resolve of Anne of Austria." [4] But comparisons of this sort, offered by supporters of the court, were the rare exception.

Another author writing in behalf of the regency explained why, in fact, the Parlement of Paris ought *not* be equated with the rebellious Parliament of England. The author feared the common people might interpret the English Parliament's action as an excuse for similar behavior by the Parlement of Paris. In a manner reminiscent of Mazarin, the author concluded that, except in name, the two bodies differed completely. In England, the Parliament was composed of representatives of all three estates of the nation; in France, "parlement" signified an assembly of one part of the third estate. Therefore a French parlement could not pretend to the same measure of authority. The author proposed that if the Parlement of Paris persisted in opposing the crown, its very name ought to be changed to clarify beyond question its real function in the state. In that case the word "parlement" ought to bear a connotation as odious as that carried by the word "tyrant." [5]

Even the *Gazette de France,* which ordinarily printed so much English news, rarely ventured comparisons of the Fronde

[4] *Question: si la voix du peuple est la voix de Dieu* (n.p., 1649), pp. 16–17, Moreau No. 2951.

[5] "Bandeau levé de dessus les yeux des Parisiens" (Paris, 1649), in *Choix de Mazarinades,* I, 244–245.

with the English Civil War. The editor of the *Gazette* occasionally hazarded the opinion that "if one allowed oneself to be governed by reason and by experience, England should be an adequate teacher to instruct the whole world by her example: kings would never yield all their authority to the people; the people would never fail in the respect due to their sovereigns." [6] But such comments were rare.

Why was it that the friends of the Queen Regent let pass an opportunity to make damaging comparisons of the Frondeurs with the English revolutionaries? Particularly when they compared them in private? Mazarin indirectly suggested a reason in his denunciation to the Queen Regent of Retz, the Coadjutor of Paris. One of Retz's crimes, he said, consisted in his publicizing the English Revolution "in order to teach the method one should employ, and to instruct them [the people] by the example of England that revolution is easy." [7] The key word here is "example." Mazarin and Queen Anne feared the English example might insinuate its way into the thinking of the general population. This probably accounts for their public silence on Anglo-French parallels, for such comparisons might boomerang.

For one brief interval the court believed that the less said about England the better. The reporting of Charles I's execution in the *Gazette de France* suggests this. Renaudot, the *Gazette's* editor, had followed the French court to St. Germain at the beginning of the troubles in Paris in January, 1649. He remained at St. Germain until the Peace of Rueil. He was at the court, therefore, when news arrived of Charles's execution, just as the first phase of the Fronde had reached a violent peak. The following announcement, under a London dateline, contains the full report about Charles printed in the *Gazette* of February 27, 1649: "The King of Great Britain, having been brought here

---

[6] *Gazette de France* (1651), "Etat général des affaires . . . 1650," p. 5.
[7] Mazarin to Queen Regent, April 10, 1651, *Lettres du cardinal Mazarin à la reine*, p. 5.

three times to Windsor Castle, was the sixth of this month condemned by the Independents to have his head cut off; it was done the 9th following; of this barbarous act, I could only relate the circumstances with horror. After the execution, all the officers of the kingdom were changed." [8] So ends the account, all the *Gazette* chose to print about the most sensational news event of the century. For an entire month, the *Gazette* maintained a complete silence on the death of Charles. Not until March 27, 1649, as negotiations for peace between the French court and the Frondeurs neared fruition, did Renaudot offer his readers a laconic report of the disposition of the English king's body.[9] Only after that did English news reappear in the *Gazette* in the accustomed volume. Proof lacks, but suspicion is strong that the *Gazette* had withheld news from England on order from the court because it was uncertain how the excitable population in France might react. Renaudot published separately from the *Gazette* an account of the King's death, but this too he delayed until some weeks after the event.[10]

Perhaps Queen Anne and her followers hesitated to speak out in public about the English Revolution for another reason too. The Queen Regent had friends in the Parlement of Paris striving to moderate the passions of the extreme faction. She was herself exerting all her influence to win over those in Parlement whose loyalties wavered. Members of Parlement and of the other sovereign courts held a range of differing opinions on the present crisis, but they nonetheless retained a highly developed *esprit de corps*. The surest way to alienate the moderates and to play into the hands of the extremists was to tar the whole body of Parlement with the brush of revolution. This

[8] *Gazette de France,* No. 21, February 27, 1649, p. 135.

[9] *Ibid.,* No. 29, March 27, 1649, p. 183.

[10] *La déplorable mort de Charles Ier* (Saint-Germain-en-Laye, 1649), Moreau No. 1005.

is why Mazarin, with tongue in cheek, flatly rejected, in public, a charge made by the spokesman of the tax farmers in 1644 that the Parlement of Paris was emulating the English Parliament.[11]

The circumstances surrounding Cardinal Mazarin's first retreat into exile in 1651 reveal the delicacy necessary in alluding to England. Before his exile, the Queen Regent had three of the then most feared enemies of the government safely locked up at Le Havre: the Prince de Condé, his brother, the Prince de Conti, and their brother-in-law, the Duc de Longueville. For months the friends of the Princes had worked for their release from prison and at last toward the end of 1650 had made promising headway. They attracted a number of those who had been Frondeurs in 1649, including many from the Parlement of Paris, and including also the Coadjutor of Paris. They judged it imperative, however, to bring the Duc d'Orléans (Louis XIV's uncle) into the cabal so that the luster of his rank would encourage still others to join. The Duke expressed interest, but he was, as usual, indecisive, hesitant to commit himself until assured the plot could succeed. He had guessed wrong so many times in the past that one can excuse his vacillation. What the plotters needed, then, was something to galvanize opposition to Mazarin and, so, overcome the Duc d'Orléans's timidity. The Cardinal's preoccupation with the English Civil War gave them their chance.

Louis XIV, his mother, his uncle the Duc d'Orléans, Mazarin, and several other important figures in the government met together early in February, 1651. At that meeting, the Cardinal, though unaware of the precise nature of the intrigues formed against him, sensed something amiss. He delivered a strong

---

[11] *Journal d'Olivier Lefèvre d'Ormesson*, I, 214. Mazarin was later accused of having underhandedly spread La Rallière's statements throughout the city in order to defame the Parlement. See *Les quarante-cinq faits criminels* (n.p., 1650), p. 6, Moreau No. 2931.

speech to those present, naming those he suspected of mischief. Accounts of exactly what he said differ, but Retz, well placed to find out, has the most plausible tale.[12]

According to Retz, while he and the other conspirators labored in vain to stiffen the resolve of the Duc d'Orléans, "Happily for us, the person *against whom* we were acting [Mazarin] was still more imprudent than the person *for whom* we were acting [Duc d'Orléans] was weak." Mazarin, he learned, had spoken "of the Parlement, of Monsieur de Beaufort, and of me as the Lower House of London, of Fairfax, and of Cromwell . . . [and] . . . he frightened Monsieur." The Duc d'Orléans stomped out of the Queen's chamber in high dudgeon, vowing he would never put himself in the hands "of that madman and of that fury," referring thus to Mazarin and to the Queen Regent, who embroidered on Mazarin's remarks. When the Duchesse d'Orléans heard what happened, she recognized how Mazarin's words, if repeated and verified by the Duke, could crystallize opposition to the crown and bring the Duke into the conspiracy. As Retz commented, "She was right!"

The Duke hesitated for a while before he would allow the incident reported, but at last hatred of Mazarin overcame his indecision. He selected Retz to inform the Parlement of Paris. The Coadjutor, happy to oblige, admitted in his memoirs that he twisted Mazarin's words to enflame the Parlement. "I embellished it with every color. I can say without exaggeration that there was never greater heat any place in the world than in everyone's mind at that moment."

Indeed, Retz did not exaggerate. The Parlement of Paris went wild when told of Mazarin's remarks. In the midst of the uproar, President Le Coigneux shouted that Mazarin deserved the death penalty, as much for the disorders he had caused in the state, as for the insult he had done Parlement in comparing it to the

---

[12] Accounts of this incident occur in a great many of the memoirs of the time. For Retz's description, see *Oeuvres du cardinal de Retz*, III, 220–233.

Parliament of England. Some of the jurists wanted to summon the Cardinal to come that very hour and render an accounting. The most temperate expected nothing less than a remonstrance of Parlement to the Queen Regent, asking for the Cardinal's removal. As the Coadjutor summed it up, "You can imagine the distress of the Palais Royal at this thunderclap."

The Parlement of Paris had company in its rage. Any number of versions of Mazarin's speech went forth, whipping up resentment everywhere.[13] Some quoted the Cardinal as having also denounced the nobles for their hatred of the King, and as having called them Fairfaxes and Cromwells. The furor helped the nobles organize an assembly of their own which subsequently expressed a desire to join with the Parlement and with the clergy to obtain the release of the Princes and a redress of wrongs.[14] This was not the first time the Cardinal's enemies had accused him of making such comparisons with England, but never before had such an outcry resulted.

Too late, the Queen Regent tried to repair the damage. She issued a conciliatory statement through the Keeper of the Seals, denying any talk whatsoever of Fairfax or of Cromwell, and any comparisons of the Parlement of Paris with the Parliament of England. Queen Anne ordered her statement read before the Parlement and called upon the Duc d'Orléans to confirm the truth of her words. But the Duke haughtily kept silent and no one believed the Queen Regent's declaration.[15] Virtually within hours, the conspirators were in control, and Mazarin rushed off

---

[13] Examples of reaction to the incident can be found in: *L'âne rouge* (Paris, 1652), p. 9, Moreau No. 85; *Les articles des crimes capitaux* (Paris, 1652), p. 6, Moreau No. 418; *Observations véritables et désintéressées* (Paris, 1652), p. 127, Moreau No. 2574; *Le secret, ou les Véritables causes* (n.p., 1651), p. 44, Moreau No. 3634.

[14] *Journal de l'assemblée de la noblesse* (n.p., 1651), pp. 4–5, 53–54, Moreau No. 1750.

[15] *Journal de Jean Vallier*, ed. Henri Courteault and Pierre de Vaissière, Société de l'histoire de France (Paris, 1912), II, 275–276.

85

to Le Havre to liberate the Princes himself, hoping for some last-minute agreement. When that failed, he had no choice but to take the road for exile.

The violent anger with which the Frondeurs reacted to Mazarin's ill-timed remarks has considerable significance. Republican propaganda was not unknown to the Fronde. And in an earlier chapter we have discussed the apprehensions of the court that the Frondeurs wished to imitate the English republicans. However, these charges ought not be taken at face value. The danger of doing so is demonstrated by the case of Robert Mentet de Salmonet.

Mentet was the man referred to indirectly by Cardinal Mazarin when the Cardinal accused Retz of circulating histories of the English Civil War among the people. Mentet, a canon of Notre Dame of Paris and a person of Scots origin, was indeed Retz's protégé. He did write a history of the English Civil War and later a remonstrance to Charles II.[16] He was *persona non grata* to the English exiles.[17] But was Mazarin's charge well-founded? An examination of Mentet's works reveals his utter hostility to the English republicans and his great sympathy for Charles I. He had nothing politically contentious to say in his book. He had alienated the English royalists because of his thesis that Protestantism brought on the English Revolution. Mentet won high praise from the distinguished writer, Guez de Balzac, for his discussion of England, and Balzac was certainly no radical.[18] Neither was Guillaume Colletet, who honored him in an epigram for his history of the English Civil

[16] Mentet de Salmonet, *Histoire des troubles de la Grande-Bretagne,* with dedication to the Coadjutor; *Remontrance très-humble au sérénissime prince Charles II* (Paris, 1652), Moreau No. 3333.

[17] Nicholas to Earl of Norwich, March 3/13, 1650/1651, *The Nicholas Papers: Correspondence of Sir Edward Nicholas,* ed. George F. Warner, Camden Society, new ser., XL (London, 1886), 226.

[18] Balzac to Conrart, July 20, 1652, Moreau, *Bibliographie des Mazarinades,* III, 102.

War.[19] Mazarin, in condemning Retz for sponsorship of Mentet, ought by the same logic to have censured himself for allowing the *Gazette de France* to fill its pages with items from England.

Despite the Frondeurs' hatred for the government of Mazarin, they regarded the English Revolution with embarrassment. Even for those few writers at the most radical fringe of the Fronde, the English example called for diffident treatment. The author of the pamphlet which Moreau termed "the most audacious"[20] of the Fronde tried his hardest to make the English republicans appear more respectable to his fellow Frondeurs. Yet he was cautious in praising them outright, saying only that he dared not judge them because he could not know their secret motives.[21]

Certainly those in the public eye as leaders of the Fronde (outside Bordeaux) repudiated republican aspirations. As one Frondeur thoughtfully observed, the conflict of the Fronde did not bring into question the King or the monarchy, notwithstand-

[19] Guillaume Colletet, *Epigrammes du sieur Colletet* (Paris, 1653), p. 59. Conrart, a staunch monarchist who knew and admired Mentet de Salmonet, confirmed that his friend's book had acquired high reputation (Conrart to Rivet, July 30, 1649, *Valentin Conrart*, p. 522).

[20] Moreau, *Bibliographie des Mazarinades*, I, 149.

[21] *Avis à la reine d'Angleterre* (n.p., 1650), p. 6, Moreau No. 471. Mr. Porshnev has cited this and several other pamphlets (taken from what he terms the radical democratic wing of the Fronde) to support his assertion that there was growing feeling of sympathy for the English Revolution in France. Although Mr. Porshnev acknowledges that such examples are few, his discussion nevertheless exaggerates the significance of a few isolated cases. Mr. Porshnev also fails to note how gingerly these authors handled the subject of the English Revolution, considering it not a praiseworthy event but an unhappy consequence of, and warning against, royal tyranny; see Porshnev, "Otkliki frantsuzskogo obshchestvennogo mneniia na angliiskuiu burzhuaznuiu revoliutsiiu," *Srednie veka*, VIII (1956), 323–324. It might be added that one will search in vain through the literature of the Fronde for a statement such as Voltaire's "Ce qu'on reproche le plus en France aux Anglois, c'est le supplice de Charles Premier, qui fut traité par ses vainqueurs comme il les eût traité, s'il eût été heureux"; see François-Marie Arouet Voltaire, *Letters philosophiques* (Rouen, 1734), pp. 34–35.

ing the "odious comparisons" being made with the English Parliament. The Frondeurs quarreled only with the "evil conduct" of the regency government.[22] Indeed, wrote another, though accused of republicanism, actually the Frondeurs were the "true royalists." [23]

Frondeur propagandists endlessly repeated that Parlement derived its glory from the majesty of the King, that members of the Parlement, far from wishing the destruction of the monarchy, wanted to protect it. Their party numbered princes of the blood and members of the aristocracy who were so tightly bound to their sovereign and so sensitive to the cries of

---

[22] *Les généreux conseils d'un gentilhomme françois* (Paris, 1649), p. 11, Moreau No. 1485. Mademoiselle de Scudéry, a supporter of the Fronde of the Princes, showed her lack of revolutionary fervor by expressing hope that those in France who wished to do what Fairfax and Cromwell had done in England would not gain control; see Dorothy McDougall, *Madeleine de Scudéry* (London, 1938), p. 74. One writer who rejected the idea that Frenchmen might imitate the English explained that "this is entirely out of the question, not only because of the natural inclination which Frenchmen have to be governed by kings, but also because such has always been their custom, which has been turned into necessity." Had Frenchmen wished to form a republic, he added, they would have done so long before, since opportunity had never lacked; see *Remède aux malheurs de l'Etat de France* (Paris, 1649), pp. 15–16, Moreau No. 3270. It can be argued of course that in virtually all revolutions critics of the régime in power have made similar disclaimers and then subsequently embarked upon revolution. Yet it would be a mistake in my opinion to discount out of hand the sincerity of such statements at the time they were made or to insist that such criticism necessarily contained in itself a revolutionary intent. Much depends on individual surrounding circumstances and on the general climate of political opinion. I expect to complete soon a book treating at length the intellectual background which helped shape political outlook during the Fronde and will consider these problems there.

[23] *Le parallèle politique chrétien du Jansénisme* (n.p., 1651), p. 15, Moreau No. 2681. Frondeurs in the provinces showed the same sensitivity as the Parisians. Opponents of the Parlement of Aix were wont to insult members of the Parlement and their friends with taunts of "Fairfax, Englishman, or enemy of the King and of the state." One outraged friend of Parlement returned the insult with a slap; see Adolphe Crémieux, *Marseille et la royauté* (Paris, 1917), p. 247.

justice from the people that "it is impossible that the misfortune of the English should fall upon France." [24]

As the leading Frondeurs wrapped themselves in a mantle of respectability, how incongruous for them, men of noble rank, dignitaries of the Catholic Church, members of the Parlement of Paris steeped in their senatorial traditions, to be linked with the revolutionary Puritans of England. Thanks to the effectiveness of English royalist propaganda in France, the Puritans appeared in the public mind as enemies of society. Could *les honnêtes gens, les hommes de bien,* to use the expressions of the time, throw in their lot with the Frondeurs if they believed the Frondeurs nursed the same ideas as the fanatics across the Channel, reputedly levelers of society and destroyers of religion? An apologist for the Ormée at Bordeaux, the most radical movement to develop in the Fronde, indicated concern about the respectability of his party when he denied the Ormistes wished to do away with the King, the Princes, or the Parlement. Nothing could be more false, he wrote. Furthermore, he asserted, the assembly of the Ormée contained a goodly number of gentlemen, lawyers, officers, and bourgeois, in short, *gens de bien.*[25] His accuracy matters less than his intent. If the Frondeurs were to win, they needed all the men of position in French society they could attract—men who could contribute the military, political, and especially economic assistance required for the defeat of the court. To attract support from *les hommes de bien,* the Frondeurs knew they must preserve an aura of respectability.

Thinking ahead, the Frondeurs trembled at the effect distorted lessons gleaned from the English Civil War might have on the impressionable young Louis XIV. They heard with dismay how Cardinal Mazarin, to whom the Queen Regent had entrusted overall direction of the King's education, acquitted himself of

[24] *Raisonnement sur les affaires présentes* (Paris, 1649), p. 6, Moreau No. 2970.

[25] *Le courrier de la Guyenne* (Paris, 1652), pp. 4–8, Moreau No. 822.

the task. Two or three times a day the King had it dinned in his ear that Monsieur le Prince was a Cromwell, the Duc de Beaufort a Fairfax, the Parlement of Paris an imitator of the Parliament of England, and the city of Paris a Whitehall preparing a scaffold for the King. One of the reasons why the Frondeurs reacted so violently to Mazarin's speech in February, 1651, was that it confirmed that he was filling his pupil with invidious comparisons of France and England. The Frondeurs believed that, by dint of repetition, these lessons would forever prejudice the King. Later events proved how well founded this apprehension was.[26]

Precisely because the Frondeurs were so self-conscious about being compared with the English rebels, they felt compelled to refer often to England. Most of the Frondeurs labored hard to disassociate themselves from the English rebels, and to instruct the French public accordingly. Many defenders of the Frondeurs vied with one another in larding their pamphlets with contemptuous and horrified allusions to Fairfax and to Cromwell. "Parricide" and "butcher" were favorite epithets to hang round the necks of these two men, who epitomized the English revolutionary movement for Frenchmen.

Conversely, the Frondeurs outdid one another in displays of sympathy for Charles I, whose condemnation they termed a massacre inflicted by a barbarous people.[27] In the earlier years of the Fronde, before Charles II forfeited his popularity through

[26] *Mémoires de J. de Saulx de Tavannes,* ed. Célestin Moreau (Paris, 1858), p. 51; *L'aveuglement des Parisiens* (n.p., n.d), pp. 29–31, Moreau No. 467; *Le secret, ou les Véritables causes* (n.p., 1651), p. 41, Moreau No. 3634; *Très-humble remontrance des bons bourgeois de Paris* (Paris, 1652), p. 6, Moreau No. 3813. The importance attached to the King's education is described by John B. Wolf, "The Formation of a King," *French Historical Studies,* I (1958), 40–72. See also Georges Lacour-Gayet, *L'éducation politique de Louis XIV* (Paris, 1898).

[27] *Avertissements aux rois et aux princes* (Paris, 1649), p. 7, Moreau No. 453; "Décision de la question du temps" (Paris, 1649), in *Choix de Mazarinades,* I, 251–252.

partisanship for Queen Anne, the Frondeurs advertised deep compassion for the English royal family. The Paris Parlement had appointed a committee to offer its condolences to Henriette-Marie on February 22, 1649.[28] The action received wide publicity. Parlement also publicly voted a pension for Queen Henriette-Marie, which permitted the Frondeurs to contrast this generous and open gesture with that of Anne of Austria, who paid the English Queen a pension from *fonds comptans* (funds for which the government gave no accounting and which in past reigns had consisted mostly of expenses the government wished to conceal). Was Anne ashamed to acknowledge helping the English queen? the Frondeurs asked.[29] Frondeurs likewise shook their heads in scorn as they observed the opulence in which Mazarin's nieces lived, at a time when the Queen Regent allowed Henriette-Marie and her sons to languish in poverty.[30]

The Parlement of Paris and its friends were especially sensitive to discussion of England. The Frondeurs agreed with Cardinal Mazarin that the Parlement of Paris and the Parliament of England differed greatly. They even agreed with the Cardinal that the Estates-General in France corresponded more closely to the English Parliament (the Paris Parlement traditionally regarded the Estates-General with jealousy). But from that point on, the Frondeurs bounded off on tangents of their own to demonstrate the superiority, rather than the inferiority, of the Paris Parlement to the English Parliament.[31]

---

[28] *Journal d'Olivier Lefèvre d'Ormesson,* I, 681; *Journal de Jean Vallier,* I, 233 and note; *Le courrier françois* (Paris, 1649), No. 6, p. 7, Moreau No. 830.

[29] *L'histoire du temps* (n.p., 1649), p. 165, Moreau No. 1644; "Manuel du bon citoyen" (n.p., 1649), in *Choix de Mazarinades,* I, 453.

[30] *Les calomnies du cardinal Mazarin* (Paris, 1649), pp. 1–6, Moreau No. 618; *Le comète royal* (n.p., 1652), p. 19, Moreau No. 716; "La Mazarinade," in *Choix de Mazarinades,* II, 248.

[31] *Les calomnies du cardinal Mazarin,* pp. 1–6, Moreau No. 618. Even an advocate for an Estates-General, though remarking that such a body

Writers praised the Paris Parlement as a disinterested arbiter of the state. They pictured it impervious to the temptations of demagoguery and incapable of irresponsibility to the crown, yet always ready to protect the people. The structure of the Parlement made this possible, they said. It was largely composed of men who had purchased their seats at great expense. Each man's investment served to impose upon him responsible behavior. If guilty of improper conduct, he knew that he might be stripped of his privileges, forfeit his investment, and so incur serious loss for himself and his heirs. England's Parliament, on the other hand, relied on an elective procedure, a method which allowed members to return home after a session, where they could not be easily punished for irresponsible acts.[32] The English institution encouraged radical, unconsidered acts. This argument of the Frondeurs sounds strangely out of tune with modern democratic attitudes, but one must bear in mind how deeply rooted was the principle of venality of office in seventeenth-century French society. Everyone of the least consequence had a stake in a purchased government office, either for himself or for someone in the family. Venality of office seemed to most people an eminently desirable practice.

The Frondeurs argued further that the Parlement of Paris enjoyed another advantage because its members came almost entirely from the ranks of *gens de justice*. These were men who spent their lives weighing evidence and examining objectively disputes brought before them. Because of their legal training, they were much better equipped for their task than their counterparts in the English Parliament. In England, Parliament recruited many of its members from the clergy and from the

---

was to France what Parliament had been to England, felt compelled to add, "I do not speak to you of that Parliament composed of the creatures of Cromwell" (*Les préparatifs de la descente du cardinal Mazarin* [Paris, 1652], p. 23, Moreau No. 2857).

[32] *Ibid.,* pp. 1–6.

nobility. These men might betray the people's interests in return for favors from the crown.[33]

The Frondeurs described the Parlement of Paris and the English Parliament as poles apart in basic outlook. The Paris Parlement loved and feared its King. It so respected the institution of monarchy, insisted one writer, that it could not condone the foundation of the Roman republic, let alone those republics which in more recent times had appeared in Switzerland, Holland, and England. Parlement repudiated any republican usurpation, regardless of the end result.[34]

The Frondeurs pronounced the fidelity to the King of Parlement and of the city of Paris all the more praiseworthy because of the contrasting material conditions in England and France. London had turned against its king at a time when the country was flourishing. Paris stoutly persevered in its loyalty to the King even though its inhabitants were starved and exhausted.[35] In contrast to the frightful outrages of the Puritans, Frenchmen had submitted themselves to be shorn and skinned by their government with patient endurance, unmoved by England's terrible example.[36]

The Frondeurs lashed out against Mazarin to prove to the public that the Cardinal, not they, was compromised by the English Civil War.[37] Writers had long indicted the Cardinal with an incredible array of misdeeds, running the gamut from sodomy to attempted assassination, and the public tended to believe the worst about him. Therefore, efforts to implicate Cardinal Mazarin in England's misfortunes were shrewdly con-

[33] *Ibid.* See also *Réponse au (Véritable) bandeau de Thémis* (Paris, 1649), p. 5, Moreau No. 3374.

[34] "Les souhaits de la France" (n.p., 1649), in *Choix de Mazarinades,* I, 86.

[35] *Les calomnies du cardinal Mazarin,* pp. 1–6, Moreau No. 618.

[36] "Décision de la question du temps," in *Choix de Mazarinades,* I, 251–252.

[37] *Exorcisme du D. Mazarin* (n.p., 1649), p. 8, Moreau No. 1331.

trived. To assign the blame for monarchy's demise in England to the Cardinal diverted attention from the Frondeurs and still further blackened Mazarin's reputation.

The attacks revealed considerable ingenuity. Rather than accuse the Cardinal of direct meddling in English affairs, some authors stressed the unfortunate example of tyrannous rule he had provided. Notwithstanding the material prosperity and the blessings of liberty enjoyed in England, the people there took fright at the example of French despotism and feared a similar despotism might come to their own land. Rather than risk it, the people of England established a republic.[38]

Other writers spoke of the effect on England of rebellion in France. Every Frondeur believed that the tyranny of Cardinal Mazarin had provoked the revolt in France. Unfortunately this rebellion, for which Mazarin bore full responsibility, encouraged the Puritans. At first the English rebels had stopped short of their final leap into revolution because the enormity and novelty of the crime troubled them. But when they saw revolt break out in France, they concluded it would likely parallel their own, and they proceeded with their horrible designs against the King of England. Mazarin had foreseen this and deliberately goaded Frenchmen into revolt so that he might accomplish the downfall of the English monarchy.[39]

Cardinal Mazarin's unpopular foreign policies furnished more grounds for criticism on the premise that they prevented the dispatch of French aid to Charles I. The Frondeurs had long accused the Cardinal of prolonging the war with Spain. That war obliged French soldiers to guard the frontiers instead of going to help Charles. The same policies of Mazarin which immobilized France also tied down the Spaniards.[40] The Cardinal,

---

[38] *Raisonnement sur les affaires présentes,* pp. 4–5, Moreau No. 2970.

[39] *La relation extraordinaire contenant le traité de Mazarin* (Paris, 1651), p. 6, Moreau No. 3167.

[40] *Le comète royal,* p. 18, Moreau No. 716.

they said, made doubly sure Spain could not assist the English royalists by stirring up Italy against the Spanish crown.[41]

Some of the Cardinal's detractors adopted a similar reasoning with regard to his domestic policies. Everything he did provoked turmoil inside France. The armies which Mazarin wickedly sent marching against Paris obviously could not be transported to England to chastise the rebels.[42] Furthermore, the Cardinal's greed caused him to divert into his own coffers funds which ought to have gone to Charles I.[43]

The Frondeurs damned the government of Cardinal Mazarin not only for incapacity to intervene in England but for positive unwillingness to help. The English rebels they said, had considered the attitude of France a crucial factor in their planning. Without assurance that they were safe from French reprisal, the Puritans would never have dared strike against the monarchy in England. The rebels had even unloosed on the Continent false reports of Charles's condemnation to test the response of France and the rest of Europe. To their great relief, the French government met the stories with complete indifference. The Puritans knew then that they could proceed in security with their revolution. The Frondeurs charged further that, when the rebels had truly killed their King, Cardinal Mazarin treated the incident as an "insignificant tale." [44]

Some writers traced the Cardinal's fine Italian hand inside England and denounced him for having fed the fires of civil war there.[45] They blamed him for supplying Charles I with ruinous advice. He counseled Charles to grant Parliament any-

---

[41] *Avertissements aux rois et aux princes*, p. 5, Moreau No. 453.

[42] *Ibid.*, p. 5; *Déclaration du duc Charles* (Paris, 1649), p. 7, Moreau No. 897.

[43] *Le comète royal*, p. 18, Moreau No. 716.

[44] *Sujet de la farce représentée par Mazarin* (Paris, 1649), p. 3, Moreau No. 3729.

[45] "Sommaire de la doctrine curieuse du cardinal Mazarin," in *Choix de Mazarinades*, I, 340.

thing it wanted and then to forget the promise as soon as Parliament ceased to sit. This counsel, the Frondeurs affirmed, had led to Charles's undoing.[46] Even the religious disquiet in England was attributed to Mazarin. His intrigues in England had placed all Catholics in England under suspicion. These suspicions gradually increased to include the English ruler. Nor was this all. Another writer recounted how the Cardinal obtained plans formulated by the Prince of Wales to aid his father and turned them over to a secret agent of Fairfax and Cromwell. This treacherous act allowed the Puritans to anticipate and frustrate the projects of the English royalists.[47] In seeming confirmation of the Cardinal's complicity, the Frondeurs explained that, when he sought a place of refuge for his exile in 1651, the Commonwealth had offered him asylum in appreciation of the services he had rendered the revolution in England.[48]

These various accusations needed some halfway plausible motives to give them credibility. However, people often heard of the Cardinal's worldly ambitions for his nieces and of his schemes to construct a network of marriage alliances with the great houses of Europe. They might easily believe the story of one Frondeur writer who said that the Cardinal had tried to marry one of his nieces to the Prince of Wales. Because the projected marriage had fallen through, a bitterly disappointed Mazarin decided to avenge himself by withholding French aid from the English royalists. Another writer explained that Mazarin had never forgotten the hospitality with which the English court had received French exiles from the régime of Cardinal Richelieu and from his own. Marie de Médicis, the Duc de Vendôme, Monsieur de Vieuville, the Duc d'Epernon, Madame

[46] *Factum pour messieurs les princes* (n.p., 1650), p. 31, Moreau No. 1367.

[47] *Avertissements aux rois et aux princes*, p. 5, Moreau No. 453.

[48] *Le déréglement de l'Etat* (n.p., 1651), p. 14, Moreau No. 1009; *La relation extraordinaire contenant le traité de Mazarin*, p. 6, Moreau No. 3167.

de Chevreuse, the President Le Coigneux, and others in disgrace in France, had found refuge in England. The English Civil War provided a convenient opportunity to pay off an old score.[49]

Other writers harked back to Mazarin's reputed avarice. They described how Fairfax and Cromwell had dangled a bribe before the Cardinal to so harass the French population as to cause a revolt and thus prevent any possibility of French interference in England. "Four millions" and a little persuasion were all it took, the Frondeurs said, for the English to win the Cardinal to their schemes. Still other writers proposed that the Cardinal had masterminded Charles's fall from the throne to show Frenchmen, by the disaster he had caused in England, what injury he might inflict upon the French monarchy if he chose. He would have the people understand that, unless they meekly submitted to his policies, he would destroy monarchy in France.[50]

In the welter of accusations, the Frondeurs implied that, had they been directing the state, they would never have permitted revolution in England.[51] Friends of the Parlement of Paris affected to reproach themselves for not having begun the Fronde sooner. If they had been more prompt, they might have thwarted the "sacrilegious designs of the English parricides that this troublemaker [Mazarin] favored." [52] The Duc de Beaufort, darling of the Paris fishwives, had wanted to help the English royalists, his apologist wrote. An offer to command the royal English army had come to him, but, alas! Cardinal Mazarin imprisoned him before he could place his military genius at the service of Charles I.[53]

Though too late to save Charles I, the Frondeurs insisted it

[49] *Apologie pour monseigneur le cardinal Mazarin* (Paris, 1649), pp. 12–13, Moreau No. 127.

[50] *Ibid.*, p. 14.

[51] *Le chevalier chrétien* (Paris, 1649), p. 15, Moreau No. 696.

[52] *Apologie de messieurs du parlement* (Paris, 1652), p. 38, Moreau No. 105.

[53] *Avertissements aux rois et aux princes*, p. 5, Moreau No. 453.

was not too late to avenge him and to restore monarchy in England. A number of writers trumpeted their desire to engage the English "parricides" in a war of revenge as soon as dissension in France abated.[54] Perhaps the Frondeurs hoped to divert the armies of the court to England to save themselves. Some pamphleteers called on the Queen Regent to abandon Cardinal Mazarin and to concentrate her fury, not on themselves, but on the rebels in England. The Prince de Condé, who served the Queen Regent in the early months of the Fronde, received a shower of admonitions to let Paris alone and to direct his attacks against the Puritans.[55] However, judging from the memoirs of the Fronde, if this was a carefully calculated strategy, no one afterward considered it important enough for mention. Rather, talk among the Frondeurs of restoring monarchy in England owed its existence to the same kind of emotional shock which struck the French and English courts. The reasons given by the Frondeurs for intervention in England are almost indistinguishable from those offered by the exiles and by persons at the French court.[56] The following examples reveal the Frondeur attitude.

As one writer put it, everyone must recognize that monarchies throughout the world were interdependent, like the stones of an arch. Remove one, and all the others would tumble after it. Revolution in one country imparted dangerous encouragement to dissident elements in neighboring kingdoms. The English Revolution posed a special peril, he added, because the English

[54] *Apparition merveilleuse de l'Ange gardien* (Paris, 1649), p. 6, Moreau No. 142; *Lettre de la reyne d'Angleterre à la reyne régente* (Paris, 1649), p. 7, Moreau No. 1943.

[55] *Les avis héroïques et importants* (Paris, 1649), pp. 10–12, Moreau No. 514; *Requête présentée à monseigneur le Prince* (Paris, 1649), p. 12, Moreau No. 3501.

[56] For a contrary view see Porshnev, "Otkliki frantsuzskogo obshchestvennogo mneniia na angliiskuiu burzhuaznuiu revoliutsiiu," *Srednie veka*, VIII, (1956), 334–338.

traveled everywhere. Their merchants and their seamen quickly learned the language of the peoples they visited. As carriers of republican contagion, they would spread it to every corner of the globe. No monarch was safe.[57]

The author went on to speak of the evil designs entertained by the Puritans against France in 1649, and he disclosed examples of their interference in the Fronde. He accused them of having hastened the trial of Charles I in order to lure Frenchmen into rebellion against their own rightful sovereign. He blamed them for having tried to subvert the Parisians with promises of men, ships, and money if they rose against their king. The author was pleased to say that Puritan overtures met with the revulsion they deserved from all sides, including the Parlement of Paris. Nevertheless, he continued, the Puritans had caused some Frenchmen to seize upon England's example to excite an already irritated French populace.[58]

Parliament in England, said some, had been the driving spirit behind the English expedition to rescue the Huguenots of La Rochelle. French Catholics were also advised of the harassment their brothers in religion suffered from the Puritans. The Puritans had thrown the Queen's altars to the ground, smashed the crucifixes, and driven the Catholic priests and friends of Henriette-Marie from the island. In contrast, Charles I, though an Anglican, had governed with tolerance. Surely, sanctity of religion cried out for retribution against a nation whose Puritan masters permitted Jews to purchase the cathedral of London, quartered troops in the churches, and persecuted Catholics and Protestants who differed from them with equal cruelty.[59]

The King of France ought to consider the affront done to him by the English rebels through their abominable treatment of his

---

[57] *Les intérêts et motifs* (Paris, 1649), pp. 3, 10, Moreau No. 1719.

[58] *Ibid.*, pp. 31–32.

[59] *L'accord passé entre les quatre empereurs* (Paris, 1649), pp. 5–6, Moreau No. 18; *L'ombre du roi d'Angleterre* (n.p., n.d.), pp. 4–5, Moreau No. 2597.

aunt and cousins in England. As a purely practical matter, the French king ought to remember his blood ties with the English royal family. One day a member of his own house might lay claim to the English throne. Of what value such a claim, however, if the republicans governed England?[60]

The French nobility received a reminder of its stake in the English Revolution. England had demonstrated that the noble class was unthinkable in a country without a king. One had only to inspect the army of Fairfax, composed of the scum of England, to realize what a mean and lowly role the Puritans had assigned the aristocracy. It was said, in fact, that the English revolutionaries had deliberated on exterminating the nobility. Some nobles had already fallen victim to Parliament along with Charles. The Marquess of Hamilton, the Earl of Holland, and Lord Capel were several who had met such a fate. Meanwhile the Puritans imprisoned ladies of high birth to snuff out the illustrious families of the country.[61]

Lest the third estate interpret the English Revolution favorably, they ought to understand that England proved how revolutions produce usurpers who surround themselves with suspicion and intrigue. The usurpers' insecurity obliges them to maintain armies in the field and to rule the country by brute force. Nor could the English Revolution be called a victory for Parliament. Fairfax had purged and packed that body until it contained only the dregs of the population, while Fairfax or Cromwell tried to seat themselves on Charles's throne. Frenchmen might expect a similar result if the Puritans succeeded in introducing a like revolution into the French kingdom.[62]

A lone dissenter to these appeals for action against the Eng-

---

[60] *Les intérêts et motifs,* pp. 7–8, Moreau No. 1719.

[61] *Ibid.,* pp. 9–10; *Almanach politique* (n.p., n.d.), p. 4, Moreau No. 62; *Lettre des milords d'Angleterre* (Paris, 1649), p. 7, Moreau No. 2074; *Réponse du nouveau roi d'Angleterre* (Paris, 1649), pp. 4–7, Moreau No. 3430.

[62] *Les intérêts et motifs,* p. 25, Moreau No. 1719.

lish republicans tried vainly to tell his fellow Frondeurs that by attacking the republicans they were playing into Mazarin's hands. They would be distracted from their struggle against the Cardinal, and they would be attacking a régime which had itself fought against royal tyranny and which might help them.[63] But this author was clearly out of step.

In expressing such forthright hostility to the English republicans, the Frondeurs still held some reservations about the causes of the Civil War. They agreed that Charles's execution was a great tragedy, but they balked at absolving the royal government in England of all blame. The Frondeurs who pled for greater moderation from the crown in France could scarcely embrace the idea that Charles's indulgence toward his subjects had precipitated the revolution. They could hardly applaud statements that the Puritan Revolution proved the crown must rule with such force as to render subjects incapable of revolt. Yet literature defending the English royalists advanced these arguments. The views of the English exiles, as well as those of Cardinal Mazarin and of the Queen Regent, were believed to accord with them.[64] A number of Frondeurs roundly denounced this interpretation of the English Civil War. Remarked Guy Joly, most could understand why the English had revolted. What they could not excuse were the excesses of the revolt.[65]

Some of the Frondeurs waved a warning finger at the English Civil War for Queen Anne's benefit. One author exclaimed that France was not alone in her fight for liberty, that Naples, Catalonia, and England had preceded her in a great movement

[63] *Avis à la reine d'Angleterre*, pp. 3–7, Moreau No. 471.
[64] *Les cautèles de la paix* (n.p., n.d.), p. 16, Moreau No. 659.
[65] "Mémoires de Guy Joly," *Nouvelle collection des mémoires*, XXIV, 7. The author of *Dialogue de Rome et de Paris au sujet de Mazarin* (n.p., 1649), p. 11, Moreau No. 1083, revealed a similar attitude when he wrote, "I have also learned of the disaster met with by the King of England and I very much blame those who have dared set hands on him, but I think that all those actions come only from a desire for liberty."

of liberation stirring the peoples of East and West.[66] Generally, though, the Frondeurs offered their warnings as counsels of moderation, which, if heeded, they said, could save the French monarchy. Indeed, wrote one apologist, only the timely barriers erected by the Parlement of Paris had thus far shielded France from the disorders and cruelties of the English Civil War.[67] Another author, who righteously disclaimed any revolutionary notions, said he feared that others, goaded by long suffering, might prove less steadfast in their loyalty. English revolutionary success, he suggested, might prompt ambitious persons in France to undertake similar violence and to perform acts they would not otherwise have dared.[68]

The same idea recurred in letters or speeches purporting to come from friends of the French monarchy (Henriette-Marie and Charles II were favorite names to attach to these fictitious pieces). They advised Queen Anne of Austria and Louis XIV how to avoid in France the holocaust of England. Other writers struck a religious note and explained the civil wars in England and France as God's punishment for sovereigns who violated the fundamental laws of the realm and despoiled their subjects of property, honor, and liberty. The Queen Regent might understand that there was yet time, however, to avoid ruin if she acted promptly and heeded English experience.[69]

---

[66] *Le TI ΘΕΙΟΝ de la maladie de l'Etat* (Paris, 1649), p. 9, Moreau No. 3775.

[67] *Réponse au (Véritable) bandeau de Thémis,* p. 5, Moreau No. 3374.

[68] *Aveuglement de la France* (n.p., n.d.), p. 17, Moreau No. 465; *La harangue des provinciaux* (Paris, 1649), p. 13, Moreau No. 1557; *Remontrance de Fairfax* (Paris, 1649), p. 7, Moreau No. 3301.

[69] Many writers invoked God's punishment as an explanation. For some of the many examples of this theory see: *Les avis héroïques et importants,* pp. 4–7, Moreau No. 514; *La conférence des députés de Son Altesse royale* (Paris, 1652), pp. 5–6, Moreau No. 741; *Discours d'un théologien* (Paris, 1649), p. 3, Moreau No. 1111; *La harangue du roi de la Grande-Bretagne* (Paris, 1652), p. 6, Moreau No. 1560; *L'heureuse captivité* (Paris, 1651), pp. 51–52, Moreau No. 1629; *Lettre de la reyne d'Angleterre,* p. 7, Moreau No. 1943; *Lettre d'un milord d'Angleterre* (Paris, [1649]), p. 4, Moreau

Sometimes these warnings were couched in brutally frank language. "Do you believe," wrote one author, ostensibly to Queen Anne, "that Frenchmen, being just as outraged [as the English], will show less resentment than those generous island- ers, and that a like cause will not produce like results? The People ask for revenge against the tax farmers and against Mazarin their protector; Heaven authorizes it; and I declare sadly to you that, if you do not act quickly, the people will take it upon themselves to act, and perhaps will bring about the ruin of those persons who have prevented such action thus far." [70]

Often these warnings carried the threat of revolution. Yet none of these authors, regardless of how outspoken his ideas about the rights of the people, urged the introduction of a re- public on the English model out of sheer admiration for it. Most of these writers probably felt a genuine concern, as they pretended, that Cardinal Mazarin might force a revolution on the country which would bring on a general catastrophe. Why doubt the sincerity of First President Mathieu Molé's anxiety for the monarchy, when, as head of the parlementary delegation to the Queen Regent after the August, 1648, riots, he told her: "We have heard voices along our route that we would not dare repeat to Your Majesty." [71] Only a handful of writers willingly

No. 1886; *Le politique chrétien de Saint-Germain à la reine* (Paris, 1649), p. 7, Moreau No. 2811; *Réponse de la reine d'Angleterre,* p. 6, Moreau No. 3395; *Lettre d'un gentilhomme à la reine* (Paris, 1649), p. 6, Moreau No. 1866. It is of interest to note that a pamphleteer for the court similarly recognized that the outbreak of revolts throughout the world could be explained as God's punishment when princes failed to observe the laws. But the author hastily added that this did not mean that God authorized subjects to judge their princes nor to treat them with insolence (*Question: si la voix du peuple est la voix de Dieu,* pp. 5–8, Moreau No. 2951).

[70] *L'esprit du feu roi Louis XIII* (Paris, 1652), pp. 18–19, Moreau No. 1287.

[71] Archives Nationales, U 336, f. 404v. The leaders of Parlement also warned Cardinal Mazarin, the Prince de Condé, and the Duc d'Orléans at an audience in early 1649 that the Fronde could produce the most serious consequences. Unless something was done to stop it, they said, some

accepted the eventuality of revolution on the English pattern in France as an alternative; and then, not because the English Revolution filled them with any enthusiasm, but because they were near despair and doubted the return of "fundamental law" under the monarchy.

The Frondeurs made it clear from their discussions of Charles I that they did not countenance regicide. They were less inhibited when speaking of Mazarin. They advised the Cardinal to reflect that if Charles I and other great men of history could meet tragic fates, certainly he was not invulnerable. If the English could kill their king, the French could surely defend themselves against the tyrant, Mazarin. An occasional Frondeur likened Mazarin to the Earl of Strafford, arguing that Strafford's villainy had caused revolution in England just as Mazarin was bringing revolution to France. The Queen Regent might ponder this example and heed the plaints of her subjects. Otherwise "she might find the crown on her head had fallen to her feet." However, this argument contained certain flaws. In the first place, it assumed a conception of the Earl of Strafford contrary to that which the friends of the English royalists had implanted in the public conscience. The French read of Strafford as a hero, in some respects second only to Charles I in the story of the Civil War. How then accept him suddenly as the villain of the piece? Furthermore everyone knew that Mazarin often compared himself with the Earl of Strafford. Thus, in a sense, the Frondeurs might lend backhanded support to the Cardinal's analogy.[72]

---

people "would follow the unfortunate example of England and would declare that all the royal authority resided in the Parlement." Mazarin affected not to be worried ("Mémoires de Omer Talon," *Nouvelle collection des mémoires*, XXVIII, 339–340).

[72] *La conférence de Mazarin avec la Fortune* (Paris, 1649), p. 14, Moreau No. 738; *La conférence des députés de Son Altesse royale*, pp. 5–6; Moreau No. 741; *Déclaration du duc Charles* (Paris, 1649), p. 8, Moreau No. 897; *Le philosophe et casuiste de ce temps* (Paris, 1649), p. 5, Moreau No. 2753.

Therefore some Frondeur writers preferred to accept the fact that Strafford had been a hapless victim of the Civil War and then show why Mazarin could *not* be compared to him. Strafford had embodied all the good qualities which so evidently lacked in Mazarin. Strafford had been innocent of wrongdoing; Mazarin was guilty. And though the English rebels had demanded Strafford's head, the Frondeurs allowed Cardinal Mazarin to leave France in safety, still in possession of all his riches.[73]

Other writers thought it more prudent to drop discussion of Strafford altogether. Perhaps they could find another "favorite" of Charles I, less popular in France than the Earl of Strafford, upon whom to load the onus of Charles's overthrow. Oddly enough, one of those picked was Fairfax. He had been a "favorite" of Charles, but had then betrayed his master and imprisoned him. Thus, Fairfax, an erstwhile favorite, had caused the tragedy in England. By analogy the Frondeurs could point to Mazarin, who they said had similarly betrayed Louis XIV and made the King his prisoner.[74] Since the Frondeurs often described Louis XIV as a prisoner of the Cardinal, the comparison had validity for them. In the final period of the Fronde, writers began to dwell on the "shameful attachment" of Henriette-Marie with Lord Jermyn. It was an attachment, they said, which stretched back through the years, and which Henriette had maintained despite the hostility of the English people toward Jermyn.[75] A writer need not spell out the parallel with Queen Anne of Austria and her "shameful attachment" with Mazarin, about which the Frondeurs so often complained.

Some of the Frondeurs, for all their aversion to the excesses of the English rebels, could not repress a certain grudging ad-

---

[73] "La vérité toute nue" (Paris, 1652), in *Choix de Mazarinades,* II, 420.

[74] *Avertissements aux rois et aux princes,* p. 7, Moreau No. 453; *La harangue du roi de la Grande-Bretagne,* p. 6, Moreau No. 1560; *Liste des empereurs et des rois* (Paris, 1649), Moreau No. 2311.

[75] *Le caducée d'état* (Paris, 1652), pp. 30–31, Moreau No. 617.

miration of their success. The Puritans had wrested control of the government from their king, even though they constituted a minority. It occurred to some of the Frondeurs that they might learn something here. They remarked that the Puritans paid their soldiery regularly and held them to a stern discipline. These were notoriously weak points in the management of the armies of the Fronde. They heard of the enthusiastic support which the middle class of London was said to have accorded the rebellion, and wished as much for France. The financial aid and willingness of the English middle class to serve in the militia had proved most important. Why could not the Parisians follow their example and raise 50,000 men for the armies of the Frondeurs? Why could not each citizen help provide for their maintenance? [76]

It is apparent that the Frondeurs differed in some of their interpretations of the English Civil War and the resulting revolution. Their inconsistencies were legion. Yet despite the worry of Cardinal Mazarin that England had become a shining beacon for republicanism in France, this was not the case. The execution of Charles I and the religious overtones to the English Revolution thoroughly discredited the Commonwealth. The English example aborted rather than stimulated the growth of republican sentiment among most Frondeurs.

The Frondeurs were not the only ones embarrassed by the Civil War in England. The Huguenots, whose peculiar position in the state kept them beyond the pale of ordinary groupings, also felt keenly the onrush of events in England. Some of the literature describing the origins of the Civil War in England had given prominent mention to the religious divisions within the British Isles. Even authors who considered the religious aims of the Independents and of the Presbyterians as so much

[76] *Raisonnement sur les affaires présentes*, pp. 4–6, Moreau No. 2970; *La réponse de messieurs les princes* (Paris, 1652), p. 17, Moreau No. 3400.

camouflage for their political ambitions, acknowledged that religious divisions had supplied the rebels with convenient pretexts. Mindful of the French religious wars, authors never lacked
who were eager to suggest a Huguenot parallel. Even some of
the English exiles distrusted the Huguenots and refused to at-
tend services in Huguenot churches. The Huguenots, they
thought, shared some of the basic tenets of the Presbyterians in
England, among them the belief that "subjects can take up arms
against their king, put him in prison, and even have him killed
by the hand of the executioner." [77]

These suspicions distressed the Huguenots. Moïse Amyraut,
distinguished theologian at Saumur, admitted in his *Apologie* of
1647 that "some persons have accused us of being enemies of
the crown . . . and object that the events now occurring in
England disclose sufficiently what of that is the essence of our
religion." [78] His colleague, Samuel Bochart, recounted the common anxiety of Huguenots that, after Charles's execution, "the
atrocity of this crime, committed by those whom most people
believe to be of the same religion as we, might draw upon our
churches a blame that time could never erase." [79]

The embarrassment was the more painful because many
prominent Huguenot churchmen had decided after the defeat at
La Rochelle to put their trust in the King. What choice had
they? The Edict of Alais, issued shortly after the defeat,
stripped them of their fortifications and of means for organizing
their defense. Unless the King protected what rights they still
retained under the edicts, they would stand defenseless against
Catholic repression. On the other hand, why expect the King

[77] Galland, "Les pasteurs français," *Bulletin—Société de l'histoire du
Protestantisme français*, LXXVII (1928), 114. W. J. Stankiewicz provides
general background on the Huguenot political position in the seventeenth
century in his *Politics and Religion in Seventeenth-Century France* (Berkeley, 1960). For the Fronde see especially pp. 136–147.

[78] Galland, "Les pasteurs français," *Bulletin—Société de l'histoire du
Protestantisme français*, LXXVII (1928), 112–113.

[79] *Ibid.*, p. 114.

to trouble himself with their protection? They must convince him that his own interest required it. They must demonstrate by word and act that the most loyal subjects in his kingdom were the Huguenots.

Huguenot leaders set a double task for themselves. They had to convince the King that he had nothing to fear from their party, and they had to insure that the rank and file did not defect from the loyalty they promised the King. That is why the Huguenots objected to some of the inferences being drawn from the Civil War in England, and why Huguenot leaders spoke out vigorously against the English Revolution.

A national synod held at Charenton in December, 1644, had set official guidelines for the Huguenot attitude toward England. The delegates, after noting reports of Independent infiltration of the maritime regions of France, enjoined all provinces to prevent the doctrines of the Independents from being absorbed into the Huguenot Church. The synod proclaimed that Huguenots must reject any doctrines from England tending to lessen their duty either to God or to the King of France.[80]

The stand of the national synod of 1644 encouraged Huguenot leaders to deny for themselves and for their coreligionists any guilt by association with the revolution in England. Moïse Amyraut had expressly published his *Apologie* of 1647 to absolve the Huguenots from charges of republicanism and of disloyalty to the crown. He emphatically condemned "the taking of arms against one's prince for whatever cause." The sea itself did not more separate the Huguenots from the revolutionaries in England than did the differences of language and sentiment, he said. No tie of secret intelligence or common outlook bound the Huguenots to the English. Unequivocally, Amyraut affirmed, [we] "blame the English for rising up against their sovereign." [81]

The execution of Charles I made it imperative to restate the

[80] *Ibid.*, p. 110. [81] *Ibid.*, pp. 112–113.

Huguenot attitude. Samuel Bochart claimed that the most cele-
brated Huguenot pastors in France gave voice, as one, to their
detestation of this act, and held it directly opposed to the word
of God. Pastors solemnly warned their flocks not to copy the
crime. Several of the pastors, including the fiery Philippe Vincent of La Rochelle and Héraut of Alençon, published denunci-
ations of the English Revolution.[82]

As mentioned earlier, all of the French translations of Charles
I's *Eikon Basilike* (excepting that of the Sieur de Marsys) were
the work of French Huguenots. Claude de Saumaise, though
a resident of Holland, retained close contacts with influential
members of the Huguenot community in France. Saumaise's
good friend, Peter du Moulin, whose *Regii sanguinis clamor* so
angered Milton, was another who, though living in Holland,
maintained important friendships with the French Huguenots.
As the son of one of the most respected Protestant theologians
in France, Pierre du Moulin, Peter's pro-royalist judgments of
England naturally received respectful attention in the Huguenot
party.[83]

The execution of Charles also prompted Moïse Amyraut to
return to a theme he had treated in his *Apologie* of 1647. His
Discours de la souveraineté des roys, published in 1650,
strengthened the arguments developed by Saumaise. Taking as
his text the Biblical passage "Touch not my anointed ones, do
my prophets no harm!" Amyraut condemned the Independents
for trying to prove they had acted according to God's command-
ments in killing their king. Did Amyraut fear some of his coreligionists might succumb to the example of England? Was
that why he chose to build his argument in religious terms which
would appeal to a Huguenot audience? Certainly he did reveal a
deep concern about the revolutionary doctrines spread in the

---

[82] *Ibid.*, pp. 114–115.
[83] Peter du Moulin, *Regii sanguinis clamor ad coelum adversus parricidas
Anglicanos* (The Hague, 1652).

"name of a great nation," authorized by the "august name of Parliament." The venom of these doctrines, Amyraut said, was infecting "so great a number of people that it is to be feared they may in time constitute a considerable sect." "Truly," he commented, "it has never been as necessary as now to give all kinds of persons a sharp and profound persuasion of the sovereign mastery of the King, since the Independents, not content with having made such a lamentable example of their own [king], seem to have openly declared war on all monarchs." [84]

As for the lesson of England's experience, Amyraut stated that the Civil War there proved that when two equal powers coexist in the state, i.e., king and parliament, inevitably the two will conflict. Just such a struggle, he wrote, produced first a civil war in England and afterward a revolution. Fortunately, France had no such problem. In France, the King had created the Parlement and the other sovereign courts; they derived their authority from him and were subordinate to him. No question of equality could trouble France as it had England. Amyraut conceded that difficulties might, and sometimes did, arise because of the absolute authority of the monarch. Kings might abuse their authority and oppress their subjects. But senates in aristocratic governments also had been known to abuse their powers; so had the people in democratic republics. A republican revolution, he argued, provided no guarantee against abuse of sovereign power. As for his fellow Huguenots, Amyraut praised them for believing obedience to their sovereign was a necessity of state and an essential tenet of the Christian religion. Huguenots would never fail their prince, Amyraut concluded. [85]

An occasional Huguenot pamphleteer sighed wistfully after

---

[84] Amyraut, *Discours de la souveraineté des roys,* pp. 3–7.

[85] *Ibid.,* pp. 143, 147, 182–183. It is of interest to note that the Cardinal de Retz conceded that the French monarchy was not limited by written laws like the English monarchy, but he emphasized the restraints imposed by tradition in France (*Oeuvres du cardinal de Retz,* I, 271–272).

England and the Puritan Revolution,[86] but the respected Huguenot leaders had taken their stand against the Revolution. Of all the lustrous names in the Huguenot community, only Philippe Vincent, pastor at La Rochelle, put limits on the obedience due a sovereign, and even he had publicly spoken out against the execution of Charles I.

[86] *Ambassade de la bonne paix générale* (n.p., n.d.), pp. 7–9, Moreau No. 68. Moreau believes this pamphlet to be the work of François Davenne, whose peculiar religious and political views can hardly be taken as representative of the Huguenot community in general. See Moreau, *Bibliographie des Mazarinades,* I, 35–43.

V

Coexistence with the
Commonwealth (1649-1650)

AN EARLIER chapter traced the mounting concern with which Cardinal Mazarin and others in the French government followed the revolutionary progress of the English Civil War and described how Mazarin's attitude toward domestic strife in France colored his interpretation of contemporary events in England. But there is another aspect of the impact of the English Revolution on France to consider: how the establishment of a republican government in England affected relations between the two neighboring states during the Fronde. How long, in other words, could or would France retain its policy of official neutrality (but unofficial partiality) toward the English royalists?

Boris Porshnev has suggested that, well before Charles I mounted the scaffold, fear of republican victory in England decided Cardinal Mazarin and his advisers to change French foreign policy. Indeed, Porshnev contends that alarm over the plight of Charles I became so keen after 1645 that the French government sought in panic to end the Thirty Years' War, at sacrifice to itself, to be free for intervention in England. In short, according to this theory, the approach of revolution in England accelerated the negotiations which led to the Peace of West-phalia in October, 1648.[1]

Unquestionably Charles's defeats caused the French government ever greater anxiety. The French advised their ambassador in England in 1646 to consider the "bad example which the subjects of other princes receive from the revolts of the English and the Scots against their king," and to remember that other princes ought not permit this "evil which could easily be imitated . . . from terminating successfully."[2] Then, as before, any number of powerful arguments supported the government's contention that a rebel victory was counter to French interests.[3] But does this mean that Cardinal Mazarin considered the fate of Charles I so vital to France that he would relinquish hard-won advantages in the Thirty Years' War to save him? If, as Mr. Porshnev affirms, Mazarin did reach this conclusion, then it must be taken into serious account in explaining the subsequent turn of Anglo-French relations.

The theory is as ingenious as it is tempting. But the evidence adduced in its support appears unconvincing. Anyone who has studied the background of the Peace of Westphalia and perused the diplomatic correspondence moving in and out of the French capital must appreciate how many different problems the Car-

[1] Porshnev, "Angliiskaia respublika, frantsuzskaia fronda i vestfalskii mir," *Srednie veka*, III (1951), 180–216. A résumé of the same argument is given in his chapter, "Angliĭskaia revoliutsiia i sovremennaia eĭ frantsiia," in *Angliiskaia burzhuaznaia revoliutsiia XVII veka*, II, 71–80.

[2] *Recueil des instructions données aux ambassadeurs, XXIV, Angleterre,* I, 16.

[3] Reasons why the French government hoped not to see a republic in England included the following: a republic would likely be hostile to the French monarchy; a republic would be more powerful, and hence more dangerous, than a monarchy in England; a republic might ally with Spain and with Holland against France; a republic would lead to suppression of Catholicism in Ireland; a republic would try to create internal disorders in France; a republic would provide a bad example to the French population; France must try to help the Queen of England and her children because of her ties to the French monarchy, etc.; see *ibid.*, I, 16–17, 33, 35–38.

dinal had to cope with at the same time. French interests were staggeringly complex, and the negotiations to end the Thirty Years' War reflect this. Furthermore, the general peace discussions, begun formally in 1644, proceeded with hostilities unabated. The changing tide of war kept talks in constant flux as the negotiators reviewed the latest battle reports. France had acquired a fairly good bargaining position by 1646, but this underwent serious erosion in 1647 and early 1648. The French campaign in Italy failed to go as well as hoped; the French missed an opportunity to exploit the Neapolitan revolt against Spain; important contingents of troops upon whom Turenne had depended for operations in the Netherlands refused to leave the Rhineland; Bavaria drifted out of neutrality and into support of the Emperor; French forces had to lift the siege of Lerida in Spain; and, most important, France's Dutch ally signed a separate peace with Spain in January, 1648, and thereby gave the Spaniards a considerable advantage in the war. It hardly seemed likely that Spain would be in a hurry to end the war with France, particularly when the Spaniards counted on domestic unrest in France to improve their chances still further.[4]

The internal crisis in France might prove a fatal weakness, and Mazarin privately admitted it. In June of 1648 the French had some misgivings that the Spaniards planned a landing in force at La Rochelle to capitalize on the discontent.[5] Meanwhile the French government's running quarrel with the sovereign courts of Paris in the spring and summer of 1648 had produced a stoppage of government credit which jeopardized all military operations. The military picture for France showed improvement later in the summer, but tension inside France remained high. Mazarin informed Servien, one of the French negotiators

[4] The complexity of the problems involved in the Peace of Westphalia has been well described by Fritz Dickmann, *Der Westfälische Frieden* (Münster, 1959).

[5] Mazarin to du Daugnon, June 14, 1648, *Lettres du cardinal Mazarin*, ed. Chéruel, III, 139–140.

at Münster, that internal pressures in France had built up so dangerously as to make an early peace imperative. Provided France secured its essential demands, this was not the time to scrutinize the other conditions of peace too closely, Mazarin wrote. It was not the foe outside which troubled him, the Cardinal emphasized, "it is the French themselves who make me apprehensive." [6] When the Prince de Condé scored a brilliant triumph against the Spaniards at Lens in August, 1648, the French were militarily able to march with greater threat on Spain's imperial ally. However, Mazarin failed to capitalize fully on that victory because its very celebration in Paris on August 26, 1648 (the occasion selected to arrest leading members of Parlement), touched off the most serious riots yet to confront the government and risked undoing everything Condé had accomplished on the field of battle. Therefore Mazarin prudently stuck to his original terms in dealing with the Emperor and used the victory at Lens chiefly to speed up the negotiations. As Mazarin saw it, the government needed peace with the Empire in order to discipline the sovereign courts. Besides, explained the Cardinal, the government was reluctant to increase its demands against the Emperor, because this would delay agreement. The Parisians, who insistently demanded peace, accused Mazarin, as it was, of prolonging the war. [7]

Enough reasons exist to explain French haste in the negotiations without any need to introduce England as a pertinent factor. Furthermore, what immediate benefit to England's king might one have expected from the Peace of Westphalia? The Queen Regent would still have Spain, considered the most powerful state in the world, as an enemy. And, as Mazarin attested in his correspondence and in his notebooks, the government was bracing for a bitter confrontation with its domestic

---

[6] Mazarin to Turenne, June 22, 1648, *ibid.*, III, 145–146; Mazarin to Servien, August 14, 1648, *ibid.*, III, 175.

[7] Mazarin to Servien, October 9, 1648, *ibid.*, III, 215.

foes. To have considered acting in Charles's behalf under these conditions would have been sheer folly.

In letters to the French ambassador in England, Mazarin frequently said that France would declare for Charles as soon as a general peace was concluded. The Cardinal even wrote to the ambassador in November, 1646, that "the principal motive of Their Majesties" in trying to arrange a general peace stemmed from consideration for the English king.[8] After the Peace of Westphalia Mazarin again expressed hope in November, 1648, that because of the Westphalian agreement and the prospect of general peace, the Puritans might abandon their revolutionary plans as they came to realize that France, Spain, and other princes would not permit the establishment of a republic in England.[9] But Mazarin intended statements like these to reach the ears of Charles I, and they must be evaluated in that light. The Cardinal obviously sought to cushion the disappointment caused by his many refusals to give Charles more aid. It cost him very little to talk grandly about what might happen in the event of a general peace. In remarks intended for other ears, the Cardinal just as earnestly denied any intention to intervene in England.[10]

It is true that the Cardinal mentioned several times in 1646 to French diplomats in Westphalia that the English problem was one of several reasons for terminating the war with Spain and the Empire.[11] But he wanted such statements used as window dressing to divert attention from the real reasons why France

---

[8] Mazarin to Bellièvre, November 12, 1646, *ibid.*, II, 336.

[9] Mazarin to Bellièvre, October 13, 1646, *ibid.*, II, 329; Mazarin to Bellièvre, December 10, 1646, *ibid.*, II, 339; Mazarin to Bellièvre, January 25, 1647, *ibid.*, II, 370; Mazarin to Grignon, November 3, 1648, *ibid.*, III, 225.

[10] Mazarin to Brasset, December 21, 1646, *ibid.*, II, 342.

[11] Mazarin to d'Avaux, March 10, 1646, *ibid.*, II, 293; Mazarin to d'Avaux, July 30, 1646, *ibid.*, II, 307; Mazarin to Bellièvre. November 12, 1646, *ibid.*, II, 336.

wanted an early peace.[12] Certainly the French government was profoundly unhappy with the state of affairs in England prior to the Fronde, but for domestic and foreign reasons France could not come to Charles's assistance. The French adopted a passive "wait-and-see" policy and did nothing.[13]

The French did perform a few last-minute token gestures in early 1649. Four days before the Parisians had themselves risen in revolt, the government published a proclamation in the name of Louis XIV, condemning the English Parliament and the Army for their attacks on their sovereign. The language of the proclamation was bold and stern. The King excoriated the Puritans as traitors to God and to the world, and forbade those responsible for the attacks to set foot in France. The King addressed a ringing appeal to neighboring states, asking them to reconcile their differences with France so that all might pool their forces to make common cause against the English rebels.[14] But the document was empty bluster.

Queen Henriette-Marie, in a frenzy to be at her husband's side, coaxed a promise from Mazarin that the French ambassador would deliver her request for a visa to the English Parliament. The Comte de Grignon obediently obeyed his instructions from Paris, but carefully refrained from adding any plea of his own for the visa. As the Parliament stubbornly refused to open the letters he brought, Henriette was thwarted.[15] Several weeks later, as Paris bristled with the soldiery of the Frondeurs, the distraught French government made one final exertion in Charles's behalf, and on February 2, 1649, ordered the Comte de Varennes to hasten to England with letters entreating Crom-

---

[12] Mazarin to Servien, August 14, 1648, *ibid.*, III, 177.

[13] Bigby, *Anglo-French Relations, 1641 to 1649*, pp. 142–155.

[14] Carte, *A Collection of Original Letters*, I, 195–197.

[15] Grignon to Brienne and Mazarin, January 14, 1649, P.R.O. transcript, 31/3/89, copied from B.N., MS. f.fr. 15997, f. 763v; Contarini to Doge and Senate, February 19, 1649, *Calendar of State Papers . . . Venice*, ed. Allen B. Hinds, XXVIII (London, 1927), 86–87.

well and Fairfax to halt the deadly designs against their king. Even this *pro forma* mission was too late. Varennes had traveled no farther than Boulogne when he learned his journey was pointless—Charles was dead! [16]

Meanwhile, in London, the Comte de Grignon had watched in numbed horror as the grisly preparations went forward for the execution of the King. Grignon endured the further torment of having to act alone, completely cut off from the counsel of his superiors. On February 4, 1649, he complained to Mazarin and to Brienne that he had had no communication from them over the past month, just when he most desperately needed instructions. He did not know then, though he would be told later, that the outbreak of the Fronde claimed the undivided attention of the government. The fact remained, however, that Grignon had to make his own decisions on what to do about the imminent execution of Charles. Since he believed Charles was beyond help, he decided he had best do nothing. How hard it was, he commented later, to contain his chagrin and to keep silent while envoys from Holland came forward to plead for the life of Charles I. Nevertheless, he felt certain his inaction best served France.[17]

After the French government weathered the hectic first days of the Fronde, communication with Grignon resumed. The day before Charles knelt on the scaffold at Whitehall, the French ambassador received at last a letter from his superiors.[18] The Fronde had settled down into an apparent stalemate, which at least permitted French officials to give some attention to England. But when the first shock of what had happened in England subsided, both Grignon in London and his government in

[16] Bigby, *Anglo-French Relations, 1641 to 1649*, p. 150.
[17] Grignon to Brienne and Mazarin, February 4, 1649; February 8, 1649, P.R.O. transcript, 31/3/89, copied from B.N., MS. f.fr. 15997, ff. 792, 803v.
[18] Grignon to Brienne and Mazarin, February 8, 1649, *ibid.*, 31/3/89, copied from B.N., MS. f.fr. 15997.

France came to a common agreement that the establishment of a republic in England need cause no basic realignment of policy. Yes, the English royalists had suffered a grievous blow, but their position was not altogether hopeless. Grignon believed that, if the Scots held firm and if Ireland united behind the new King, there was still some hope for the future.[19]

Other considerations militated against a change of policy. Queen Anne and Cardinal Mazarin risked losing the few friends they still had in France if they suddenly threw over the English royalists. With some of the Frondeurs loudly calling for an expedition to restore monarchy in England, the Frondeur press would have had a field day if the government abandoned the English royalists. Furthermore, the Queen Regent might seem to condone regicide and revolution at a most awkward moment. For many compelling reasons, then, the government could not forsake the English royalists; but neither did the government wish to provoke the Independents in England, now stronger than ever, while France had to confront civil war at home. The dilemma which had plagued the French in their relations with England since the start of the English Civil War remained as perplexing as before.

Gradually the continuity of French policy toward England became clearer. A delegation of notables, which the Queen Regent sent into Paris, presented official condolences to Queen Henriette-Marie; the government accorded recognition to Charles II, then in Holland; and statements, soon widely broadcast, gave assurance France would not recognize the English republic nor accept its ambassador.[20] In May of 1649, the French ambassador in London was, after some hesitation, called home. There remained only his secretary, Monsieur de Croullé,

[19] Grignon to Brienne and Mazarin, February 25, 1649, *ibid.*, 31/3/89, copied from B.N., MS. f.fr. 15997, f. 837v.

[20] *Mémoires de Nicolas Goulas,* III, 74; Grignon to Brienne and Mazarin, March 18, 1649, P.R.O. transcript, 31/3/89, copied from B.N., MS. f.fr. 15997, f. 890.

to represent France in England. Croullé had only the vaguest unofficial status, but the French hoped his residence in London might permit *de facto* relations to continue with the Commonwealth while avoiding a formal recognition of the new régime.[21]

People in England saw through the waiting game played by the French. Many believed France ought to be made to reveal its true intentions toward the Commonwealth. If the French had committed their support to the English royalists, it were better to find out at once rather than at a moment of French choosing. Not everyone in England agreed; but certainly everyone regarded the French with suspicion. Despite the minimal activity of the Comte de Grignon during the trial of Charles I, the Puritans resented what little he had done. The French government's recognition of Charles II increased the distrust.[22] English newspapers reminded their readers of the cordial manner in which the French court received and entertained the English exiles. René Augier, the Parliamentary agent in Paris, regularly sent home reports from France, filled, as the French government thought, with "quantities of the most infamous and most pernicious lies." [23] Augier could hardly have assumed a contrary attitude, for, as one foreign observer in Paris remarked, the French spoke constantly about Charles's death with such a passion "that if God grants peace one day, as is so ardently desired, it seems likely that they would in a moment divert all their forces for the destruction of that barbarous people." [24]

[21] Grignon to Brienne and Mazarin, April 15, 1649; May 4, 1649, P.R.O. transcript, 31/3/89, copied from B.N., MS. f.fr. 15997, ff. 940, 952v.

[22] Grignon to Brienne and Mazarin, February 25, 1649, *ibid.*, 31/3/89, copied from B.N., MS. f.fr. 15997, f. 837v; Croullé to Mazarin, June 7, 1649, *ibid.*, 31/3/89, copied from A.E. Angleterre, LIX, ff. 223–236.

[23] Croullé to Mazarin, August 19, 1649, *ibid.*, 31/3/89, copied from A.E. Angleterre, LIX, ff. 251–254.

[24] Morosini to Doge and Senate, June 8, 1649, *Calendar of State Papers . . . Venice*, XXVIII, 103–104. Feeling was so aroused in France that sometimes the English royalists were liable to attack because, as Englishmen, they shared the stigma of being from a country of "regicides." See the letter of John Foss at Nantes written to Sir Ralph Verney at Blois

The friends of Charles II in France contributed to this talk and "with more zeal than discretion" loudly bawled their predictions of French aid for Charles II. So many reports of French sympathy for the royalists arrived in England that Croullé found it pointless to deny to Commonwealth officials that France would have preferred a royalist victory.[25]

The French were not the only ones nervously eyeing the new régime in England. None of England's Continental neighbors displayed enthusiasm to recognize the "Puritan regicides." Almost a year elapsed before Spain cautiously permitted its ambassador, Cardeñas, to present his credentials—and Spain was the first state to take that limited step toward recognition. But though the English republicans bitterly resented the diffidence with which all European governments treated them, they reserved their greatest anger for the French.

Ironically, some of the English republicans believed more strongly than their royalist foes that only French distractions prevented French intervention. Indeed, some of the Puritans feared that, distractions notwithstanding, France might still help Charles. That is why a shiver of alarm shot through England when Charles II left Holland to enter France in early 1649.[26] The more gullible swallowed all kinds of fanciful stories. According to a report of November, 1650, the French government planned to release the Prince de Condé from prison and to set him at the head of an invasion force aimed against England.[27] When that report proved totally false, the republican

---

in which he says, "Pray, Sir, write not in the superscription *anglois* for that nation is so much in hatred that he cannot pass the streets in safety." Cited in *Memoirs of the Verney Family during the Civil War*, ed. Frances P. Verney, II (London, 1892), 403.

[25] Croullé to Mazarin, September 19, 1650, P.R.O. transcript, 31/3/90, copied from A.E. Angleterre, LIX, ff. 443–449.

[26] Grignon to Brienne and Mazarin, April 26, 1649, *ibid.*, 31/3/89, copied from B.N., MS. f.fr. 15997, f. 949v.

[27] Croullé to Mazarin, November 7, 1650, *ibid.*, 31/3/90, copied from A.E. Angleterre, LIX, ff. 470–477.

press, none dismayed, publicized another imaginary French plan to land an army in the West of England.[28]

Probably persons of authority in England took these predictions of French invasion lightly. Even the press had to admit that France could not do England much harm. However, the stories suggest the prevailing suspicion of French motives. From France, Cardinal Mazarin tried his best to reassure the Puritans. His government wished nothing more than a cordial relationship with the Commonwealth. He categorically denied that France, once at peace, would rally behind Charles II. These reports, he said, were utterly without foundation, concocted by persons of little sense or else by persons of malicious intent.[29] Grignon (and, after his departure, Croullé) repeated these assurances in as many ears as they could reach, but English distrust was too deeply imbedded to be eliminated by a few gentle phrases. Too many signposts of French hostility stared the Puritans in the face.

They smarted from the strictures which the French government had clamped on English trade in France in the fall of 1648: the French forbade the entry of English woolens and silks.[30] The English had always fretted about the health of their cloth trade and even before the embargo worried that the French cloth industry was growing at the expense of their own.[31] Curiously, the Parlement of Paris had included the embargo among the demands which it thrust upon the Queen Regent in the riotous summer of 1648. The Queen Regent accepted the embargo along with the other demands on October 22, 1648. The embargo was designed to protect and to encourage

[28] *The Weekly Intelligencer,* No. 9, February 18/28–February 25/March 7, 1650/1651, p. 68.

[29] Mazarin to Croullé, May 28, 1649; September 18, 1649, P.R.O. transcript, 31/3/89, copied from A.E. Angleterre, LX, ff. 58, 145.

[30] *Articles proposées et arrestées en la chambre S. Louis par les deputez des quatre compagnies* (Paris, 1648), article No. 22.

[31] Historical Manuscripts Commission, *The Manuscripts of His Grace the Duke of Portland,* I (London, 1891), 405.

the French textile industry. It affected Normandy [32] and the Paris region in particular where fear of competition had a long history. In 1630 and 1632 riots had broken out in Rouen, sparked by workers in the cloth industry unemployed because of the importation of competing English cloth. An angry mob had pillaged an English ship in the port, and then vented its fury on merchants engaged in the cloth trade with England.[33] The competition from England had continued, and its dampening effect on the manufacture of French cloth was felt keenly. When the Parlement of Paris formulated its demand for an embargo against English cloth, it explained the injury French manufacturers of woolens and silks had received by reason of importations from Holland and England. These imports had reduced "an infinite number of the little people, who were employed in the manufacture of cloth, to beggary, or has obliged them to change their domicile to foreign countries, besides resulting in the transfer of immense sums." [34] In its search for friends, Parlement had good reason to be solicitous about the cloth industry.[35]

[32] "Mémoire des instructions nécessaires pour le Sr. Salomon" [before December 10, 1650], P.R.O. transcript, 31/3/90, copied from A.E. Angleterre, LX, ff. 446–447. The memoir indicates that Normandy would oppose repeal of the ban on English textiles.

[33] Porshnev, *Les soulèvements populaires en France de 1623 à 1648,* p. 265.

[34] B.N., MS. f.fr. 16423, f. 13. French merchants had long complained that the English would permit only manufactured goods to leave England but would accept none from France, to the prejudice of French workers and of French manufacturing; see Lafosse to Séguier, February 4, 1645, *Lettres et mémoires adressés au chancelier Séguier* (1633–1649), ed. Roland Mousnier, Publications de la Faculté des Lettres et Sciences Humaines de Paris, Série "Textes et Documents," VII (Paris, 1964), Fascicule 2, Part 2, 753. Mercantilists were becoming increasingly upset by the evils of foreign competition. For an excellent study of the problem as a whole see Lionel Rothkrug, *Opposition to Louis XIV: The Political and Social Origins of the French Enlightenment* (Princeton, 1965), especially pp. 182–187.

[35] Mme Cubells, "Le parlement de Paris pendant la Fronde," *Dix-septième siècle,* No. 35 (1957), 192.

The Queen Regent later disregarded most of the stipulations in the agreement of October, 1648, but she allowed the cloth embargo to stand. The act had not been aimed exclusively at the English, however. It included Dutch silks and woolens as well as lace from Flanders and needlework from Spain, Genoa, Rome, and Venice. It was pure and simple protectionist legislation. The Puritans, however, chose to read it as a measure intended for their punishment as republicans.

The embargo played havoc with English trade to France. French officials confiscated English cloth; English merchants found themselves isolated from French markets because their French factors refused to communicate with them for fear of prosecution. The English complained that the embargo violated a series of Anglo-French treaties extending back many years, which had guaranteed freedom of trade between the two countries. The Company of London merchants trading in France angrily petitioned Parliament for retaliation. The Company suggested that all French wines, wool, silk, and linen cloth be barred from entry into England and Ireland. Parliament balked at the request on linen, but accepted the other demands. In September, 1649, not quite a year after the French embargo had begun, Parliament formally prohibited the import of wines, manufactured woolens, and silks from France and posted severe penalties for transgressors.[36]

The English retaliation caught the French by surprise. Though Croullé had listened to grumbling in Parliament against the French embargo, he failed to gauge its seriousness. Rather belatedly, he endeavored to persuade members of Parliament that the French embargo was without political meaning. Croullé was plainly mystified at the uproar in England. The English, he wrote, had themselves blocked the importation of French woolen cloth, beaver, and various other products for protec-

[36] *Journals of the House of Commons from November 8, 1547 to December 31, 1800,* VI ([London], n.d.), 284–285.

tionist reasons even before the French embargo. Why, then, should they work themselves into such a passion when the French adopted similar measures? [37]

Preliminary estimates about the English embargo differed. The Venetian representative in London informed his government that if both England and France strictly enforced their embargoes, people in both countries would suffer.[38] The French crown, for its part, had trouble deciding what to do and considered revoking its embargo. Croullé advised against it, however, for he believed the economic implications of the English embargo signified less than the hostile spirit which underlay it. He expected the English to fall victim of their own embargo. "A prodigious number of families" in England subsisted from commerce with France, Croullé informed the Cardinal. The public treasury in England obtained £200,000 in duties on French wines alone. Croullé doubted that the English would enforce the embargo and deprive themselves of the lucrative profits in that trade, not to mention the pleasure of drinking French wines.

The French merchants in England had prepared a memorandum for Croullé, reviewing the situation as they saw it, and advocating a strong stand against England. Rather than meekly submit and repeal the French embargo in hope the English would follow suit, the merchants wanted a re-examination of the trading position of French merchants in England. They described the discrimination which the English practiced against them. The English imposed higher duties on French merchants in order to concentrate French trade in the hands of their own nationals. Before negotiating a suspension of the trade embargoes, discrimination ought to be discussed too. Since the

[37] Croullé to Mazarin, September 2, 1649; September 6, 1649, P.R.O. transcript 31/3/89, copied from A.E. Angleterre, LIX, ff. 262–271.

[38] Contarini to Doge and Senate, September 24, 1649, *Calendar of State Papers . . . Venice*, XXVIII, 118.

English had to have French wines, salt, and grain, the French merchants believed they had powerful leverage. When the English realized their dependence and made some concessions, then was the time to lift the French embargo.[39]

Croullé's confidence received a jolt a few weeks later. He reported wryly that the English jokingly remarked to him that "men get accustomed to everything, and that as they were getting along well without a king, they could also get along well without French wine." Nevertheless Croullé continued in his belief that the French embargo should remain in force, unless the English agreed to remove theirs at the same time. Otherwise the English would attribute the concession to weakness. Croullé's view prevailed, and in November, 1649, Mazarin told him the government had dropped its plan to revoke the embargo.[40]

The English Parliament had every intention of enforcing its own embargo. When the Ambassador of Holland applied in September, 1649, for special permission for Dutch ships to transport French wines into England, he learned no exceptions were admissible.[41] Not until 1651 did the Commonwealth relent ever so slightly. An illegal traffic shortly developed in which the Dutch, as intermediaries, concealed the origins of prohibited French products and brought them into England. Similarly, they loaded forbidden English cloth for delivery at French ports. This was a hazardous trade, especially the bringing of

[39] Croullé to Mazarin, September 2, 1649; September 6, 1649; October 18, 1649, P.R.O. transcript, 31/3/89, copied from A.E. Angleterre, LIX, ff. 262–271, 283–286. French merchants had been urging a re-examination of trade arrangements with England for some years. See Lafosse to Séguier, February 4, 1645, *Lettres et mémoires adressés au chancelier Séguier*, II, 753. Jean Eon had similarly complained about English discrimination in his *Le commerce honorable, ou considérations politiques* (Nantes, 1646), pp. 68–73.

[40] Croullé to Mazarin, October 4, 1649; October 25, 1649, P.R.O. transcript, 31/3/89, copied from A.E. Angleterre, LIX, ff. 285–288, 297–300.

[41] *Commons Journals*, VI, 297.

contraband into England, and the Puritans discovered and arrested at least some of those who tried it.[42]

Another irritant troubled Anglo-French understanding. The English republicans were incensed at the many kinds of harassment which their shippers and merchants received from the French, quite apart from the embargo. At almost the same time the French had invoked their embargo, the English Parliament debated what to do about the frequent seizures of English property in France. So persistent was the problem that Parliament passed an act calling for the voluntary contribution by English merchants trading in France of 5s. on every £100 value of merchandise and 6d. per tun of wine. Parliament proposed to create a fund from which to defray the expense of litigation in the French courts.[43]

Responsibility for the harassment is hard to establish in view of the long standing rivalry between the two countries. In 1645 (prior to the French capture of Dunkirk), French merchants complained that corsairs from Dunkirk were taking captured French ships into English ports for sale, unopposed by the English authorities. They complained further that ships of Parliament and of Charles I were seizing French vessels, trading with England, on the charge that they were carrying contraband to the other side. French merchants and shippers were angered at the behavior of both the royalists and the Parliament men in this period. But, since the English Parliament had a much larger number of ships at sea, the injury to French commerce was much greater from this quarter and hence aroused greater resentment in France.[44]

The French retaliated under various guises. Sometimes they confiscated Puritan ships and cargoes on pretext of debt, some-

[42] Croullé to Mazarin, January 2, 1651, P.R.O. transcript, 31/3/90, copied from A.E. Angleterre, LIX, ff. 502–503.

[43] *Commons Journals*, VI, 52.

[44] Lafosse to Séguier, February 4, 1645; July 9, 1645, *Lettres et mémoires adressés au chancelier Séguier*, II, 754, 760.

times because the ships were said to have contraband Spanish cargo aboard, sometimes simply in open reprisal for injuries inflicted on French shipping. Much of the activity at sea was performed by French vessels operating under English royalist commission.[45] Gradually the scope of the attacks at sea increased. In the summer of 1650 some twenty-five French ships joined Prince Rupert's squadron in battle against the Commonwealth fleet of Admiral Blake.[46] Prince Rupert subsequently led his English royalist raiders into the Mediterranean and used Marseille and Toulon as bases in which to provision his ships and to dispose of his prizes. The Puritan press, even the *Gazette de France,* reported this.[47]

These assaults on English trade and shipping caused real hurt. Commonwealth trade with the Levant suffered the greatest damage, because Commonwealth shipping was most vulnerable to attack in the Mediterranean. In March, 1649, the merchants of the Levant Company were already complaining of attacks by French warships. By the fall of 1650 they calculated their losses over the preceding eighteen to twenty-four months at seventeen ships and a thousand men, plus the huge financial loss of £550,000.[48] They believed further that the intrigues of the French consul at Constantinople, who sided with the English royalist representative there and who did all in his power to embarrass the Puritans,[49] were undermining their position in the

[45] Croullé to Mazarin, December 27, 1649, P.R.O. transcript, 31/3/89, copied from A.E. Angleterre, LIX, ff. 328–330. For incidents in the period before the Fronde see S. Elliot Hoskins, *Charles the Second in the Channel Islands* (London, 1854), II, *passim.*

[46] *Mercurius Pragmaticus,* May 21/31–May 28/June 7, 1650, sig. Hhh2v; *Portland Manuscripts,* I, 531–532; *Nouvelles ordinaires de Londres,* No. 4, August 1/11–8/18, 1650, p. 14; *ibid.,* No. 25, December 19/29–December 26/January 5, 1650/1651, p. 100.

[47] *Gazette de France,* No. 98, August 5, 1651, p. 789.

[48] Croullé to Mazarin, October 3, 1650, P.R.O. transcript, 31/3/90, copied from A.E. Angleterre, LIX, ff. 451–454.

[49] Basadonna to Doge and Senate, December 11, 1650, *Calendar of State Papers . . . Venice,* XXVIII, 163.

Near East. Though the English had established supremacy over the French in the Levant earlier in the century, the Puritans had misgivings about the future.

To the complaints registered by Augier in Paris, and by members of Parliament to Croullé in London, the French government drew from a bottomless well of excuses and promises. At first they told the English that any seizure of property was for legal cause and in strict accordance with regular judicial process.[50] As this explanation failed to cool tempers in England, Mazarin tacitly admitted some wrongs might have been committed, but that the government, to prevent their repetition, had renewed standing orders against illegal seizure of English ships and was directing reparation for damages. "It will be seen whether there is any artifice and dissimulation in our words," the Cardinal wrote.[51] A number of orders on record seemed to bear out the Cardinal. The French government had on July 10, 1643, ordered French ports opened equally to ships of both parties in the English rebellion but forbade either side to sell prizes. On May 27, 1647, the government had issued regulations to prevent "pirates" who hid behind commissions of Charles I from entering French ports. More orders had gone out to make good the losses inflicted on Parliamentary ships since 1643. In March, 1648, the government singled out several ships and some goods for return to their English owners.[52] But as late as September, 1649, no clear-cut prohibition existed to prevent French sailors from serving Charles II, nor any prohibition to prevent them from entering French ports.[53]

On September 7, 1649, the government did finally forbid

---

[50] Mazarin to Croullé, June 23, 1649, P.R.O. transcript, 31/3/89, copied from A.E. Angleterre, LX, f. 75.

[51] Mazarin to Croullé, November 15, 1649, *ibid.*, 31/3/89, copied from A.E. Angleterre, LIX, ff. 306–310.

[52] *Gazette de France,* No. 41, March 20, 1648, pp. 353–360.

[53] *Factum pour Messire Henry d'Anglure de Bourlemont* (n.p., n.d.) in B.N., MS. f.fr. 18592, ff. 346–355.

French subjects to accept commissions from foreign princes. However, months passed before this injunction became generally known. The ponderous judicial machinery moved slowly. An ordonnance embodying the provisions of the letters patent was not drafted until December 8, 1649, nor its existence advertised by the public crier at Paris until February 1, 1650. Only on March 8, 1650, did it receive appropriate publicity at Toulon.[54] The ordonnance had negligible effect, anyway, for want of enforcement. In the meantime the distraught Monsieur de Croullé tried to explain away the confiscations of English property by attributing them to the internal disorders in France. Certain individuals, he said, attacked the English, not only without the knowledge or permission of the King, but contrary to his wishes.[55]

Unquestionably the maritime disputes suffered from the confusion of authority and jurisdiction in France. Parlements claimed the right to issue letters of reprisal against the English without need of approval from the crown. Chancellor Séguier was warned as early as 1645 that such unconsidered acts by the Parlement of Rouen might cause the English to retaliate by more seizures of French property.[56] Several times the crown attempted to countermand orders of the Parlement of Rennes by which certain English mariners and merchants had been imprisoned, though with what result is unknown. In defiance of the King's Council, the Parlement of Paris sought to adjudicate seizures of English property. An English royalist admiralty court on the Isle of Jersey claimed the right to dispose of prizes brought to France by privateers acting under commission of Charles

---

[54] *Déclaration du roy portant reglement sur le fait de la navigation . . . extrait, greffe de l'admirauté de Toulon* [March 8, 1650] in B.N., MS. f.fr. 18592, ff. 32–37.

[55] Croullé to Mazarin, December 27, 1649, P.R.O. transcript, 31/3/89, copied from A.E. Angleterre, LIX, ff. 328–330.

[56] Lafosse to Séguier, July 9, 1645, *Lettres et mémoires adressés au chancelier Séguier,* II, 760.

II.[57] The total result was a legal tangle which made justice almost unobtainable for the Puritan merchant or shipper.

Cardinal Mazarin, less exposed to the hot blast of English wrath than Croullé in London, continued to deny well into 1650 that any French subjects preyed on English shipping under license of Charles II.[58] However, in May, 1650, the Cardinal at last admitted his error. Though rejecting any notion that the French government had profited from the attacks, he promised to stop them.[59] The unfortunate Croullé, whose thankless task it was to repeat the excuses of his government to irate officials of the Commonwealth and to London merchants, reached the end of his own patience. Wearily, he reminded the Cardinal and Secretary Brienne that until French attacks on English shipping ceased, or until some sort of restitution occurred, matters were sure to get worse.[60]

In the spring of 1649 Londoners muttered angrily about the need to furnish the merchants with letters of marque to recoup their losses. Croullé considered such talk bluff,[61] but in July of that year Parliament authorized the issuance of the letters. Parliament did not specifically name France, but none doubted that France was an intended target.[62] After learning the French had seized a particularly valuable ship, the "Apollo," the Puritans delivered an ultimatum in August. Unless they obtained

[57] B.N., MS. f.fr. 18592, ff. 346, 430, 434.

[58] Mazarin to Croullé, January 8, 1650, P.R.O. transcript, 31/3/90, copied from A.E. Angleterre, LX, f. 221.

[59] Mazarin to Croullé, April 6, 1650; May 16, 1650, *ibid.*, 31/3/90, copied from A.E. Angleterre, LX, ff. 266, 272–273.

[60] Croullé to Mazarin, December 29, 1649, *ibid.*, 31/3/89, copied from A.E. Angleterre, LIX, ff. 328–330. Also Croullé to Mazarin, May 16, 1650; June 7, 1650, *ibid.*, 31/3/90, copied from A.E. Angleterre, LIX, ff. 372–376, 385–387, 433–437.

[61] Croullé to Mazarin, June 7, 1649, *ibid.*, 31/3/89, copied from A.E. Angleterre, LIX, ff. 223–226.

[62] Croullé to Mazarin, July 12, 1649, *ibid.*, 31/3/89, copied from A.E. Angleterre, LIX, ff. 240–242.

satisfaction within forty days, letters of marque against French ships would follow. The French did nothing.[63] By December, 1649, the Commonwealth had distributed several letters of marque; by February, 1650, at least one English captain prowled the seas looking for French ships on the strength of such a letter.[64]

This was only the beginning. Four months later, English merchants and shippers pressed their government for protective naval vessels. They appreciated that letters of marque were of little real use to most of them.[65] Commonwealth Admiral Popham had his orders in April, 1650, to proceed against French shipping; [66] in September of that year, instructions to the English navy permitted attacks on French naval ships as well as merchantmen.[67] Systems of convoy came under study in 1650. By November, Parliament approved convoys for the Levant trade.[68] Croullé summed it up in September, 1650, when he admitted that he saw no difference between a war at sea and what the English were about.[69] Things looked much the same in France, where people talked excitedly of the "war" which English ships had declared on French shipping.[70]

[63] Morosini to Doge and Senate, August 10, 1649; September 14, 1649, *Calendar of State Papers . . . Venice*, XXVIII, 111, 117.

[64] Croullé to Mazarin, December 20, 1649, P.R.O. transcript, 31/3/89, copied from A.E. Angleterre, LIX, ff. 325–327; also Croullé to Mazarin, February 14, 1650, *ibid.*, 31/3/90, copied from A.E. Angleterre, LIX, ff. 346–349.

[65] Croullé to Mazarin, June 20, 1650, *ibid.*, 31/3/90, copied from A.E. Angleterre, LIX, ff. 394–397; *Commons Journals*, VI, 466.

[66] John Thurloe, *A Collection of the State Papers of John Thurloe* (London, 1742), I, 144.

[67] *Commons Journals*, VI, 466; *Portland Manuscripts*, II, 69.

[68] Senate to Contarini, February 5, 1650, *Calendar of State Papers . . . Venice*, XXVIII, 135; *Gazette de France*, No. 176, November 26, 1650, p. 1542.

[69] Croullé to Mazarin, September 19, 1650, P.R.O. transcript, 31/3/90, copied from A.E. Angleterre, LIX, ff. 443–446.

[70] J. Loret, *La muze historique, ou recueil des lettres en vers*, ed. J. Ravenel and Ed. de la Pelouze (Paris, 1857), I, 32.

The deteriorating relations with the Commonwealth aroused a deeper concern in France that Spain might entice the republic into full-scale war with France. For a long time the English capital had buzzed with rumors of an Anglo-Spanish entente in the offing. The Comte de Grignon, and later Monsieur de Croullé, faithfully reported them in their dispatches home. In February, 1649, Grignon wrote as if the slightest French affront to the Puritans might precipitate an Anglo-Spanish alliance.[71] Croullé speculated in the fall of 1649 that a secret league might already exist, that England only awaited the pacification of Ireland and Scotland to announce it.[72] Some normally well-informed persons said Spain had recognized the Commonwealth. Croullé conceded that signs of a *rapprochement* with Spain were unmistakable. Spain had accorded more favorable treatment to merchants from the Commonwealth. The Puritans allowed Spaniards in Catholic religious orders, residing with the Spanish ambassador in London, to practice their religion without interference. When in January, 1650, Croullé reported that the Spanish ambassador had formally presented his credentials on the sixth of that month, this gave added confirmation of Anglo-Spanish friendship in the making. At virtually the same moment, Commonwealth authorities ordered a raid on Croullé's house, ostensibly because he permitted Catholic religious services there, and threatened him with expulsion. The meaning seemed painfully clear.[73]

Thus far Cardinal Mazarin had remained reasonably unperturbed. Secret informants in Madrid described for him the indecision of the Spanish king's Council vis-á-vis the Commonwealth. The Spaniards, like the French, were stalling for time to see

[71] Grignon to Brienne and Mazarin, February 25, 1649, P.R.O. transcript, 31/3/89, copied from B.N., MS. f.fr. 15997, f. 837v.

[72] Croullé to Mazarin, September 20, 1649; September 27, 1649, *ibid.*, 31/3/89, copied from A.E. Angleterre, LIX, ff. 276–279, 280–284.

[73] Croullé to Mazarin, January 6, 1650, *ibid.*, 31/3/90, copied from A.E. Angleterre, LIX, ff. 331–332.

whether Charles II might establish himself in England.[74] Mazarin, meanwhile, tried to sow doubt about Spain in the minds of the Puritans. He directed Croullé to tell the English of the Spanish king's recently expressed wish to help Charles II. The King had said that Charles's cause was "the common cause of all kings." He promised to give Charles substantial aid if he could secure a peace with France.[75] But Mazarin's efforts to poison Anglo-Spanish relations were unsuccessful.

Rumor persisted of Anglo-Spanish designs against France. Dunkirk, the bastion on the Channel which the French had captured from the Spaniards in 1646, figured prominently in such talk. Croullé heard in the spring of 1650 that the Commonwealth was readying a fleet, loaded with troops, to sail in April to help the Spaniards retake Dunkirk. The fleet actually sailed for Lisbon, but Croullé's informants told him its original destination had indeed been Dunkirk. They said another naval force would leave later for Dunkirk.

Archduke Leopold, who commanded Spanish operations in the Low Countries, had actually promised Dunkirk to the English if they helped capture it, so Croullé heard. Croullé found it hard to believe, however, that the Spaniards would offer the English a chance to throttle shipping through the Channel. Toward the end of the year, rumor had it that the Commonwealth had definitely decided, once it dealt Scotland a final blow, to dispatch troops to the Continent to aid the Spaniards in Flanders.[76] These stories caused the Cardinal a twinge of

[74] The deliberations of the Spanish Council of State reveal the uncertanties in the minds of Spanish councilors about England. See Guizot, *History of Oliver Cromwell*, I, 377–382, 385–391, 404–406, 419–421, 424–426.

[75] Mazarin to Croullé, January 28, 1650, P.R.O. transcript, 31/3/90, copied from A.E. Angleterre, LX, ff. 230–231.

[76] Croullé to Mazarin, February 21, 1650; November 14, 1650; November 21, 1650, *ibid.*, 31/3/90, copied from A.E. Angleterre, LIX, ff. 350–355, 478–481, 482–484.

uneasiness, and he ordered Croullé to alert French commanders in Dunkirk and Calais of any forthcoming attack by the English or the Spanish.[77]

A greater potential danger was the possibility that England, like Spain, might lend the Frondeurs a hand. Just as the English republicans felt certain of the enmity of the French crown, so the Queen Regent's government sensed the hostility of the Puritans. Evidently the Puritans wanted to overturn monarchy everywhere. The Comte de Grignon recounted for his superiors in February, 1649, how those in the Puritan army, even the ministers in their pulpits, praised revolution and took pride in the example England had set for the rest of Europe.[78] Croullé confirmed that the ordinary talk in England was against monarchy, especially the French monarchy.[79]

Actually, the English had so many preoccupations in closing out their own monarchical régime in the early months of 1649 that they were slow to exploit the Fronde. According to the Spanish ambassador in London, Parliament had instructed its agent in Paris to offer the Frondeurs help from the English fleet and to promise them succor of other sorts in early 1649.[80] If such an offer was made, nothing came of it. Grignon reported on March 4, 1649, that Parliament was about to send an agent to France with letters to the Parlement of Paris as well as to the King of France.[81] From France, report had it that a republican agent from England had arrived but had been apprehended

[77] Mazarin to Croullé, November 29, 1650, *ibid.*, 31/3/90, copied from A.E. Angleterre, LX, f. 352.

[78] Grignon to Brienne and Mazarin, February 15, 1649, *ibid.*, 31/3/89, copied from B.N., MS. f.fr. 15997, f. 815.

[79] Croullé to Mazarin, September 26, 1650; November 7, 1650, *ibid.*, 31/3/90, copied from A.E. Angleterre, LIX, ff. 447–449, 470–477.

[80] Guizot, *History of Oliver Cromwell*, I, 379.

[81] Grignon to Brienne and Mazarin, March 5, 1649, P.R.O. transcript 31/3/89, copied from B.N., MS. f.fr. 15997, f. 856v.

by the crown and taken to St. Germain before he could communicate with the Paris Parlement.[82]

Some Frondeurs urged their chiefs at that time to seek foreign aid when they sensed victory was not in sight. However, massive opposition to that strategy developed within the Fronde. Some Frondeurs even boasted that they would *not* appeal for help from England or anywhere else.[83] When several of the Frondeur leaders in Paris attempted to wreck peace negotiations with the Queen Regent (leading to the Peace of Rueil in April, 1649) by holding out hope of foreign assistance, the majority of the Frondeurs refused to take them seriously. A person purporting to be a messenger from Holland with a packet for the Parlement was simply hooted at; the cry went up that it was all part of the "old game." Mathieu Molé, First President of the Paris Parlement, commented that "there will be one next from England and then another from Turkey." Parlement refused to accept the packet. Obviously, few then either wanted, or could welcome, help from the infamous "regicides." [84]

Some months later, when the English republicans had more time to devote to troubles in France, Bordeaux rather than Paris attracted them. Bordeaux had been the scene of uprisings against the fiscal demands of the crown, and the region remained in ferment even after the royal governor suppressed overt opposition. The tactless, authoritarian Duc d'Epernon, who governed Guyenne at the beginning of the Fronde, had alienated virtually all of Bordelais society. After Paris rebelled against the Queen Regent in 1649, Bordeaux staged a new revolt against its hated governor. The city continued in revolt for most of 1649 until finally Mazarin brought the city and the Duc d'Epernon together

[82] Patin to Spon, February 18, 1649, Guy Patin, *Lettres du temps de la Fronde,* ed. André Thérive, Collection des chefs d'œuvre méconnus (Paris, 1921), p. 70.

[83] "Décision de la question du temps," in *Choix de Mazarinades,* I, 250, 252.

[84] *Journal d'Olivier Lefèvre d'Ormesson,* I, 712.

in a peace which, like the Peace of Rueil at Paris, was more a truce.

Thus, from the outset, Bordeaux had a reputation for rebellion. From the English point of view, the city possessed additional interest because it served as the entrepôt of a region which for centuries had maintained close trade ties with England, principally through the wine trade. When the Commonwealth invoked its embargo on French wine in 1649, Englishmen assumed the Bordelais would suffer. The Puritans believed, for economic reasons, the Bordelais would pressure the French court for a revocation of the French embargo; or, failing that, the Bordelais might proceed to "a greater extremity" against their government. Either alternative looked promising in England.[85]

Bordeaux had yet another attraction for the Puritans. The city was located in an area populated by significant numbers of Huguenots and in close proximity to Protestant citadels like La Rochelle. All through the English Civil War reports had come to the French court from agents in Great Britain and from officers in Normandy that the Puritans were trying to excite the Huguenots to rebellion. Nothing important had occurred so far, but as early as 1646 the government in Paris speculated that with a Puritan triumph in England the Huguenots, "seeing themselves aided by such a great power, . . . would perhaps have considerable difficulty in containing themselves." [86] With

[85] Croullé to Mazarin, September 13, 1649, P.R.O. transcript, 31/3/89, copied from A.E. Angleterre, LIX, ff. 272–275.

[86] *Recueil des instructions données aux ambassadeurs, XXIV, Angleterre,* I, 37. Warren C. Scoville, in *The Persecution of Huguenots and French Economic Development, 1680–1720* (Berkeley, 1960), pp. 7–12, provides some interesting estimates of the size of the Huguenot population in various parts of France prior to the revocation of the Edict of Nantes. He indicates Guyenne, Saintonge, and the géneralité of Bordeaux probably had between 150,000 and 200,000 Huguenots. He estimates one fifth of the population around La Rochelle and Rochefort were Protestant. About 10 per cent of the population of Poitou was Huguenot. Upper and lower

the English Revolution now an accomplished fact, French agents in Britain believed that the Commonwealth would lean heavily on Huguenot support for a strike against France.

Just before leaving England, the Comte de Grignon advised his government to nip these projects in the bud. He thought he knew the way. French Huguenot ministers in London, he wrote, made no secret to him of their hostility to the republican doctrines disseminated in England. English soldiers had already closed one Huguenot church in London because the pastor dared voice his disapproval of republicanism. The French government ought to persuade the Huguenots in France to express similar condemnation of republicanism and of the crime committed against Charles I. Such declarations could block a *rapprochement* of the Puritans with the Huguenots.[87] What, if anything, the French government did about Grignon's suggestion is unknown. However, as previously noted, Huguenot leaders did publicly condemn the English Revolution.

Nevertheless, tongues continued to wag that the English republicans were up to mischief in Bordeaux, though solid proof lacked. The Venetian ambassador in Paris speculated in June, 1649, that attempts to squelch revolt in Bordeaux might provoke the city to appeal to England. Although he believed a few months later that the Bordelais had received an offer of help from England, he suspected they wanted mostly to frighten the Queen Regent with such talk.[88] From London, Croullé wrote to Mazarin and to Brienne that he suspected the

---

Normandy had between 60,000 and 100,000 Huguenots, with some estimates running as high as 200,000. The city of Bordeaux, whose population he estimates at about 30,000 to 40,000, had approximately 2,000 Huguenots.

[87] Grignon to Brienne and Mazarin, February 15, 1649, P.R.O. transcript, 31/3/89, copied from B.N., MS. f.fr. 15997, f. 815.

[88] Morosini to Doge and Senate, June 8, 1649; November 23, 1649, *Calendar of State Papers . . . Venice*, 103, 126; Contarini to Doge and Senate, September 24, 1649, *ibid.*, XXVIII, 118.

Commonwealth had received a request for aid from Bordeaux. Evidently the city had not sent a special envoy, but this meant nothing. Bordeaux merchants, both Huguenot and Catholic, were in England and could conduct the negotiations. The English might not be ready to assist the Bordelais openly, Croullé thought, but certainly they wished to foment disorder in France to prepare the way for a later invasion. Agitators, passing themselves off as Normans, had slipped into France from Jersey and Guernsey, he said, and were wooing the Huguenots with promises of aid. Croullé wondered if the ships collected by the Commonwealth to battle against those of Charles II might be diverted to Bordeaux. He heard that Cromwell's brother-in-law was assuring the Bordelais that England would not fail them. Croullé assumed Cromwell must be behind this anti-French activity.[89]

The French press published reports that Bordeaux looked to England for rescue.[90] The English royalist press told of promises by the Commonwealth to dispatch 10,000 cavalry and infantry to Bordeaux under command of General Skippon.[91]

What was the substance behind these rumors? Croullé admitted in more reflective moments that much of the talk about Cromwell's hostility toward France originated with persons who wanted to worsen French relations with the Commonwealth—i.e., the English royalists. He acknowledged that many of the opinions ascribed to Cromwell were so patently false that he did not bother to repeat them.[92] A French agent in Scotland had also

[89] Croullé to Mazarin, November 22, 1649, P.R.O. transcript, 31/3/89, copied from A.E. Angleterre, LIX, ff. 311–312; Croullé to Mazarin, November 29, 1649, *ibid.*, 31/3/89, copied from A.E. Angleterre, LIX, ff. 313–315; Croullé to Mazarin, December 6, 1649, *ibid.*, 31/3/89, copied from A.E. Angleterre, LIX, ff. 316–321; Croullé to Mazarin, December 27, 1649, *ibid.*, 31/3/89, copied from A.E. Angleterre, LIX, ff. 328–330.

[90] *Le courrier bourdelois* (Paris, 1649), Part I, p. 6, Moreau No. 811.

[91] *Mercurius Pragmaticus*, January 1/11–8/18, 1649/1650, sig. Nn4v.

[92] Croullé to Mazarin, October 25, 1649, P.R.O. transcript, 31/3/89, copied from A.E. Angleterre, LIX, ff. 297–300; Croullé to Mazarin,

written the Cardinal that reports Cromwell would essay an overthrow of the French monarchy came from disgruntled English royalists.[93] As for the Huguenots in the Bordeaux area, the Cardinal had a letter in October, 1649, telling him the Huguenots had been ready earlier to take up arms in support of the Parlement of Bordeaux but had heeded warnings to act prudently. Admittedly, the Maréchal de La Force, the most powerful Huguenot lord in the region, had displayed great curiosity about the Fronde in Guyenne, but curiosity by itself was not criminal, the Cardinal was reminded.[94]

Mazarin's information did not therefore cause him too much anxiety. When Croullé wrote in October, 1649, that Cromwell said he was coming to France as soon as he finished with Ireland,[95] the Cardinal replied with a confident, mocking air, "If, after the Irish expedition, Monsieur Cromwell comes to France, he will be well received here, since he is a person of merit; assuredly everyone will go to receive him wherever he disembarks; but I do not believe he is being advised to undertake such a journey soon." More bluntly, the Cardinal wrote in December, 1649, that he doubted the English republicans would proceed lightly against the French crown.[96]

Why, then, did he warn the Duc d'Epernon, Governor of

November 15, 1649, *ibid.*, 31/3/89, copied from A.E. Angleterre, LIX, ff. 306, 310.

[93] Graymond to Mazarin, November 3, 1649, *ibid.*, 31/3/89, copied from A.E. Angleterre, LX, ff. 178–181.

[94] Du Plessis-Praslin to Mazarin, October 27, 1649, *Archives historiques du département de la Gironde*, IV(Paris, 1863), 435. The Duc d'Epernon had written to Chancellor Séguier earlier in the year that he had assurances of loyalty from the Huguenot pastors and from other leading Huguenots. D'Epernon believed at that time that they would serve the King (d'Epernon to Séguier, February 6, 1649, *Lettres et mémoires adressés au chancelier Séguier*, II, 1,004).

[95] Croullé to Mazarin, October 18, 1649, P.R.O. transcript, 31/3/89, copied from A.E. Angleterre, LIX, ff. 293–295.

[96] Mazarin to Croullé, November 6, 1649; December 11, 1649, *ibid.*, 31/3/89, copied from A.E. Angleterre, LX, ff. 177, 201.

Guyenne, on December 19, 1649, that prospects of English aid might strengthen the Bordelais in their resistance? The Cardinal tells why in another letter the same day to another correspondent. He wished to frighten the unpopular governor and to make him more accommodating for peace. Actually no danger of English interference at Bordeaux existed, he remarked. The Cardinal dismissed further thought of English troublemaking at Bordeaux from his mind after the agreement concluded between the Bordelais and the Duc d'Epernon at the close of the year. He assured Croullé he need worry no more about the English.[97]

In the span of a few weeks, revolt overtook France again and Mazarin lost some of his complacency about England. The arrest of the Princes had sent their families and friends into the provinces to organize an attempt to liberate the Princes. The Vicomte de Turenne, the most renowned military commander in France, after Condé himself, joined the revolt and headed the Princes' army in the east of France. The Prince de Condé's wife and young son, along with the Duc de La Rochefoucauld and others, fled to the southwest and made for Bordeaux. They obtained admission into the city in May, 1650, and persuaded the municipal authorities, still unhappy with their governor, to join the uprising. Bordeaux became the principal center of revolt in the west of France.

With Bordeaux in revolt, the specter of England returned. The Duc d'Epernon commented nervously about suspicious Huguenot activity in the spring of 1650 and spoke of certain individuals who regretted the *douceur* of England's rule over Guyenne centuries before.[98] The Comte de Brienne expressed

---

[97] Mazarin to d'Epernon, December 19, 1649, *Lettres du cardinal Mazarin,* ed. Chéruel, III, 431, 437; Mazarin to Croullé, January 8, 1650, P.R.O. transcript, 31/3/90, copied from A.E. Angleterre, LX, f. 221.

[98] *Lettre de Monsieur le duc d'Epernon à un de messieurs du Parlement de Paris* (n. p., 1650), p. 5; d'Epernon to Mazarin, April 4, 1650; April

disquiet at the synods of Huguenots which met in 1650 in the upper Guyenne and the upper Languedoc region, contrary to the edicts.[99] Probably the government knew that the Princes' party was carefully testing the mood of the Huguenots in April. Lenet, the trusted agent of the Prince de Condé at Bordeaux, began later to negotiate with the Huguenot Maréchal de La Force and with other Protestants of the area. As early as May, 1650, friends of the Princes considered asking for aid from England or from Spain.[100] The city of Bordeaux communicated with the English Parliament in May.[101] From London, Croullé fretted again about the Puritan fleet stationed off Lisbon, still wondering if it might receive orders for action at Bordeaux.[102] Cardinal Mazarin probably knew of rumors circulating in the Spanish capital in July that the English fleet would definitely come to Bordeaux. According to some reports, ten Commonwealth ships had already sailed into the mouth of the Gironde.[103]

Mazarin believed Bordeaux had probably asked the English for help, but he felt confident that England's involvement with the Scots prevented them from acting. He recognized that the Bordelais population was exposed to radical political doctrines. He personally thought most of the inhabitants would welcome a republic; but he also believed that those acting for the Princes would prevent the population from embarking on too radical a

---

18, 1650; May 12, 1650; May 14, 1650; May 31, 1650, *Archives historiques du département de la Gironde*, III, 399, 413, 419–421, 440–443.

[99] "Mémoires du comte de Brienne," *Nouvelle collection des mémoires pour servir à l'histoire de France*, ed. Joseph F. Michaud (Paris, 1838), XXV, 126.

[100] "Mémoires de Pierre Lenet," *ibid.*, XXIV, 255.

[101] Mairet to Frondeurs of Burgundy, May 30, 1650, *Archives historiques du département de la Gironde*, XIII, 539.

[102] Croullé to Mazarin, July 4, 1650, P.R.O. transcript, 31/3/90, copied from A.E. Angleterre, LIX, ff. 404–407.

[103] Basadonna to Doge and Senate, July 27, 1650; August 30, 1650; September 7, 1650, *Calendar of State Papers . . . Venice*, XXVIII, 151, 154–155.

course. Radicalism in Bordeaux could harm the Princes as much as the crown, he reasoned.[104]

The Cardinal kept his fences mended with the Huguenots. Ignoring the illegal synods, the Cardinal allowed the Huguenots to send deputations to the King. He carefully rewarded locally prominent Huguenots with government posts at Bergerac, Nîmes, and Castres,[105] and tried to force the Duc d'Epernon into a more yielding attitude toward the Maréchal de La Force. Mazarin probably exaggerated his confidence in Huguenot loyalty for the benefit of Puritan consumption. Nevertheless there is a ring of sincerity to his statement to Croullé that the Huguenots "are not simply content in obeying exactly and serving in the armies, and their pastors in preaching obedience, but they have not mixed in the movements which trouble this state at any place or upon any occasion, although solicited to do so; also we treat them well and respect precisely what has been accorded to them by the edicts." [106] Croullé had already said much the same thing in London.[107]

The Cardinal assessed the situation correctly. Condé's lieutenant at Bordeaux, Pierre Lenet, discounted English intervention in the summer of 1650. He had reached much the same conclusion as Mazarin. England had too many other preoccupations to allow herself the luxury of intervention in France. Lenet took greater interest in seeing that merchant vessels from England and other states called at Bordeaux.[108]

Though some persons, like President Charon of the Bordeaux

---

[104] Mazarin to Le Tellier, July 16, 1650; August 25, 1650, *Lettres du cardinal Mazarin,* ed. Chéruel, III, 604, 735, 742.

[105] D'Epernon to Mazarin, May 12, 1650, *Archives historiques du département de la Gironde,* III, 417.

[106] Mazarin to Croullé, August 2, 1650, P.R.O. transcript, 31/3/90, copied from A.E. Angleterre, LX, f. 343.

[107] Croullé to Mazarin, July 18, 1650, *ibid.,* 31/3/90, copied from A.E. Angleterre, LIX, ff. 415–418.

[108] Mémoires de Pierre Lenet," *Nouvelle collection des mémoires,* XXIV, 308, 322, 335.

Parlement, hoped for a Huguenot coalition with the Princes, they were a minority.[109] A Huguenot synod of representatives from Saintonge, Angoumois, and Aunis held at Marans enjoined pastors to exhort all Huguenots to keep faith with the King.[110] Some of the rumors about Huguenot discontent were clearly false and deliberately planted. Croullé dismissed reports that the Huguenot Duc de Bouillon and his brother the Vicomte de Turenne had asked the Puritans for help.[111] Lenet's experience in bargaining with the Protestant Maréchal de La Force convinced him the Marshal and his friends wanted primarily to frighten the crown into purchasing their loyalty at a higher price.[112]

Many friends of the Princes, Lenet included, felt uneasy about seeking Huguenot support. As Catholics, they feared a political quarrel might balloon into a religious war if the Huguenots joined the revolt en masse. The Princes would lose in the long run, because Catholic clergy and Catholic *gens de bien* would drop out. Lenet described the dismay in Bordeaux at a rumor the Princess de Condé had visited the Huguenot Maréchal de La Force.[113]

The wavering revolt at Bordeaux reached another brief halt in October, 1650. But, as the Princes remained in prison, it was a foregone conclusion that their friends would renew the struggle. They pounced on every sign of discontent to fashion new plots in behalf of the Princes. This constant domestic tension

[109] *Ibid.*, XXIV, 303.

[110] Original Drafts or Copies of the Dispatches of Sir Richard Browne, British Museum, Additional MS. 12186, II, f. 163.

[111] Croullé to Mazarin, July 4, 1650, P.R.O. transcript, 31/3/90, copied from A.E. Angleterre, LIX, ff. 404–407.

[112] "Mémoires de Pierre Lenet," *Nouvelle collection des mémoires*, XXIV, 308.

[113] *Ibid.*, XXIV, 290, 308, 340, 403. Although the Archbishop of Bordeaux remained loyal to the crown, many of the clergy of Bordeaux were in the front ranks of the Fronde. See Louis Bertrand, *La vie de Messire Henry de Béthune, archevêque de Bordeaux*, I (Paris, 1902), 276–324.

within France became increasingly important in determining the Commonwealth attitude toward France. Thus far the Cardinal had assumed a rather detached view of English threats, but how much longer could he afford to do so?

He realized that Anglo-French relations followed a broader pattern than the day-to-day ups and downs might indicate. As long as France was united at home and as long as England confronted hostile armies in Ireland and Scotland, England was limited in what it could do.[114] Conversely, the nightmare of French diplomats and officials was a France torn by civil war, attacked by an England triumphant over Ireland and Scotland. So far none of these latter three conditions had existed simultaneously, but even partial fulfillment had a noticeable effect.[115] Toward the end of 1650 the tide seemed to be running in England's favor. The French domestic scene could blow up at any moment; Cromwell had already broken the back of Irish resistance in 1649; his victory at Dunbar over the Scots in September, 1650, though not decisive, suggested he held the upper hand there too.

Consequently the halt of the Bordeaux revolt in October, 1650, failed to stop rumors of English invasion. The reported timing of invasion remained vague. Some predicted it for the following spring, others for summer.[116] War talk was everywhere. Croullé reported it from London. Predictions of English invasion were publicly bruited in France.[117] Foreign diplomats

---

[114] Croullé to Mazarin, July 7, 1650; October 10, 1650; November 7, 1650, P.R.O. transcript, 31/3/90, copied from A.E. Angleterre, LIX, ff. 408–410, 455–457, 470–477.

[115] Croullé to Mazarin, September 6, 1649, *ibid.*, 31/3/89, copied from A.E. Angleterre, LIX, ff. 268–271. Also Croullé to Mazarin, January 17, 1650, *ibid.*, 31/3/90, copied from A.E. Angleterre, LIX, ff. 333–336.

[116] Croullé to Mazarin, September 12, 1650; September 19, 1650; November 7, 1650, *ibid.*, 31/3/90, copied from A.E. Angleterre, LIX, ff. 439–442, 443–446, 470–477.

[117] *Second avertissement à messieurs les prévost des marchands et échevins de Paris* (Paris, 1652), Part II, pp. 7–8, 11–13, Moreau No. 446.

expected it.[118] The Cardinal began now to repeat with real concern remarks attributed to Cromwell after the battle of Dunbar. Cromwell supposedly told his followers that once they had conquered the Scots they ought to address themselves to the conversion of all monarchies into republics.[119] Mazarin suggested to the Secretary of State for War that he procure additional troops in view of "the hostile intentions of the English." [120]

By the end of 1650 the French scrutinized their relations with the Commonwealth in fresh appraisal. A memorandum submitted to the Council of the Queen Regent described what had happened to French trade. The Fronde, coupled with hostility abroad, had, in the words of the memorandum, "completed our ruin by taking away the courage of the merchants." As long as France had confronted only Spain, the merchants had gotten along fairly well, the memorandum continued, but since the English had declared their sea war, the condition of the merchants had become desperate. France lacked naval forces to stand up to those of the Commonwealth; cessation of commerce reduced the revenue coming into the royal treasury; domestic troubles prevented the government from finding money to arm a fleet. "It is difficult to see how commerce can be re-established as long as this disorder continues and as long as we endure the reprisals which the English inflict upon us." [121]

The Frondeurs accused Mazarin of responsibility for the paralysis of trade. The Cardinal's greed to obtain "immense sums" from the capture of English and Dutch ships, they said, had provoked the English reprisals in the first place. The Frondeurs also flailed the Cardinal for his inadequacies in ob-

---

[118] Morosini to Doge and Senate, January 3, 1651, *Calendar of State Papers . . . Venice*, XXVIII, 166.

[119] Mazarin to Le Tellier, October 13, 1650, *Lettres du cardinal Mazarin*, ed. Chéruel, III, 865.

[120] Mazarin to Le Tellier, September 28, 1650, *ibid.*, III, 824.

[121] *Lettres, instructions et mémoires de Colbert*, ed. Pierre Clement, I (Paris, 1861), 487–488 and editor's note.

taining the return of French ships captured by England.[122] That the Frondeurs also blamed the Cardinal for his friendliness with the English republicans was one of those contradictions which evidently bothered no one.

The Venetian ambassador in Paris expressed astonishment that the French merchants failed to complain as a body to their government.[123] However, a pamphlet printed in 1650 provides a somewhat different impression.[124] The author said complaints over the sea war with England had arisen all over France and were presented to the court but failed to accomplish anything. Citizens of Bordeaux spoke to members of the government in 1649 about their losses to the English, the author said, but the officials simply advised them to arm themselves and seize English ships. "This is fine consolation for ruined persons who have lost their property and their credit and who are, besides, incapable of sending ships out to sea," the author commented sarcastically. Besides, he added, people who made their living from commerce considered privateering an alien business.

The author of this pamphlet blamed the French government for indifference to the cupidity of certain persons who abused the good intentions of the King and used his commissions to pillage friend and foe. He claimed that the King's own warships attacked French merchant vessels. The capture of English shipping simply drove the Commonwealth to step up their attacks against French merchant shipping. Like the official memorandum referred to previously, the author described in black terms the effects of the "war caused by us Frenchmen" against

[122] *Journal de la Lettre de (madame) la princesse douairière de Condé* (n.p., 1650), pp. 32–33, Moreau No. 1751; *Journal des délibérations* (n.p., 1650), pp. 7–8, Moreau No. 1759; *Lettre de madame la princesse douairière,* p. 29, Moreau No. 1954; *Les sentiments des François* (n.p., 1650), p. 4, Moreau No. 3653.

[123] Morosini to Doge and Senate, July 18, 1651, *Calendar of State Papers . . . Venice,* XXVIII, 193.

[124] *Plainte publique sur l'interruption du commerce* (Paris [1650]), Moreau No. 2784.

the English. The English embargo on wine he termed unbearable for Guyenne and the provinces watered by the Loire. The attacks on French shipping were bringing the kingdom to ruin. From Dunkirk to Bayonne, no French ships could leave port without danger of capture by the English. French shippers might have to stand by and watch the Dutch take over their commerce. And what was to become of the French colonies?

The author emphasized that the interruption of commerce was a problem which the whole nation shared with the shippers and the merchants. The King suffered loss of revenue from duties on merchandise entering and leaving the kingdom. The economic ruin of French maritime centers would depress the rest of the economy. The cumulative effect might cause sedition in the principal towns. The most important families in Paris and in the provinces would feel the economic collapse. If the maritime provinces believed themselves "abandoned to the violence of the English," they might in despair revolt, for which "there is always only too much disposition among the people."

What ought the government do to improve relations with England? Most important, this author said, the King must revoke all confiscations of English goods and restore them. Captains guilty of seizures ought to be punished. If these actions proved ineffective, then the government might use royal funds to reimburse the English, or cause the people to contribute. In short, this self-appointed spokesman for the merchants and the shippers urged conciliation.

Clearly, then, some people in and out of the French government believed it necessary to improve relations with the Commonwealth toward the end of 1650. But all of the issues at dispute required careful negotiation. Yet negotiation was blocked by the absolute refusal of the French government to bestow official recognition on the republican régime in England and by the equally adamant refusal of the Commonwealth to start talks before and until recognition. Neither Croullé in

London nor Augier in Paris could persuade either government to budge from its position. Without prospect of settlement, relations steadily worsened, and it seemed impossible to break out of the vicious circle.

For a brief time a face-saving device for negotiating the economic and maritime disputes brightened prospects. Perhaps the English and French merchants and shippers could settle their differences without directly involving their governments. The English merchants selected one Hugh Morel to represent them in Paris. Morel, a merchant himself, had spent much time in France, knew conditions there, and made important French contacts in late 1650. He sought out French merchants who had sustained losses from the Commonwealth to get their help for a settlement. He sounded out the Coadjutor of Paris, a man of great influence, but failed to obtain his support. However he gained access to the Duc de Vendôme, Admiral of France, a key man in any discussion of maritime disputes, and he obtained audiences with Cardinal Mazarin.[125]

The Council of State in England expressly forbade Morel to represent himself as an official agent of the Commonwealth but almost before he knew it, Morel was discussing affairs of state. He set a figure of twenty-two million crowns to the losses which England had sustained, to justify English reprisals. He thought in this way he could force France to recognize the Commonwealth.[126] Mazarin interpreted Morel's activity as indication the Commonwealth was ready to bargain without insisting on prior recognition. Consequently the Cardinal appointed Salomon de Virelade, of a Parlementary family of Bordeaux, to undertake a mission to England to conclude an agreement.[127]

[125] Original Drafts or Copies of the Dispatches of Sir Richard Browne, British Museum, Additional MS. 12186, III, ff. 194v, 198v, 201v.

[126] *Ibid.*, III, f. 198v.

[127] *Ibid.*, III, f. 201v. Mazarin was all the more prone to believe this as he had heard the English were sending a man to France on pretext of complaining of losses at sea but actually to discuss broader subjects

His appointee promptly arranged to call on merchants and members of the *bourgeoisie* in Paris, to assure them of Mazarin's concern for their prosperity. He also made himself accessible to Hugh Morel, who presented him with the complaints of the English merchant community.[128]

However, Salomon misunderstood Mazarin's intentions, just as Mazarin had misinterpreted the mission of Morel. Salomon bubbled over with grand sounding but chimerical projects for a total overhaul of Anglo-French relations. The long list of recommendations and questions which he forwarded to his government before he was due to leave shows the extent of his ambitions.[129] His rosy vision soon faded. Mazarin would not let him carry official accreditation. Yet without it, Salomon learned through a note from an official of the English government, England refused to receive him.[130] Croullé had warned that this might happen when he first heard of Salomon's mission.[131] Naturally, the mission had to be cancelled.

Hugh Morel's conversations also bogged down. The Duc de Vendôme contended that any ship carrying enemy goods (Spanish cargo, for example) was automatically subject to seizure along with the goods. Many English ships fell in this category. Morel doubted that the Council of the Queen Regent would overrule Vendôme.[132] To complete his sorrow, Morel received

(Mazarin to Le Tellier, October 13, 1650, *Lettres du cardinal Mazarin,* ed. Chéruel, III, 865).

[128] Salomon to Mazarin, December 19, 1650, *Archives historiques du département de la Gironde,* XIII, 507.

[129] *Ibid.,* XIII, 506–507: "Mémoires des instructions nécessaires pour le Sr. Salomon" [before December 10, 1650], P.R.O. transcript, 31/3/90, copied from A.E. Angleterre, LX, ff. 446–447.

[130] Frost to Salomon, December 11/21, 1650, *ibid.,* 31/3/90, copied from A.E. Angleterre, LX, f. 442.

[131] Croullé to Mazarin, November 14, 1650, *ibid.,* 31/3/90, copied from A.E. Angleterre, LIX, ff. 478–481.

[132] Morel to Speaker, April 10, 1651 (O.S.?), Henry Cary, *Memorials of the Great Civil War in England from 1646 to 1652* (London, 1842), II, 264.

a scolding from the Commonwealth for having meddled in things of no concern to him.[133] Backdoor diplomacy to resolve Anglo-French differences had failed.

[133] Croullé to Mazarin, December 26, 1650, P.R.O. transcript, 31/3/90, copied from A.E. Angleterre, LIX, ff. 498–501.

VI

The Rising Cost of
Puritan Enmity (1651-1652)

THE French government continued to pay a higher price for its aversion to republicanism in England with every passing month. A dispatch from Croullé in London, dated January 9, 1651, curtly announced official Spanish recognition of the Commonwealth.[1] This could mean only one thing: the Spaniards had written off Charles II as a lost cause. Croullé had preceded his letter on this subject with another, a few days earlier, describing a raid on his house by English soldiers, almost identical to the one they had made the year before. Again the authorities told him that, as he had no official diplomatic status, he could not have Catholic services conducted in his house. The Commonwealth ordered him to leave England[2] and this time the order stood. Before the end of January, Croullé boarded ship and headed for home. A few weeks prior to this, the English government recalled its man, René Augier, from Paris.[3] Now, with Croullé's departure, the last vestige of diplomatic tie between

---

[1] Croullé to Mazarin, January 9, 1651, P.R.O. transcript, 31/3/90, copied from A.E. Angleterre, LIX, ff. 504–505.

[2] *Recueil des instructions données aux ambassadeurs, XXIV, Angleterre,* I, 88.

[3] *Notes on the Diplomatic Relations of England and France,* p. 14.

France and the Commonwealth snapped, just as Spain and England moved closer together.

Agitation within the French government to break the deadlock with England increased. According to one report, someone had proposed recognition of the Commonwealth to thwart Spanish plans for an English alliance. The Council postponed deliberation on the proposal, but a significant shift in policy toward England seemed to be under study.[4] A memorandum which Secretary of State Servien submitted to the Queen Regent sometime in January, 1651, probably triggered the speculation. A very curious document, the memorandum deserves careful reading because of Servien's close working relationship with Cardinal Mazarin. The Secretary of State concisely reviewed all the familiar perils which awaited if England, victorious in Ireland and Scotland, turned next against France. He concluded that the government ought to recognize republican England, even though, as he delicately phrased it, "the King of England will complain of it and will no doubt display a resentment which will be painful." Servien qualified his proposal in one important respect. Unless the Commonwealth agreed in advance to certain concessions, there was no point in recognizing it. Without a prior commitment, Servien feared the Commonwealth might continue hostile acts *after* recognition, leaving the French in more awkward stance than before.[5]

Servien knew that Commonwealth officials repeatedly had said they would discuss nothing until recognized. Evidently he believed that a really serious offer of recognition, even though tied to prior conditions, might bring them around.

Hardly had Servien's memorandum come under discussion than the French capital buzzed with sensational news. Cardinal

[4] B.N., MS. f.fr. 25025, f. 361.

[5] "Mémoire de Servien touchant la république d'Angleterre," P.R.O. transcript, 31/3/90, copied from A.E. Angleterre, LX, ff. 448–449. Croullé had given similar advice to Mazarin in his letter of November 7, 1650, *ibid.*, 31/3/90, copied from A.E. Angleterre, LIX, ff. 470–477.

Mazarin had been forced into exile, and the Princes, freed from their prison at Le Havre, were jubilantly headed for Paris. This event occurred in early February, 1651. When, or if, the Cardinal might return, no one could say. The composition of the new government and its policies, foreign and domestic, lay under a shadow of uncertainty.

Hugh Morel sprang back into action. Thinking to resume the conversations he had conducted earlier in the winter, Morel appealed directly to the Queen Regent and to Louis XIV. He laid the blame for English losses at sea on the exiled Cardinal. Let the government designate the Duc d'Orléans or the Princes to investigate past attacks on English shipping, he advised. Let the government entrust them with the prevention of new attacks.[6] But Morel's appeal went unnoticed. He misjudged the extent of the shake-up in the French government. As week succeeded week, the triumph of Mazarin's foes appeared much less complete than first presumed.

In his exile, Mazarin corresponded frequently with the Queen Regent and his advice carried weight with her. Many persons retained their posts of government, including Servien and Brienne. Despite the return of the Princes, despite the greater influence of the Duc d'Orléans and the improved standing of some of the "Old Frondeurs" (veterans of the revolt of 1649), divisions among them prevented any person or faction from filling the void left by Mazarin's exile. Continuity of administration was not abruptly shattered, especially in the conduct of foreign affairs.

Queen Anne and her new government determined to act upon Servien's memorandum of the month before. The Sieur de Gentillot, a Huguenot and former native of Bordeaux, was picked

---

[6] B.N., MS. f.fr. 18592, f. 410. Morel had also tried once again to enlist the aid of the Coadjutor but was rebuffed. Morel was described as being "at his wits' end." (Letter from Paris, March 10, 1651, Carte, *A Collection of Original Letters*, I, 425).

to go to England. His instructions confirmed willingness to recognize the Commonwealth, providing advance agreement was reached on reprisals, reparations, and trade embargoes.[7] Gentillot soon departed for England; but hardly had he arrived in London, in March, than he discovered the worthlessness of his detailed instructions. Commonwealth officials refused to talk to him until *after* recognition. Authorities in London likewise refused to bandy pleasantries. They believed Gentillot had come only to spy, and they summarily ordered him to leave.[8] The sharpness of the rebuff left officials in Paris perplexed and unable to decide on another venture of the sort. For some months to come, Anglo-French affairs continued their dangerous drift.

The war at sea between France and the Commonwealth intensified. French ships, sailing under commission of Charles II, still swarmed out of French ports, despite all the vaunted prohibitions by the Queen Regent and the provincial authorities.[9] If anything, the marauders became more audacious. When the Commonwealth dislodged the Channel islands of Guernsey and Jersey from royalist control in late 1651, Sir George Carteret, the royalist lieutenant governor of Jersey, simply retired to St. Malo. From there he fitted out and put to sea some six or seven ships. Based at St. Malo and at Brest, the ships, under commission of Charles II, hunted after Puritan vessels. The French governor of Brest set an example by sending a frigate at his own expense to prey on Commonwealth commerce, under cover of a commission from the English king.[10] Although French attacks hit the English hardest in the Mediterranean, as before, the English coastal trade, including the traffic of coal ships to London, came under more frequent assault. The more adventurous raiders made forays onto English soil for plunder

[7] *Recueil des instructions données aux ambassadeurs, XXIV, Angleterre,* I, 94–104.

[8] *Ibid.,* I, 105.   [9] *Calendar of the Clarendon State Papers,* II, 110.

[10] *Nouvelles ordinaires de Londres,* No. 97, May 6/16–13/23, 1652, p. 338; *The Weekly Intelligencer,* No. 72, May 4/14–11/21, 1652, p. 451.

and hostages to bring back to France. The privateers continued to dispose of their prizes in France without difficulty.[11]

English reprisals naturally increased. Even so, the French government claimed that French losses were lighter than those of England. Officials argued that English ships ordinarily carried more valuable cargoes which rendered the loss of one English ship and cargo equivalent to the loss of as many as thirty French ships.[12] But officials could not gloss over the fact that French shippers suffered great hurt.

French encouragement of privateering against the Puritans rebounded in unexpected fashion. According to the Puritan press, those who manned the French privateers were "men of forlorn and dangerous fortunes [who] thirst daily after blood, having no respect either of friend or foe." "All's fish that comes in their piratical net," one writer explained.[13] An international nest of pirates plied the Channel waters and, when challenged, produced commissions from Charles II. Their numbers in some areas amounted to several hundred vessels.[14]

But it was the Commonwealth navy and privately owned English ships, supplied with letters of marque from the Commonwealth, which inflicted the most crippling blows on French shipping. Hardly a week passed in the summer of 1651 without news of serious French losses at sea due to attack by Commonwealth ships. The Channel was extremely risky, but French ships bound to and from more distant points, Newfoundland and Portugal for example, risked capture. English sea power pushed into the Mediterranean, and French ships as far away

[11] *French Intelligencer,* No. 11, January 27/February 6–February 4/14, 1651/1652, p. 78; *ibid.,* No. 21, April 6/16–13/23, 1652, p. 160.

[12] *Recueil des instructions données aux ambassadeurs, XXIV, Angleterre,* I, 103.

[13] *French Intelligencer,* No. 20, March 30/April 9–April 6/16, 1652, p. 150.

[14] *Ibid.,* pp. 150–152.

as Genoa, even those in Greek waters, were no longer safe.[15] When Admiral Penn steered his squadron home from a cruise in the Mediterranean in the fall of 1651, he boasted at least sixteen French ships in his squadron's catch.[16] An English squadron even sailed into the harbor of Toulon and fired upon ships as they lay at anchor.[17]

To avoid the perils of their sea war, French and English merchants used Dutch carriers almost exclusively for trade across the Channel. However, the Navigation Act, passed by the English Parliament in October, 1651, halted that traffic. Henceforth only English ships or the ships of the country from which goods originated could bring cargoes into England. French products not subject to the English embargo, such as salt, brandy, vinegar, hides, and fruit had to be carried in either French or English ships if they wished to reach English markets. But to comply with the Navigation Act exposed the merchandise to the hazards of the Anglo-French sea war. Thus the merchants of both countries came to share more fully the distress of the ship owners.[18]

Although the Navigation Act prevented French merchants from

---

[15] Morosini to Doge and Senate, August 16, 1651, *Calendar of State Papers . . . Venice*, XXVIII, 195; Corner to Doge and Senate, May 20, 1652, *ibid.*, XXVIII, 236.

[16] Morosini to Doge and Senate, December 19, 1651, *ibid.*, XXVIII, 207–208.

[17] Morosini to Doge and Senate, May 2, 1651, *ibid.*, XXVIII, 179–180.

[18] *Commons Journals*, VII, 66–67, 89. Sir Henry Puckering wrote from Rouen to his friend Sir Ralph Verney at Blois, "You shall have notice of the first Dutch ship that goes for England. English bottoms there are none since those that went when I was last here." The merchants, he added, were waiting "till either public war or peace be proclaimed" (Puckering to Verney, December 10/20, 1650; January 9/19, 1650/1651, Claydon House MSS.). For a study of the Navigation Act of 1651 and its effects see J. E. Farnell, "The Navigation Act of 1651, the First Dutch War, and the London Merchant Community," *Economic History Review*, 2d ser., XVI (1964), 439–454.

chartering Dutch vessels for the English trade, they might still hope to employ the Dutch to carry French goods safely to other world markets. Unfortunately, trouble soon arose here too. Commonwealth ships began halting Dutch ships suspected of having French cargo aboard, regardless of destination. The practice was extremely serious for the French, but it also vitally affected the Dutch. Holland had built its phenomenal prosperity around the carrying trade and its ability to perform the function of middleman in the world market. The Dutch had too much at stake to submit tamely to English seizure of the French cargoes on their ships. They protested sharply in the latter part of 1651, but the Puritans refused to desist.[19] This dispute was one of several irritants which goaded Holland into an unofficial belligerency at sea with the English, similar to the sea war between France and England. By early summer 1652, antagonisms ripened into open conflict, and the first of the Anglo-Dutch wars of the mid-seventeenth century began. The French might draw some grim satisfaction from England's engagement in war by so great a naval power as Holland. But, as a practical matter, war between Holland and England reduced still further the security of French goods transported on Dutch ships. Only a well-protected convoy might expect to run the gauntlet of hostile English ships.

The already piteous plight of the French economy worsened when the Prince de Condé sent out his call for a renewal of the Fronde in the summer of 1651. Omer Talon, in a speech to the Paris Parlement on June 20, 1652, graphically described the continuing enfeeblement of French commerce. Merchants told their correspondents not to send goods or letters of exchange because of the lack of security. The economic com-

[19] *Letters and Papers Relating to the First Dutch War, 1652–1654,* ed. Samuel R. Gardiner. Navy Records Society, Vol. XXX ([London], 1906), 58–59, 79–81. In 1651 almost all international trade with Bordeaux, for example, depended on Dutch bottoms; Théophile Malvezin, *Histoire du commerce de Bordeaux,* II (Bordeaux, 1892), 355.

munities of Italy, Germany, the Low Countries, the North, and the Levant had lost confidence in France. Manufacture had just about ceased. Money lacked to pay the wages of the day laborers who earned their living in the fabrication of silk, wool, and linen cloth. Because of general unemployment, Paris had absorbed a quantity of beggars whose number Talon estimated at nearly 100,000, and the figure rose every day. Rouen, Nantes, Bordeaux, Montpellier, Marseille, and Lyon all shared in the depression.[20]

Renewal of the Fronde in 1651 increased suspicion that the Commonwealth might supplement economic retaliation against the French government with political and military harassment. Invasion fever spread again in France. Perhaps the Puritans might land in Normandy. The Duc de Longueville, the most influential person in Normandy, had actively supported the Frondeurs in 1649; he had shared a prison with his brother-in-law, the Prince de Condé, in 1650–1651; the Duke's wife, an inveterate intriguer, was one of the prime movers in this latest outbreak of the Fronde. Nobody could decide what the Duc de Longueville intended. Condé tried to secure his support in the summer of 1651, but for several months the Duke's behavior had been a model of ambiguity.

Before Condé had fairly begun his revolt, Louis XIV's Council (the King was declared of major age in September, 1651, at age thirteen) discussed reports that the Duc de Longueville had reached a secret understanding with the Huguenots of Dieppe and was plotting with the Commonwealth a general Huguenot revolt in Normandy.[21] The rumors changed several months later, as the Commonwealth took over Guernsey and Jersey from the English royalists. In December, the ap-

---

[20] "Mémoires de Omer Talon," *Nouvelle collection des mémoires*, XXVIII, 490–491.

[21] Morosini to Doge and Senate, September 19, 1651, *Calendar of State Papers . . . Venice*, XXVIII, 198–199.

pearance of large Commonwealth fleets cruising off the Norman coast in support of that operation threw Normandy into a panic.[22] English merchants reported that the Duc de Longueville was holding consultations with other regional leaders to decide on defense measures. They said the Duke had petitioned the King for permission to fortify strategic points in Normandy. Though his request was denied, the Duke went ahead anyway, they said, and, with the backing of the Parlement of Rouen, ordered a general mobilization of the male population from ages sixteen to sixty for military service. He also helped himself freely to royal revenue to pay for it.[23]

Rumors of English invasion of Normandy lacked all basis. No doubt the Duc de Longueville shrewdly played on general nervousness to stiffen his own military posture and to strengthen his bargaining position with the French crown. The Puritans thought so, at least. But as late as March, 1652, the French court still apprehended an English invasion of Normandy. Not until the Duke reached an agreement with the crown that spring did Mazarin feel more secure.[24]

Uneasiness about English intentions toward southwestern France, particularly around the Bordeaux and La Rochelle areas, replaced the anxiety about Normandy. As in the previous revolt, Bordeaux became a focal point of resistance to the crown. The Prince de Condé directed the rebellion from Bordeaux in the winter of 1651–1652, and the city also sheltered inside its walls the Prince de Conti and the sister of the two Princes, Madame

[22] Morosini to Doge and Senate, November 14, 1651, *ibid.*, XXVIII, 203–204; *Le courrier de l'armée* (Paris, 1652), p. 7, Moreau No. 819.

[23] *French Intelligencer,* No. 3, December 2/12–9/19, 1651, p. 21; *The Weekly Intelligencer,* No. 44, November 4/14–11/21, 1651, p. 246; *ibid.,* No. 50, December 9/19–16/26, 1651, p. 287; *ibid.,* No. 54, December 30/January 9–January 6/16, 1651/1652, pp. 299, 311; *ibid.,* No. 65, March 16/26–March 23/April 2, 1651/1652, p. 395.

[24] Morosini to Doge and Senate, March 18, 1652, *Calendar of State Papers . . . Venice,* XXVIII, 217; Paul Logié, *La Fronde en Normandie* (Amiens, 1952), III, 116.

de Longueville. Though the King, and Queen Anne, spent the winter with an army in this general sector, when Cardinal Mazarin joined them at Poitiers in April, 1652, the court then returned to the vicinity of Orléans. The Prince de Condé also left Guyenne in April of 1652 to assume personal direction of his troops in the Loire valley and to oversee the intrigues of his friends in Paris. Bordeaux and Guyenne then receded somewhat in importance, though not for long.

Unquestionably, England took renewed interest in the revolt potential of France. In the summer of 1651, just prior to the beginning of Condé's revolt, Colonel Sexby left England for France on order of a secret committee of the Council of State. The committee directed him to give an account of the country and of the affections of the people. Colonel Sexby, a well-known "Agitator" in the Puritan army, was a man of decided Leveller opinions. He had departed from the army under a cloud, but he retained enough credit with Cromwell and the Commonwealth to receive his present appointment and a grant of £1,000 a year for himself and the four gentlemen who accompanied him. Sexby headed for southwestern France and made Bordeaux his base. From there, he reported back to his chief, Thomas Scot, the head of the Commonwealth Intelligence Service, and to the Council of State, writing twice a week for the almost two years of his stay. Scot dispatched another agent, a Lewis de Bourgogne, into France about the same time. Bourgogne started at Calais, went through the Channel ports, and finally reached Bordeaux, where he, too, elected to stay, that area, as Scot testified afterward, being thought most likely "to have given a footing to the English had there been occasion ministered of attempting them by land." [25]

[25] Charles H. Firth, "Thomas Scot's Account of His Activities as Intelligencer during the Commonwealth," *English Historical Review*, XII (1897), 116–126. The Venetian ambassador, Morosini, reported that the English encouraged the Bordelais with substantial promises of help

England and the Fronde

England rejoiced in the anguish of the French government, but the Puritans hesitated about aiding the Frondeurs. Before making a commitment, they wanted to be sure the Frondeurs could win. They also wanted assurance that contributions of ships and troops for Condé would result in the betterment of the Huguenot position and in a change of political structure in keeping with the republican ideology they themselves professed. On none of these points did the first reports from France give them satisfaction. It looked in England as if Condé and his aristocratic friends might execute a *volte-face* and come to terms with the French crown whenever it suited them.[26] Furthermore, despite the factions which Condé had rallied behind him, his total strength was uncertain. Henry Vane the Younger, extremely influential in the Commonwealth, visited Paris, probably in October, 1651, to sound out the Coadjutor of Paris on the new revolt and to win his friendship for the Commonwealth. But Retz, bedazzled with visions of the cardinal's hat which Louis XIV's government held out to him, and then on poor terms with Condé, showed disinterest in the revolt. Vane returned from his interview with polite but empty phrases—no commitment.[27] As the leader of the Francophobes in England, Vane must have felt a bitter disappointment. Regarding Louis XIV's uncle, the Duc d'Orléans, no one could predict what he might do. The Huguenot Vicomte de Turenne, who had joined the Fronde in earlier outbreaks, opted this time to stand with the government. Furthermore the Parlement of Paris, for all its hatred of Mazarin, exuded little enthusiasm for Condé.

Condé appeared at this time an unlikely instrument for the realization of Commonwealth religious and political ideals in

(Morosini to Doge and Senate, May 2, 1651, *Calendar of State Papers . . . Venice*, XXVIII, 179–181).

[26] "Mémoire d'un inconnu" [March 4, 1652], P.R.O. transcript, 31/3/90, copied from A.E. Angleterre, LXI, ff. 38–39.

[27] *Oeuvres du cardinal de Retz*, III, 115–116. For the date of this visit see Gardiner, *History of the Commonwealth*, II, 155n.

France. The editor of one of England's most important newspapers, the *Weekly Intelligencer*, summarized the general feeling: "I cannot well for the present see which way the liberty of the people . . . should advance itself."[28] He stated his distrust of Condé more explicitly a few days later. Discussing the struggle between Louis XIV and the Prince de Condé, he wrote, "But let Caesar or Pompey get the conquest, I know not what the liberty of the people shall obtain by it, which is the reason that so seldom I adventure upon the affairs of the French nation, the interest of the great ones there . . . being to magnify their moving humors and to uphold monarchy in any descent of the royal blood."[29]

However, the Prince de Condé appreciated the usefulness of English aid, and he lost little time in sending an agent, the Chevalier de La Rivière, to England, probably in October, 1651, to obtain it. Cromwell made La Rivière cool his heels for three days before condescending to receive him. When at last La Rivière was ushered into the Puritan leader's presence, he foolishly opened the discussion with a preposterous request for £100,000 and an expeditionary force of 6,000 infantry and 2,000 cavalry. Cromwell laughed in his face and replied facetiously that "this was a trifling matter." He would come in person with 40,000 infantry and 12,000 cavalry at his own expense. Then Cromwell added meaningfully, "provided the Prince would give his hand to reduce France to the state in which England now is." La Rivière, stung by the sally, left without a word. But, as the Venetian agent in London commented, Condé had no choice but to ask again for English aid, because, without foreign help, "he is obviously going to destruction."[30]

Almost simultaneously, October 16, 1651, Cromwell granted

[28] *The Weekly Intelligencer*, No. 39, September 23/October 3–September 30/October 10, 1651, pp. 303–304.
[29] *Ibid.*, No. 45, November 11/21–18/28, 1651, p. 355.
[30] Morosini to Doge and Senate, October 24, 1651, *Calendar of State Papers . . . Venice*, XXVIII, 202.

an audience to an agent of the Comte du Daugnon. The Count, who governed Brouage, a naval base whose location allowed him to police the waters around La Rochelle, had already communicated with Parliament in England as early as April, 1651.[31] He supported the Prince de Condé in the current crisis. However, he pursued a course of some independence, more as an ally than as a subordinate of the Prince. The Count's agent, Conan, a native of La Rochelle, brought to England a proposal that the Commonwealth garrison the towers guarding the port of La Rochelle. The Count could guarantee English admittance to the towers. Cromwell called for a map and seemed favorably impressed. However, the proposal died in Council, where the members probably voted it premature.[32]

But as the Venetian agent correctly surmised, Condé and his friends needed English help too badly to accept these rebuffs as final. The Prince opened a second round of discussions in early 1652, this time under conditions more favorable. By then, Condé had a treaty of assistance from Spain, concluded November 6, 1651. The Duc d'Orléans had ended his most recent bout of indecision by declaring for Condé. The Fronde began to look really formidable.

Present for talks in London were: the Sieur de Barrière, a native of Bordeaux representing Condé; the Marquis de Cugnac, grandson of the powerful Huguenot Maréchal de La Force in Guyenne; and a third agent, Saint-Thomas, who acted for the Comte du Daugnon. Their presence started a new flurry of reports that persons high in the Commonwealth had promised men, money, and ships for the Bordelais "if they will no more be in subjection unto monarchy but declare themselves a free state." [33]

[31] *Commons Journals*, VII, 133.

[32] Morosini to Doge and Senate, October 24, 1651, *Calendar of State Papers . . . Venice*, XXVIII, 202.

[33] *The Weekly Intelligencer*, No. 70, April 20/30–April 27/May 7, 1652, p. 435.

Condé wanted help, but without ideological strings attached. His agent, Barrière, tried to side-step discussions of religious or of political change for Bordeaux. In a speech to Parliament shortly after his arrival, Barrière alluded vaguely to the matter by remarking "what a great honor will it be besides for the Commonwealth of England, after it hath so happily and so gloriously established the precious liberty at home" to help their neighbors. He urged the Commonwealth to act against "those who ever opposed this Commonwealth and are still of the same mind when they shall be in power to do it." [34]

Though Barrière reiterated Condé's need for help and exclaimed that "the greatest trust of all that country next unto God is in some help from hence," he scaled down his request to a more modest dimension. His immediate concern was Bordelais commerce. As Barrière admitted, the Prince de Condé "hath not other subsistence, only by way of the trade of the said city." Barrière hoped for an agreement of free commerce for Bordeaux and Guyenne with the Commonwealth. Guyenne had never committed piratical acts against English shipping, he said, and Guyenne had consistently ignored the embargo proclaimed by the French crown against English cloth. The Bordelais treated English merchants as their best friends, Barrière continued, even permitting English ships to carry their cannon when sailing past the city—an extraordinary mark of trust.[35]

Barrière recognized that a broad trade agreement with England might take time to negotiate, and so he pushed instead for immediate permission to transport five or six thousand tuns of Bordeaux wine to England. This represented possibly 10 per cent of Bordeaux's annual wine export. Sale of the wine could materially ease Condé's money worries and could ease

---

[34] Barrière to Parliament, [April 6 (?), 1652] (O.S.?), *Portland Manuscripts,* I, 640–641.

[35] Barrière to Council of State, [April 6, 1652] (O.S.?), *ibid.,* I, 639–641.

anxiety in Bordeaux. If the wine were not shipped quickly, the summer heat would make it impossible to transport without danger of spoilage. The proposal encountered opposition in Parliament, however. Objectors said that to purchase wine from Bordeaux could drain England of specie. Probably this was a pretext for delay to allow the government more time to decide what to do. Barrière told the Puritans that the Prince would accept goods in exchange for the wine in place of specie. But whether he obtained the agreement, we cannot be sure.[36]

Barrière continued to work for a treaty of commerce with England through the summer, on Condé's instructions. The Prince received warnings from Pierre Lenet in Bordeaux that the city's trading position vitally affected their plans. Lenet described how the approach of Vendôme's fleet in the summer of 1652 frightened the Bordelais merchants. People who had promised to lend money to keep the revolt going suddenly refused.[37]

The Prince replied that a commercial agreement with England was the only solution. Freedom of trade would bring English merchant shipping to Bordeaux. Then the English would have to protect them with naval escort. The fleet of Admiral Vendôme could not dispute passage with English sea power. The Prince wrote to Barrière, telling him, "it is necessary to work incessantly for this result and to get the English to resolve the question of liberty of commerce." [38] Barrière responded with a show of energy. He spent liberally to grease the way (by September he claimed to have disbursed 2,000 ja-

[36] Barrière to Council of State, [April 6, 1652, O.S.?]; May 4, 1652 (O.S.), *ibid.*, I, 639–640, 647; Barrière to Parliament, [April 6(?), 1652, O.S.?], *ibid.*, I, 640–641.

[37] Lenet to Condé, August 8, 1652, "Mémoires de Pierre Lenet," *Nouvelle collection des mémoires*, XXIV, 559; Condé to Lenet, August, 1652, *ibid.*, XXIV, 564; Barrière to Conti, September 12, 1652, *ibid.*, XXIV, 571.

[38] Condé to Lenet, August, 1652, *ibid.*, XXIV, 564.

cobuses for the purpose). But by the end of August he still lacked a commitment from England.[39]

Barrière also sought to raise troops for Condé's armies. Individuals in England told him they could organize the recruiting if Parliament granted safe-conduct for ferrying the troops to France. Irish troops disembarked in the Bordeaux area in the summer of 1652, but, since Spain constantly procured Irish mercenaries for its own service, it is uncertain whether these were soldiers Barrière had obtained.[40]

On balance, the net result of the Prince's efforts to obtain English help during the first year of the new revolt appeared unimpressive. The Commonwealth listened attentively to Condé's proposals but could not put aside suspicions about him. Reports dispatched by English agents in the Bordeaux area fanned the suspicion. Condé knew this, and in the summer of 1652 he asked Lenet to find out the English agent in Bordeaux responsible and to devise some way to get him out of the city without antagonizing England.[41] If the agent was Colonel Sexby, as seems likely, Lenet failed to get him to leave.

Discouragement over prospects of obtaining English assistance settled over the Princes' party. Condé's friends in Bordeaux doubted that England had any intention of accepting Barrière's proposals. Foreign observers agreed that the English "do not build much on the domestic troubles of France." Obviously the Commonwealth would have preferred to deal more directly with the Huguenots in Guyenne than with the Prince de Condé. A highly placed member of Parliament, perhaps even Cromwell, said that the Huguenot Marquis de Cugnac in London had "more bacon in his mouth" than Barrière.[42] However,

[39] Barrière to Conti, September 12, 1652, *ibid.*, XXIV, 571.

[40] For discussion of Irish troops recruited for the Fronde, see pp. 211–213.

[41] Condé to Lenet, [probably July, 1652], "Mémoires de Pierre Lenet," *Nouvelle collection des mémoires*, XXIV, 557.

[42] Paulucci to Morosini, May 23, 1652, *Calendar of State Papers . . .*

Condé held the upper hand at Bordeaux and it was through Condé that the negotiations had to be conducted.

The Commonwealth acted cautiously in response to Condé's appeals for another reason. As Barrière informed the Prince on April 15, 1652, astounding as it appeared, the Commonwealth was negotiating an alliance with the French crown.[43] Strange news indeed! Considering the sea war and strained relations between the two countries, an apparently absurd notion. Yet Barrière spoke the truth.

The strategic Channel port of Dunkirk was the consideration, it appeared, which might cause the two governments to overlook their mutual distrust. Dunkirk seemed likely to fall back into Spanish hands. The re-opening of the Fronde diverted French military strength and made reinforcement difficult. The French toyed with the idea of transferring the city to Dutch sovereignty as an alternative preferable to Spanish capture, but when they approached the Dutch in November, 1651, the Dutch shied away. The Dutch feared that they might call down Spanish wrath upon their heads if they ran off with the prize Spain wanted so badly. Meantime, persons in the Commonwealth interested themselves in Dunkirk's fate and calculated the advantages England might derive from ownership of the city. They soon put out feelers to test French reaction.[44]

Late in December, 1651, Cardinal Mazarin learned that the Comte d'Estrades, French governor and military commander at Dunkirk, had received a visit from someone from England on this question. The Cardinal considered the idea of ceding Dunkirk to the English repugnant. He wrote the Count on December 26, 1651, that he considered him too good a French-

---

Venice, XXVIII, 237–238; "Mémoire d'un inconnu" [March 4, 1652], P.R.O. transcript, 31/3/90, copied from A.E. Angleterre, LXI, ff. 38–39.

[43] Samuel R. Gardiner, "Cromwell and Mazarin in 1652," *English Historical Review*, XI (1896), 505.

[44] *Ibid.*, 480.

man to receive such a proposition, whatever personal advantage d'Estrades might obtain. The Cardinal's hostility resulted in part from a suspicion that d'Estrades might be preparing some treachery for personal profit. No one's loyalty could be taken for granted in the Fronde. But, before another two months passed, the Cardinal apparently dismissed his apprehension about d'Estrades and evidenced interest of his own in the English proposition.[45]

The absence of regular diplomatic channels between France and the Commonwealth obliged the discussion of Dunkirk to follow circuitous routes. For this reason the English first talked to d'Estrades, and, for the same reason, someone sought out the Sieur de Gentillot, who had just returned from a second unsuccessful trip for his government to London.

S. R. Gardiner and J. J. Jusserand have described in great detail the story of the establishment of contact between the two governments and the negotiations about Dunkirk.[46] A full account is too complex to go into here. It is enough to say that by mid-February Mazarin had before him concrete proposals. Gentillot said an English gentleman of the Leveller party assured him the English would support the interests of the French crown if France relinquished Dunkirk to the Commonwealth. Mazarin learned at the same time from the Comte d'Estrades that a certain Colonel Fitzjames, acting for Cromwell, had discussed Dunkirk with d'Estrades since the preceding November. The Colonel said England would pay 1,500 livres for the port and seal the purchase with a treaty of alliance.

[45] I am inclined to accept the interpretation of J. J. Jusserand, "Le maréchal d'Estrades et ses critiques," *Revue historique,* CLVIII (1928), 225–254, on this point rather than Gardiner's interpretation. The latter believes d'Estrades to have been engaged in traitorous dealings with Cromwell.

[46] In addition to the articles of Gardiner and Jusserand cited above, see also Clyde L. Grose, "England and Dunkirk," *American Historical Review,* XXIX (1933), 1–27.

Assuming Spain opposed the arrangement, the English prom-ised to send 10,000 infantry and 100 vessels to fight the Spani-ards, provided France dispatched 3,000 cavalry to the nearby city, Gravelines, to reinforce it against Spanish attack. Both Gentillot and d'Estrades sympathized with the proposals they transmitted. Gentillot pointed out to the Cardinal the possibility of paying off English claims for losses at sea with Dunkirk. If Dunkirk were to pass from French sovereignty anyway, why not collect some benefit rather than surrender the city to the Span-iards? [47]

Other persons in France urged the Cardinal to consider an English alliance. Several memoranda in February, 1652, of anonymous authorship, pleaded the case. The authors reasoned that the one foreign power best able to help or to hurt France at that moment was England. To obtain English assistance against the Frondeurs, or to dissuade the English from aiding the Prince de Condé, ought to be the goal of the crown. The authors omitted reference to Dunkirk. Perhaps they were unaware of the soundings taken by the Commonwealth. They based their arguments on other considerations, but these meshed nicely with the current discussion of Dunkirk.[48]

According to the memoranda, new representatives ought to go to England; but, if they were to receive better treatment than Gentillot and his predecessors, the English must see some profit for themselves. The English liked one to believe that they acted out of religious conviction, the authors continued, therefore why not flatter this conceit? Why not draw them into an alliance by showing them evidence of the favored treatment of their coreligionists in France? If necessary, why not, indeed, confer upon the Huguenots the same rights they possessed in

[47] Gardiner, "Cromwell and Mazarin in 1652," *English Historical Review,* XI (1896), 482–500.

[48] "Avis touchant les affaires d'Angleterre," [February 13, 1652], and [February 24–25, 1652], P.R.O. transcript, 31/3/90, copied from A.E. Angleterre, LXI, ff. 6–8, 9.

1619? This suggestion had the double advantage of creating English friendship for the French crown and of inducing those Huguenots who presently supported the Prince de Condé to switch. No doubt, the writers added, France must cede a point of territory, temporarily at least, to engage the Puritans to send troops and monetary help. The authors avoided naming names, but the transfer of Dunkirk could have fulfilled this requirement.[49]

Cardinal Mazarin probably knew the Spaniards were holding talks of their own with Commonwealth leaders, trying to persuade England to assist them in reducing Dunkirk. The Spaniards, similarly aware of the Anglo-French conversations, held out attractive bait to the Puritans. If England helped them capture Dunkirk, Spain would help the English take Calais.[50]

The Cardinal learned that influential people in England were split into three groups regarding France. The Levellers, he heard, were friendly toward France and preferred to have England at war with Spain. Sir Henry Vane the Younger led the opposite faction, the Francophobes, who preferred a war with France. A third group, headed by Cromwell, occupied a middle ground, ready to throw its support to either of the other two factions, depending on which course seemed most profitable. The Cardinal might infer that if France spurned an English alliance, England would ally with Spain.[51]

The Cardinal was in a quandary. He worried about the fate of Dunkirk and worried about the tenor of Anglo-Spanish conversations. Yet an *alliance* with a régime of "regicides," thus far unrecognized by France, placed him in a dilemma. At

[49] *Ibid.*

[50] Leopold to Philip IV, February 6, 1652, *Correspondance de la cour d'Espagne sur les affaires des Pays-Bas au XVIIe siècle,* ed. Henri Lonchay, continued by Joseph Cuvelier, IV (Brussels, 1933), 313; Philip IV to Cardeñas, April 27, 1652, *ibid.,* IV, 327.

[51] Gardiner, "Cromwell and Mazarin in 1652," *English Historical Review,* XI (1896), 490.

times Mazarin seemed willing to accept an English alliance and to transfer Dunkirk to them. Perhaps it was partly for this reason that the crown made a new bid for Huguenot goodwill (and hence the goodwill of the Puritans) in May, 1652. The King promulgated a declaration which confirmed the Huguenots in the enjoyment of rights conferred by the Edict of Nantes and other edicts and declarations concerning the free and public exercise of their religion in previously designated localities, "notwithstanding all letters and judgments both of our Council as of the sovereign courts . . . contrary to this." [52] The practical meaning of this declaration is unclear. If the government issued it with an eye to its psychological effect on the Commonwealth, the Puritans needed more than this. The authors of the memoranda mentioned before had emphasized the need to transfer a strong point to the English. Thus the Cardinal still had to make up his mind about Dunkirk.

At the beginning of March, Mazarin envisaged a joint Anglo-French occupation of Dunkirk through the medium of a Swiss garrison with allegiance sworn both to England and to France. But on March 12, 1652, the Comte d'Estrades informed Colonel Fitzjames that the court had decided against any transfer of Dunkirk. Several more changes of heart occurred. Then on May 1, 1652, the crown prepared instructions providing for the cession of Dunkirk to England if the Puritans agreed to help France defend Gravelines against the Spaniards. The Sieur de Gentillot was named to undertake his third mission to England to convey these new proposals. [53]

Just as an Anglo-French alliance appeared within reach, almost everything went wrong. The anti-French group in England raised a storm, saying Dunkirk was not France's to give, that

[52] Pierre Blet, *Le clergé de France et la monarchie* (Rome, 1959), II, 350–351.

[53] Gardiner, "Cromwell and Mazarin in 1652," *English Historical Review*, XI (1896), 498–508, 509.

it rightfully belonged to Spain, a country friendly to England. Because England and Holland were rapidly drifting into war in the late spring of 1652, sentiment in England grew that this was no time to provoke Spain into a war. Interest in the French alliance cooled markedly in England. On the French side, some argued that, even with the cession of Dunkirk, the Commonwealth probably would insist on payment for its losses at sea from French attack. Those losses were believed to run to several million pounds. Furthermore, Gravelines fell to the Spaniards at the close of May. It was too late for English help to change that. Finally, Mazarin decided against bartering Dunkirk to the Commonwealth. France would try to hold the city.[54]

That decision rendered Gentillot's mission to England a futile effort. He now had little more to offer the Puritans than on previous occasions: no recognition without preliminary agreement on the other disputes. In July, for the third time in less than a year and a half, the Commonwealth told Gentillot to leave. A blunt spoken ex-musketeer, Gentillot minced no words in reporting his failure to the Comte de Brienne. He was highly annoyed, as much with his own government as with the English. Ruses and inventions of the imagination could not lull the Puritans, he warned Brienne. Unconditional recognition was the *sine qua non* for friendship with England. "One must not imagine, chimerically, that there were other ways to choose." French domestic troubles would make the Puritans inflexible in their deliberations. It could be expected, he went on, that they would wait while "our confusions" in France worsen. Gentillot concluded his warning, saying, "We ought not doubt that they will fall upon us and that your empire will be overturned." [55]

[54] Morosini to Doge and Senate, June 11, 1652, *Calendar of State Papers . . . Venice*, XXVIII, 244.

[55] *Recueil des instructions donnée aux ambassadeurs, XXIV, Angleterre*, I, 123.

Gentillot's warning went unheeded as the French government concentrated on the defense of Dunkirk. Reports in early summer of 1652 from the city's commander, the Comte d'Estrades, contained all the usual descriptions of a city under close siege. Provisions had run low; troops lacked; time was running out.[56] But how to break through the Spanish siege ring consisting partly of troops pressing on the land side and partly of ships patrolling the waters outside? Cardinal Mazarin believed the sea route held the key. If Admiral Vendôme detached an adequate squadron to collect troops and supplies at Calais, and then escorted the transports safely past the Spanish blockaders, the city could hold out. The continued presence of French naval units might allow the government to keep a supply line into the city indefinitely. Orders sent to Brest, where Vendôme's fleet was harbored, directed the Admiral to detach a squadron to Calais as quickly as possible.[57]

Nothing happened! The Cardinal dispatched courier after courier to Brest, always with the same negative result. Perhaps Vendôme hesitated because he had heard for two years that the Commonwealth was about to send its navy to help the Spaniards take Dunkirk. More likely, Vendôme was too deeply involved readying his fleet for operations against the Spaniards and the Frondeurs in the La Rochelle-Bordeaux area to want to split his force. Ships of the Frondeur Comte du Daugnon, together with Spanish vessels, blocked entry to La Rochelle and protected the sea route to Bordeaux for the Frondeurs. Therefore, ignoring his orders, Vendôme sailed his fleet southward from Brest. The Admiral inflicted a limited defeat on the enemy and unblocked La Rochelle, while badly frightening the mer-

[56] *Relation inédite de la défense de Dunquerque* (1651–1652), ed. Philippe Tamizey de Larroque, Collection méridionale, III (Paris, 1872).

[57] Mazarin to d'Estrades, September 30, 1652, *Lettres du cardinal Mazarin*, ed. Chéruel, V, 309; Mazarin to Vendôme, September 30, 1652, *ibid.*, V, 311.

chants of Bordeaux, as noted before; but the engagement, which occurred on August 9, 1652, was not decisive.[58]

Meanwhile the beleaguered garrison of Dunkirk waited. Cardinal Mazarin was beside himself with anger and frustration. He addressed more orders to the Admiral at La Rochelle, and complained bitterly that "we are in a time when many people feel free to ignore the orders of the King." If only Vendôme had followed orders, the Cardinal explained, Dunkirk would be relieved and the Admiral back sweeping the sea clear of the enemy off Brouage and Bordeaux. Just as the Cardinal had despaired of help from Vendôme, the news arrived that the Admiral had detached ships for the Channel operation. The Cardinal's spirits rose. The detachment was small, only eight vessels, but Mazarin believed that "there is great appearance that the naval force will accomplish the mission we have set for ourselves." [59]

Unknown to the French, the Spanish ambassador in London profited from the renewed chill between France and the Commonwealth to secure the Puritans' assistance for Dunkirk.[60] Admiral Blake was ordered to employ his powerful fleet to keep the French relieving vessels from reaching Dunkirk. Consequently, when the French squadron set out from Calais with its covey of supply and troop ships headed for Dunkirk, it ran into the Spaniards *and* the English fleet of Blake. In the battle which followed, the French lost seven of their eight naval vessels to Blake. All their transports were sunk, captured, or turned away from their destination. The defeat inflicted by Blake was as overwhelming as it was unexpected. Two days later, on September 16, 1652, the Comte d'Estrades surrendered to the Spaniards, as he had promised to do if reinforcements failed to

[58] Cosnac, *Souvenirs du règne de Louis XIV*, IV, 368–392.

[59] See Mazarin's letters written in August and September, 1652, *Lettres du cardinal Mazarin*, ed. Chéruel, V, 146–147, 157, 170, 198–200, 226–229, 312.

[60] Guizot, *History of Oliver Cromwell*, I, 269.

175

reach him by that date. Spanish troops marched into Dunkirk! [61] The French government was stunned. Almost by reflex, Mazarin and Vendôme sought first to absolve themselves from blame. The Admiral recalled how he had long opposed sending a squadron to Dunkirk. Mazarin riposted that the Admiral's tardy compliance with orders had ruined the operation. If he had sent the squadron when first asked, the English would not have caused trouble, because Blake's fleet had then been off chasing Dutch herring boats and the Spaniards had not yet persuaded the Commonwealth to attack the French relief squadron.[62] The Cardinal's argument has some justification, but obviously he was caught completely off guard by the English attack. He had disregarded warnings that the English might intervene at Dunkirk. However, as those warnings had been repeated so often in the past without result, no wonder he ignored them.

What mattered now, however, was to find out what the English attack might portend. Perhaps Blake had acted on his own initiative and would be disavowed. Admiral Vendôme wrote on September 23, 1652, both to Blake and to Blake's superiors in London, expressing disbelief that the English government could have authorized the attack. Vendôme demanded restitution of the captured ships.[63] For two and a half months the Council of State in London did not deign to reply. When at last it did, it endorsed Blake's action fully, explaining that the attack was in reprisal for injuries English shippers and mer-

---

[61] Henri Malo, *Les corsaires dunkerquois et Jean Bart* (Paris, 1913), I, 420–422; "Avis de la prise des vaisseaux du roi par les anglais," [September 17, 1652], P.R.O. transcript, 31/3/90, copied from A.E. Angleterre, LXI, ff. 88–89.

[62] Mazarin to Ondedei, September 21, 1652, *Lettres du cardinal Mazarin*, ed. Chéruel, V, 265; Mazarin to d'Estrades, September 30, 1652, *ibid.*, V, 309; Mazarin to Vedôme, *ibid.*, V, 311.

[63] Vendôme to Blake, [September 23, 1652], P.R.O. transcript, 31/3/90, copied from A.E. Angleterre, LXI, f. 91.

chants had borne from the French.[64] Well before this note reached France, everyone realized Blake must have had official backing. On September 24, 1652, Gentillot had advised from Calais that the English Parliament, though planning to return captive French sailors, would keep the ships.[65] Mazarin commented indignantly that "the English have raised their masks against us."[66] "The King must adopt some good resolution in regard to the English," he thought, "because the consideration we have had for them so far has only served to make them bolder in acting against us." Vendôme urged the Cardinal on and suggested the seizure of all English property in France. Many on the King's Council supported Vendôme's suggestion.[67]

An order went out to confiscate three English ships at Honfleur whose cargoes were valued at four or five hundred livres. However, the governor of the place, a supporter of the Duc d'Orléans, disobeyed it.[68] The town of St. Malo, without waiting for an order, confiscated all English merchant ships and goods in port.[69] Immediately the Commonwealth press published reports of wholesale confiscation of English property in France. For good measure, the press speculated that Admiral Vendôme was assembling a fleet to avenge the loss of Dunkirk. Sir George Carteret, the English royalist, was to participate and

[64] Le conseil d'état d'Angleterre au duc de Vendôme, [December 2/12, 1652], *ibid.*, 31/3/90, copied from A.E. Angleterre, LXI, f. 118.

[65] Gentillot to Servien, [September 24, 1652], *ibid.*, 31/3/90, copied from A.E. Angleterre, LXI, ff. 92–95.

[66] Mazarin to Le Tellier, September 27, 1652, *Lettres du cardinal Mazarin*, ed. Chéruel, V, 298; Mazarin to Vendôme, September 30, 1652, *ibid.*, V, 313.

[67] Hyde to Nicholas, October 12, 1652 (O.S.?), *Clarendon State Papers*, III, 105–106.

[68] "Avis de la prise des vaissaux du roi par les anglais" [September 17, 1652], P.R.O. transcript, 31/3/90, copied from A.E. Angleterre, LXI, ff. 88–89.

[69] *Nouvelles ordinaires de Londres*, No. 116, September 16/26–September 23/October 3, 1652, p. 464.

to command the ships of Charles II based at Brest and at St. Malo.[70] Never had an Anglo-French war seemed so close as after the fall of Dunkirk.

[70] *The Weekly Intelligencer,* No. 95, October 19/29–October 26/ November 5, 1652, p. 643; No. 96, October 26/November 5–November 2/12, 1652, p. 648.

VII

What Will England Do?
(1652-1653)

NOTWITHSTANDING the flashes of temper which Blake's attack provoked among top officials of the French government, the imminence of war with England sobered them. The recommendation of the Duc de Vendôme and others for wholesale seizure of English property in France was not acted upon. In the few instances where local authorities had acted against the English, as at St. Malo, other authorities countermanded the action. The Parlement of Rennes, for example, forbade any molestation of the English. Though the Puritan press observed certain persons in France trying to contravene the order, nevertheless the gesture caused satisfaction in England.[1]

Calmer counsels came to Paris, and these finally prevailed against the bellicose urgings of Vendôme's group. Among those advising prudence was the Sieur de Gentillot. As a man three times expelled from England and as one who had recently helped arrange for the ill-starred relief squadron for Dunkirk, Gentillot bore no love for the Puritans. But, as a realist, he urged against replying to Blake's attack with a counter display of force. The

---

[1] *Nouvelles ordinaires de Londres,* No. 124, November 11/21–18/28, 1652, p. 496.

better course, he thought, was to exercise patience and to demonstrate a genuine desire to improve relations—and this for the very good reason that France could not fend off a concerted attack from England. The governors of the Channel ports were doing what they could, he said, but, considering the limited means at their disposal, they could do little more than protect themselves against insult. They certainly could not withstand a siege of more than twelve days' duration.[2]

Another development highlighted the embarrassment which might ensue from full-scale war with England. In September–October, 1652, the revolt of the Frondeurs in the Paris area drew to a close. As the Frondeurs fell out among themselves, agents of the crown had ample opportunity to conduct secret talks for peace. More and more persons expressed disenchantment with the Fronde. In October, Louis XIV and his court returned to Paris in triumph. Just prior to the collapse of the Fronde in Paris, the Prince de Condé departed to continue the fight with the army of his Spanish ally in the East, but most of the Frondeurs in Paris, including the Duc d'Orléans and the Duc de Beaufort, meekly submitted. The re-entry of Louis XIV into Paris marked the end of fighting there, but the Fronde continued in the Bordeaux area, which now became the principal center of rebellion in France.

Past experience had demonstrated time and again that as long as revolt blazed somewhere in France, it could be re-ignited elsewhere. Presumably, if France went to war with England over its humiliation by Blake, the Puritans would help the Frondeurs at Bordeaux. The same individuals now humbly making their peace with the crown in Paris might then rejoin the revolt.

Furthermore, the Fronde at Bordeaux had some months before taken an ominous turn. In the past, the Princes had co-

---

[2] Gentillot to Servien, September 24, 1652, P.R.O. transcript, 31/3/90, copied from A.E. Angleterre, LXI, ff. 92–95.

ordinated their opposition to the court with elements of the traditional power structure of Bordeaux. This had meant working
through dissatisfied members of the Parlement of Bordeaux and
through the *jurats* of the Hôtel de Ville. However, in the summer of 1652 a group called the Ormée displaced the Parlement
and the Hôtel de Ville as the dominant local political force in
Bordeaux.

The rise of the Ormée to a position of power at Bordeaux is
one of the most fascinating developments of the Fronde. The
full history of the Ormée is yet to be written, however, and the
circumstances surrounding its rise are little understood.[3] It seems
to have originated as a kind of brotherhood for the artisan
groups of the city, an organization for mutual protection and
assistance. The published articles of union for the Ormée provided for such things as arbitration of disputes among members,
assistance in finding employment, and certain kinds of financial
help. However, the Ormistes also addressed themselves to
political questions. Since the Ormée eventually counted as many
as 12,000 persons in its membership, it was a group to be reck-
oned with.[4] The Ormistes criticized the privileged and relatively
conservative *jurats* of the Hôtel de Ville and the *noblesse de
robe*, represented in the Parlement of Bordeaux, just as they
criticized Mazarin and the court. An early objective of the
Ormée had been to control the local government in Bordeaux.
In June and July of 1652 they succeeded in mobilizing enough
popular support and shunted aside the old established leadership.

It would be a mistake, however, to imagine the Ormée as a
bloc solidly united in its goals. Internal disagreement weakened
it. Catholics and Huguenots both belonged to it. The published

---

[3] One of the best surveys at present is in H.N. Brailsford, *The Levellers
and the English Revolution* (London, 1961), pp. 671–692.

[4] *Mémoires de Daniel de Cosnac,* ed. Jules de Cosnac, Société de
l'histoire de France (Paris, 1852), I, 72–73.

articles of union [5] promised obedience to the King and service to the Governor, but some Ormistes dreamed of a republic. Some Ormistes were pro-English; others leaned to Spain. Lines blurred even more because sympathizers of Parlement and of the Hôtel de Ville infiltrated the Ormée in order to steer the organization. Regardless of how radical the Ormistes might be, though the Princes had to work through the Ormée, henceforth, in defending Bordeaux and Guyenne.

It was widely known in France that the Ormée had eclipsed the Hôtel de Ville and the Parlement of Bordeaux in the summer of 1652. The Venetian ambassador in Paris attributed it to English influence.[6] Loret, the private news gatherer of Mademoiselle de Longueville, wrote of the intentions of the Bordelais to set up a republic.[7] French officials, who were equally well informed—doubtless far better informed, in fact— worried about English influence there, present and future. The French court doubtless knew of Barrière's boasting in September that the English Parliament had concluded a treaty of commerce with Bordeaux.[8] Barrière had broadcast the news widely. He discovered a few days later that his announcement was premature and had to admit that Parliament still withheld final

[5] *Articles de l'union de l'Ormée* (Paris, [1652]), p. 2, Moreau No. 408.

[6] Morosini to Doge and Senate, May 28, 1652, *Calendar of State Papers . . . Venice,* XXVIII, 238. The ambassador wrote that the opportunity enjoyed by the English of going yearly to Bordeaux in order to ship wines had given them ample means not only of establishing connections there but, under conditions then existing, of impressing their own opinions on the inhabitants of the city. The people, he said, assembled daily at a certain spot, more to hear the news at first than from any idea of insurrection. However, in meeting there they began to discuss the badness of the times and contrasted it with the prosperity of England. That kind of talk then led to speeches in favor of liberty, the expulsion of the parlement and the formation of a more popular one. In short, they began to talk of governing themselves, the ambassador reported.

[7] Loret, *La muze historique,* I, 249.

[8] Barrière to Conti, September 12, 1652, "Mémoires de Pierre Lenet," *Nouvelle collection des mémoires,* XXIV, 571.

approval. However, the cause appeared to be only a technicality: how many other regions in France to include with Guyenne in the treaty. Presumably Barrière could straighten this out shortly, and, when he did, the treaty might be even more damaging to the French crown.[9]

The naval victory of Blake amply proved to all Frenchmen the vital role of English sea power. Because of it, Dunkirk had fallen; but the diversion and subsequent loss of the French squadron also had immediate impact on Bordeaux. The Duc de Vendôme had to postpone his plan to seal off the water route to Bordeaux. The Prince de Condé and Pierre Lenet both chortled over the implications. New confidence flowed into the previously disheartened mercantile community of Bordeaux. Thanks to the English, they told one another, Vendôme could not disturb them for a while at least.[10]

Condé and his confederates circulated stories about new Commonwealth action to be directed against France. Cromwell, they said, had promised the Comte du Daugnon that he would support an attack on La Rochelle and would send 10,000 infantry and 4,000 cavalry against the city by the end of December. The London press picked up the report under Paris datelines and embellished it with assertions that the Count would deliver the isles of Ré and Oléron into Cromwell's hands.[11] The news stories did have some substance. Du Daugnon's agent in London affirmed in private letters that England was ready to make a treaty for the reduction of La Rochelle, provided the

[9] Barrière to Council of State [October 25, 1652, O.S.?], *Thurloe Papers,* I, 216.

[10] Lenet to Condé, September 30, 1652, Cosnac, *Souvenirs du règne de Louis XIV,* V, 56–57; Marigni to Lenet, September 22, 1652, "Mémoires de Pierre Lenet," *Nouvelle collection des mémoires,* XXIV, 574.

[11] *French Occurrences,* November 1/11–9/19, 1652, pp. 199–200; *The Weekly Intelligencer,* No. 98, November 9/19–16/26, 1652, pp. 665–666; Mazarin to Le Tellier, October 2, 1652, *Lettres du cardinal Mazarin,* ed. Chéruel, V, 322.

Count turned over a port to guarantee the security of English ships in that area. Whatever might come of it, the Commonwealth promised to let the Count have Irish mercenaries at twelve livres a head—as many as 1,000 if he could pay for them.[12]

Also of concern to the French crown were rumors of a peace in the making between England and Holland, and the arrangement of an alliance between England and Spain. If either or both of these things came to pass, Paris could expect more aggressive action from the Commonwealth. With Dunkirk still a burning memory, French officials were reluctant to write off Puritan threats as bluff.

In fixing upon a strategy, the French government assigned top priority to the suppression of the Fronde in Bordeaux, before the Puritans overcame their indecision and jumped in on the side of the Frondeurs. Instructions sent to representatives of the crown entrusted with the reduction of Bordeaux conveyed a sense of haste. Subdue the Frondeurs before England upsets everything: this was the refrain heard from Paris.[13] To keep the English off balance in the meantime, the French government made increasingly friendly advances to the Dutch and fostered talk of a Franco-Dutch alliance. Careful not to go too far, the French government kept the conversations alive to frighten the Commonwealth and to prevent an Anglo-Dutch peace.[14] If all else failed and the Puritans invaded France, the

[12] Saint-Thomas to du Daugnon, December 2, 1652, "Mémoires de Pierre Lenet," *Nouvelle collection des mémoires,* XXIV, 584.

[13] Mazarin to Bishop of Tulle, June 2, 1653, *Lettres du cardinal Mazarin,* ed. Chéruel, V, 626; Sagredo to Doge and Senate, July 8, 1653, *Calendar of State Papers . . . Venice,* XXIX, 95.

[14] Mazarin to Le Tellier, September 30, 1652, *Lettres du cardinal Mazarin,* ed. Chéruel, V, 306–307. For reports carried in the English press see: *French Occurrences,* No. 34, December 6/16–13/23, 1652, p. 220; *The Weekly Intelligencer,* No. 99, November 23/December 3–November 30/December 10, 1652, p. 710; *ibid.,* No. 119, May 3/13–10/20, 1653, p. 849; *Nouvelles ordinaires de Londres,* No. 126, November

French could push the alliance with Holland to a swift conclusion.

Simultaneously, the French government strove for a more amicable relationship with England. If successful, this policy could forestall Commonwealth aid to the Frondeurs and block an English alliance with Spain, while relieving French trade of the crippling blows inflicted by England. But how to improve relations? All previous efforts snagged sooner or later on the question of recognition. The answer, if distasteful, was evident. The French grimly steeled themselves to waive all prior conditions. The alternative, they believed, was war with England and disaster at Bordeaux.

The Cardinal passed over Gentillot and selected Monsieur de Bordeaux, an intendant in Picardy, prominent jurist, and member of a wealthy family of merchants and tax farmers, to represent the government in England. After oral briefing, the new envoy received his formal written instructions, dated December 2, 1652.[15] Less than two weeks later, Monsieur de Bordeaux was settling down in London, bracing himself for his critical task.[16]

The envoy's instructions indicated a prudent optimism. The government in Paris believed that if the recognition issue could be eliminated for once and for all, then Monsieur de Bordeaux might obtain restitution of the ships captured by Blake. If successful there, Monsieur de Bordeaux could range on to more general disputes about trade and shipping. However, the in-

---

25/December 5–December 2/12, 1652, p. 502; *ibid.*, No. 147, April 14/24–April 21/May 1, 1653, p. 588. See also Vendôme to Mazarin, June 28, 1653, *Archives historiques du département de la Gironde*, VIII, 470; Thurloe to Whitelocke, December 2/12, 1653, Sigismund von Bischoffshausen, *Die Politik des Protectors Oliver Cromwell in der Auffassung und Thätigkeit seines Ministers, des Staatssecretärs John Thurloe* (Innsbruck, 1899), pp. 146–147.

[15] *Recueil des instructions données aux ambassadeurs, XXIV, Angleterre*, I, 152–157.

[16] Bordeaux to Brienne, December 22, 1652, P.R.O. transcript, 31/3/90, copied from B.N., MS. f.fr. 16008.

structions emphasized that, if necessary, France would continue to endure English "piracy," provided England did not join Spain and the Frondeurs. Therefore Monsieur de Bordeaux's primary objective was to keep England from meddling in the Fronde.[17]

London gave Monsieur de Bordeaux a mixed reception. Some in the English capital had never expected him to arrive at all. They assumed talk of his mission in Paris was just another artifice. When he did arrive, opinion split as to why he had come, some of it friendly, some hostile. However, when he agreed forthwith to recognize the Commonwealth without a quibble, the atmosphere noticeably improved.[18]

Monsieur de Bordeaux's first speech before a special committee of the Parliament on December 31, 1652, marked the end of one phase in the "cold war" between Puritan England and the French crown. The French envoy assured his listeners that his government absolutely rejected the necessity of ideological conflict with England. After all, he said, past treaties between the two countries had aimed at the common good and concerned primarily the peoples of the two states, rather than the princes. Necessities of commerce and understanding between the two neighbors remained, regardless of changes in the form of government. For its part, the French government believed that England and France could profit mutually from commercial exchange.[19]

The first positive result of the re-establishment of diplomatic

---

[17] *Recueil des instructions données aux ambassadeurs, XXIV, Angleterre,* I, 155.

[18] Bordeaux to Brienne, December 30, 1652, P.R.O. transcript, 31/3/90, copied from B.N., MS. f.fr. 16008; Paulucci to Sagredo, December 20, 1652; December 27, 1652, *Calendar of State Papers . . . Venice,* XXVIII, 321–323, 325–326. For English comment see: *French Occurrences,* November 29/December 9–December 6/16, 1652, p. 216; *The Weekly Intelligencer,* No. 101, December 7/17–14/24, 1652, p. 717; *Nouvelles ordinaires de Londres,* No. 126, November 25/December 5–December 2/12, 1652, p. 504; *ibid.,* No. 128, December 9/19–16/26, 1652, p. 510.

[19] *Portland Manuscripts,* I, 666–667.

relations was the appointment by the Commonwealth of five commissioners to meet with Monsieur de Bordeaux, beginning in January, 1653. The meetings failed to resolve the dispute over the ships captured by Blake. As a matter of fact, Monsieur de Bordeaux learned that the English had ordered those ships in repairable condition sold at Dover shortly after his arrival in England.[20] Paris officials fretted about it, principally because they believed it involved French honor. However, despite that, Monsieur de Bordeaux felt encouraged by the general tone of his conversations with the Puritans. Numerous English merchants wanted to resume commerce with France, and said so publicly. The Commissioners airily dismissed the desire of the merchants when talking to Monsieur de Bordeaux, and assured him that "we amuse ourselves with the merchants here; that is not the crux of the affair." They tried to tell him that the English government was guided by higher interests than the concerns of the merchants. But Monsieur de Bordeaux remarked that Parliament invariably sounded out the opinion of the merchants before concluding any agreements, which seemed to belie the Commissioners' nonchalance.[21]

Before long the hopelessness of recovering the ships taken by Blake became so apparent that this aspect of the problem faded from view, and Monsieur de Bordeaux concentrated on the larger issues. In March and April of 1653 discussion turned on an agreement for temporary cessation of reprisals on both sides, which could then lead to a permanent agreement. The negotiators disagreed over the time limit for the cessation of the sea war. The Puritans wanted to hold it to an initial maximum of three months, while Monsieur de Bordeaux objected that French ships could not complete their business and return to France in safety should hostilities resume at the expiration of the third month.

[20] Bordeaux to Brienne, March 10, 1653, Cosnac, *Souvenirs du règne de Louis XIV*, VI, 434–437.

[21] Bordeaux to Servien, January 20, 1653, *ibid.*, VI, 198–200.

For this reason he insisted on a six-month truce, and he picked up considerable support from the English merchants, who said the same thing to their own commissioners.[22]

In general, English merchants and shippers maintained a flexible attitude about compensation for losses, in the belief that their own government would pocket the settlement. They were interested primarily in insuring the future security of their commerce. Traders in the Mediterranean, whose losses were particularly heavy, felt less disposed to waive claims, it is true, but Monsieur de Bordeaux was confident he could dispose of the reparation issue. Parliament had designated René Augier, former Parliamentary agent in Paris, to study the reparation dispute and to draw up figures on English losses. Bordeaux wrote that Augier had come to see him several times and had hinted that, for the proper personal consideration, he could keep the figures low. Monsieur de Bordeaux assured him that the French government would reward him "according to his merit." [23]

Lack of co-ordination and lack of unanimity in France on how best to deal with the English hampered Monsieur de Bordeaux's negotiations. Economic pressures were heavy on French shippers and merchants to achieve a *modus vivendi* with the Puritans. By 1653 even fishing vessels could not leave port in Brittany, Normandy, and Picardy.[24] But when local officials requested directives from Paris on how to meet these and other problems, the government sometimes found it easier not to reply than to commit itself.[25] French shippers, no less than the English, noticed the contrast between the stern sounding ordon-

---

[22] Bordeaux to Brienne, March 20, 1653, *ibid.*, VI, 442–446.

[23] Bordeaux to Brienne, March 17, 1653, *ibid.*, VI, 440–442.

[24] *Mémoire pour les marchands de Paris, Rouen, S. Malo, Nantes, Morlay, Le Havre, & Dieppe, traffiquans en mer* (n.p., n.d.), in B.N., MS. f.fr. 18592.

[25] Sagredo to Doge and Senate, May 27, 1653, *Calendar of State Papers . . . Venice*, XXIX, 77.

nances against attacks on English shipping and the complete disregard with which those ordonnances were treated by local governors. French merchants and shippers continued to be confused as well by attacks of French naval ships against their own vessels.[26]

A printed *Mémoire pour les marchands de Paris, Rouen, S. Malo, Nantes, Morlay, Le Havre, & Dieppe, traffiquans en mer* (1653) urged the government to put a stop to commerce raiding against the English, yet advised the government not to return confiscated English goods. If the English continued their attacks, the King ought to bar English ships from French ports. In the next breath, the author advised against breaking diplomatic relations with England; yet he also advised that the King might grant letters of marque for recovery of losses inflicted by the English.[27]

Some of the French Channel ports, impatient with the government's handling of relations with England, undertook negotiations of their own with the Commonwealth. Monsieur de Bordeaux complained from London that the Sieur de Montigny, Governor of Dieppe, had requested passports from the Commonwealth for ships of that port without bothering to submit the request through him. The envoy icily termed it a procedure which "has appeared extraordinary and has even cast suspicion on his [Montigny's] loyalty to the service of the King, since he acted on his own without the participation of the ministers of His Majesty." [28] The Governor of Dieppe had similarly applied to the English Parliament to allow the fishermen of Dieppe to fish off the coast of Sussex. These requests were steered through Parliament by persons who stressed the "good understanding"

[26] *Mémoire pour les marchands de Paris, Rouen, etc.,* in B.N., MS. f.fr. 18592.

[27] *Ibid.*

[28] Bordeaux to Brienne, February 10, 1653, Cosnac, *Souvenirs du règne de Louis XIV,* VI, 208–212.

said to exist between England and the port of Dieppe because of the many services received by Englishmen from the Governor.[29]

In January, 1653, the Council of State in London learned that St. Malo wished to trade with England and would accept English cloth regardless of the French embargo, provided it could export to England items of French origin such as linens, sailcloth, and other naval stores. The Parliament was reminded of St. Malo's importance as supplier to the islands of Guernsey and Jersey. Several London merchants, claiming support from most of the ports of western England, filed petition for a suspension of letters of marque against the ships of St. Malo. They petitioned that St. Malo receive the same protection granted to the ships of Dieppe and Calais, thereby indicating that Dieppe and Calais had concluded agreements with the Commonwealth. Unfortunately for St. Malo, Parliament set the petition aside because it wished to determine how negotiations with Monsieur de Bordeaux might develop. If those negotiations terminated successfully, St. Malo would fall under the general treaty.[30]

Monsieur de Bordeaux complained that his task was made harder by uncomplimentary reports about the Commonwealth which appeared in the *Gazette de France*. Could not the *Gazette* be muzzled? [31] He also complained of the highhanded behavior of local port officials in France against the Puritans. The English took particular offense when authorities at Nantes allowed Prince Rupert to bring in several English prizes from his recent West Indies cruise.[32] Officials of the marine at Calais permitted

[29] *Calendar of State Papers, Domestic Series, 1652–1653*, ed. M. A. E. Green (London, 1878), pp. 53–54, 152, 177. See also André L. Simon, *The History of the Wine Trade in England*, II (London, 1909), 65–69.

[30] *Ibid.*, pp. 62–63, 93, 195.

[31] Bordeaux to Brienne, February 27, 1653, P.R.O. transcript, 31/3/90, copied from B.N., MS. f.fr. 16008.

[32] Bordeaux to Brienne, March 24, 1653, *ibid.*, 31/3/90, copied from B.N., MS. f.fr. 16008.

seizure of English property, Bordeaux wrote, making it difficult for him to convince the Puritans of French good faith.[33] He recounted how English merchants came to him for help in obtaining the release of cargoes confiscated in France, of how he wrote letters in their behalf to the local authorities which the officials simply ignored.[34] Paris assured Monsieur de Bordeaux that in the future his recommendations would be honored, but time proved otherwise.[35]

The English royalists confirmed the state of confusion regarding French treatment of Puritan shipping and property. By winter's end in 1652, the exiles were unaware of any order from the French crown against ships sailing under commission of Charles II. If the Lieutenant Governor of Brest pretended such an order, the exiles said, he did it to make the exiles pay him for permission to sell their prizes.[36]

In spite of everything, Monsieur de Bordeaux appeared near an agreement with the Commonwealth. On April 19, 1653, he informed his government that the Puritans wanted a treaty immediately and were willing to settle reparation claims and other questions later. Monsieur de Bordeaux assumed their haste came because the Frondeurs at Bordeaux seemed close to defeat.[37] The French envoy shortly received back word that his government would approve a treaty.[38]

Probably even before that letter arrived in London, a new

---

[33] Bordeaux to Brienne, April 10, 1653, Cosnac, *Souvenirs du règne de Louis XIV*, VII, 355–358.

[34] Bordeaux to Brienne, May 15, 1653, P.R.O. transcript 31/3/90, copied from B.N., MS. f.fr. 16008.

[35] Bordeaux to Brienne, June 5, 1653, *ibid.*, 31/3/91, copied from B.N., MS. f.fr. 16008; Bordeaux to Brienne, July 10, 1653, Cosnac, *Souvenirs du règne de Louis XIV*, VII, 433–436.

[36] Hyde to Nicholas, February 27, 1652/1653 (O.S.?), *Clarendon State Papers*, III, 145.

[37] Bordeaux to Brienne, April 19, 1653, Cosnac, *Souvenirs du règne de Louis XIV*, VII, 367–368.

[38] Bordeaux to Brienne, April 24, 1653, *ibid.*, VII, 369–371.

coup de théâtre in the English Revolution scrambled all plans. On April 30, 1653, Cromwell made his famous appearance before Parliament to announce its dissolution. The same afternoon, he summarily dismissed the Council of State. Cromwell and the Puritan Independents, who backed him, now ruled England. The French naturally wondered how the political reshuffling might affect the treaty negotiations. At the very least, delay was inevitable, to give the new English government a chance to take stock.

In these same months leading to Cromwell's assumption of power, the position of the Frondeurs in Bordeaux had steadily deteriorated. The respite which Admiral Blake's action gave them lasted briefly. For a while the Frondeurs imported grain from Brittany, and, despite the lack of formal agreement with England, several English ships loaded cargo at Bordeaux.[39] But in December, 1652, the economic outlook darkened. Cardinal Mazarin ignored advice to have merchants from Rouen and Paris buy up all grain stocks to keep it from going to Bordeaux.[40] Instead, he adopted a more practical plan and ordered Vendôme to enforce a blockade by sea, in conjunction with the attack by land of the royal armies.

Toward the end of the year, the Duc de Vendôme resumed more aggressive action against the Frondeurs. Pierre Lenet at Bordeaux admitted to the Prince de Condé that traffic into Bordeaux by sea had virtually ceased.[41] The fleet which Spain had sent to aid the Frondeurs proved lamentably ineffective. Instead

[39] Vivens to Mazarin, September 16, 1652, *Archives historiques du département de la Gironde,* VIII, 412; *Le journal contenant ce qui se passe,* p. 130, Moreau No. 1740; *Relation véritable contenant tout ce qui s'est fait et passé à Bordeaux* (n.p., 1652), p. 5.

[40] Pontac to Mazarin, January 1, 1653, *Archives historiques du département de la Gironde,* VII, 258.

[41] Lenet to Condé, December 12, 1652, "Mémoires de Pierre Lenet," *Nouvelle collection des mémoires,* XXIV, 586.

of the thirty ships required to hold open the access route by sea, the Spanish commander had but half that number and used those poorly.[42]

Before Vendôme could sail up the Gironde, however, the Frondeurs received a reprieve in the form of a Dutch convoy. The convoy, shepherded by Admiral van Tromp and headed for Bordeaux, dropped off merchant vessels here and there at French ports all along the way, including Rouen, St. Malo, Nantes, and La Rochelle. Van Tromp proposed to wait for the merchantmen to unload and to load cargoes, then escort them home again, picking up en route Dutch vessels stranded in French ports by the hostilities with England. The Dutch were bent on trade with anyone and everyone in France and plainly indifferent to the political niceties created by the Fronde.[43]

When a major portion of van Tromp's convoy reached St. Martin on the Isle of Ré, a sloop headed out from La Rochelle to announce to the Dutch commander Vendôme's astonishment and displeasure that so great a fleet was bound for rebellious Bordeaux.[44] But, as Vendôme lacked enough power to stop the Dutch, the message failed to deter them. When the convoy reached Bordeaux, it must surely have been a delightful sight to the Frondeurs. Lenet had just about given up hope for it in early December.[45] Now the holds of the Dutch ships disgorged

[42] Conti to Chouppes, February 15, 1653, *ibid.*, XXIV, 596.

[43] Tromp to States-General, December 17, 1652, *Letters and Papers Relating to the First Dutch War, 1652–1654*, ed. Samuel R. Gardiner, Navy Records Society, Vol. XXX ([London], 1906), 137–138; see also *ibid.*, p. 215. The Dutch had aided the Bordeaux Frondeurs before. The Duc d'Epernon had complained in 1649 that Dutch merchants had furnished vessels and munitions to the Bordeaux rebels (d'Epernon to Séguier, May 27, 1649, *Lettres et mémoires adressés au chancelier Séguier*, II, 1015).

[44] *Letters and Papers Relating to the First Dutch War*, XXX, 217.

[45] Lenet to Condé, December 12, 1652, "Mémoires de Pierre Lenet," *Nouvelle collection des mémoires*, XXIV, 586.

enough grain and other supplies to provision the city until the following July or August.[46] This windfall boosted Frondeur morale considerably.

In other respects, the result of the Dutch visit to Bordeaux disappointed the Bordelais and the Dutch themselves. For one thing, the Dutch found trade in the region much disrupted by the troubles inside France. For another, the Dutch were caught in a crossfire of customs claims. The city of Bordeaux attempted to collect custom duties, and at the same time Vendôme demanded payment of custom before the fleet left the Gironde. Because of the wrangle, a third of the Dutch ships sailed from the city, their holds empty. Those which did load at Bordeaux sailed past Vendôme's fleet without bothering either to pay or to salute.[47]

Probably, as the Puritans believed, the Dutch subsequently came under strong pressure from the French government not to repeat their visit to Bordeaux.[48] Probably, too, the Dutch were soured on trade with the city anyway. In any case, this was the last Dutch convoy to put into Bordeaux during the Fronde. Toward the end of June, 1653, a large Dutch fleet of approximately one hundred ships sailed northward from La Rochelle with cargoes of wine, vinegar, brandy, and paper, but none of it came from Bordeaux.[49]

Once the Dutch departed, Vendôme tightened his control of

[46] Vivens to Mazarin, March 22, 1653, *Archives historiques du département de la Gironde,* VII, 296.

[47] *Nouvelles ordinaires de Londres,* No. 137, February 10/20–February 17/27, 1653, p. 544; Bishop of Tulle to Mazarin, February 13, 1653, *Archives historiques du département de la Gironde,* VII, 268–269; see also *ibid.,* VII, 271–272; Tromp to States-General, January 24, 1653, *Letters and Papers Relating to the First Dutch War,* XXXVII, 27; see also *ibid.,* XXX, 218; XXXVII, 24.

[48] *The Weekly Intelligencer,* No. 103, March 8/18–15/25, 1652/1653, p. 770.

[49] Letter of intelligence from La Rochelle, June 26, 1653, *Thurloe Papers,* I, 296.

the seaway to Bordeaux and wrote confidently to the Cardinal, February 25, 1653, that he was now master of the river.[50] The Duke was jubilant because he believed that only an effective naval blockade could bring the rebels to their knees. Vendôme had no fear of dislodgement by the inferior Spanish fleet. Nonetheless, as late as July, 1653, the Duke admitted that the Bordelais still had one avenue of escape—English intervention. If naval units from England joined the fleet of the Frondeurs and the Spanish, he could not maintain the blockade.[51]

Condé and his lieutenants reached the same conclusions, and they redoubled their efforts to obtain help from the Puritans. In London, Barrière tried to use the arrival of the Dutch convoy at Bordeaux as a prod. With a feigned air of confidence, Barrière explained to the Council of State in February, 1653, that everything was going so well for the Prince de Condé that he really did not require their help. But what a pity, Barrière added slyly, that the English allowed their Dutch rivals to reap the benefit of trade with Bordeaux. As Barrière told the story, the Dutch had laden six hundred ships at Bordeaux or vicinity. The value of the traffic from that area, he said, exceeded that of all the rest of France, since from Bordeaux came salt, wine, and an infinite variety of products. If the English hesitated to trade with the Frondeurs out of respect to the French crown, Barrière pointed to the example of the Dutch.[52] Notwithstanding Barrière's arguments, the treaty of commerce with England continued to hang fire.

The Comte du Daugnon at Brouage handed the Frondeurs a further disappointment. Following a familiar pattern, the Count

[50] Vendôme to Mazarin, February 25, 1653, *Archives historiques du département de la Gironde*, VII, 275–276.

[51] Vendôme to Mazarin, February 25, 1653, *ibid.*, VII, 275–276; Vendôme to Mazarin, March 20, 1653, *ibid.*, VII, 290; Vendôme to Mazarin, July 9, 1653, *ibid.*, XV, 335.

[52] Barrière to Council of State, February 1 [11 ?], 1653, *Thurloe Papers*, I, 225.

had bargained with all sides since his involvement in the Fronde. The Count and his agent in London agreed in December, 1652, that no treaty ought to be signed with the Commonwealth until the last possible moment.[53] Mazarin's correspondence reveals that the Count was also making peace overtures to the court in December.[54] No dupes, the Puritans gave up hope on the Count in February, 1653. They predicted that, before Vendôme's fleet attacked Brouage, the Count would abandon Condé and the Frondeurs in return for good terms from Louis XIV.[55] The prediction proved accurate. For a marshal's baton, a dukedom, and other considerations, he made his peace with the King.

Barrière tried to persuade the English that the Comte du Daugnon's defection had resulted because of his despair of receiving English aid. Barrière intimated the city of Bordeaux might be overcome by the same despair unless England acted promptly. Officials of the Commonwealth retorted that unless Barrière had more specific proposals to make than those they had listened to so far, England could do nothing for the Frondeurs.[56]

The Comte du Daugnon's reversal caused wavering among some of the Frondeurs present in London. Monsieur de Bordeaux received a visit from an unnamed "man of honor" who claimed he could arrange for the submission of the powerful La Force family in Guyenne and for the transfer of places held by the family to the royal armies closing in on Bordeaux.[57] The Marquis

[53] Saint-Thomas to du Daugnon, December 2, 1652, "Mémoires de Pierre Lenet," *Nouvelle collection des mémoires*, XXIV, 584.

[54] Mazarin to Le Tellier, December 22, 1652, *Lettres du cardinal Mazarin*, ed Chéruel, V, 509; Mazarin to Servien, December 22, 1652, *ibid.*, V, 511.

[55] *The Weekly Intelligencer*, No. 105, February 8/18–15/25, 1652/1653, p. 740.

[56] Barrière to Condé, April 11, 1653, Musée Condé, Chantilly, MS. série P, XIII, f. 49.

[57] Bordeaux to Brienne, April 3, 1653, P.R.O. transcript, 31/3/90, copied from B.N., MS. f.fr. 16008; Bordeaux to Brienne, April 17, 1653, Cosnac, *Souvenirs du règne de Louis XIV*, VII, 361–365.

de Cugnac, the late Maréchal de La Force's grandson, must have been responsible for the offer. Nothing came of it, but the proposal reveals the pessimism of the Frondeurs in England.

Restlessness pervaded Bordeaux in late winter and spring of 1653, providing an ideal climate for plots and counterplots. Among them was a plot conceived by the Huguenot faction within the Ormée, with the backing of English agents. The plot threatened the Princes as much as it did the crown, it seemed. The Duc de Saint-Simon, from his listening post close by at Blaye, reported to Cardinal Mazarin in February, 1653, that the conspirators planned to declare Bordeaux a republic toward the end of March, and to expel the Prince de Conti (Condé's brother) from the city. Monsieur de Théobon, who enjoyed considerable popularity in Huguenot circles of Bordeaux, was said to be one of the leaders. Another Huguenot, Monsieur de Labadie, brother of the well-known Huguenot pastor Jean de Labadie, labored for the conspiracy at La Rochelle and Montauban, whose populations consisted of a significant Huguenot element. The conspirators expected powerful assistance from England.[58]

Pierre Lenet learned of the republican plot too and informed the Prince de Condé about it. Condé cynically advised his lieutenant in a letter of March 10, 1653, to avoid hasty action. They must always side with the strongest faction in Bordeaux, he counseled. If the Huguenots succeeded in bringing off their coup, obviously they could dominate the city. The best way to provide for that risk, Condé thought, was to join them, taking care to control them. They might talk about the establishment of a republic in Bordeaux, but the Prince felt sure Lenet could prevent it. Meanwhile the republican discussion might serve to give the rebellion new life. A "guilt by association" would mark all the Frondeurs vis-à-vis the crown, making it harder to with-

[58] Intelligence from Saint-Simon, February, 1653, *Archives historiques du département de la Gironde*, VII, 264–265.

draw from the rebellion. Therefore Condé advised Lenet to work with the Huguenot republicans.[59]

Even before Lenet received the Prince's reply, he evidently anticipated the answer. He began to reach a friendly understanding with the republican Huguenots. He did his work so well that the English Colonel Sexby and his associate, Arundel, were encouraged to submit to the Prince de Conti two of the most remarkable documents to emerge from the Fronde. The first bore the title, "L'accord du peuple." As students of the English Civil War might guess, it derived, title and all, from the English Levellers' famous "Agreement of the People" of 1649. The French version, presented to the Prince de Conti, differed in some respects, however. Approximately half of the articles of the original Leveller statement were deleted, and additional cuts were made in some of the remaining articles. Sexby and his assistants had attempted to adapt the document for a French milieu, but they had evidently edited it in haste. A number of references and provisions applicable to England were quite inappropriate for France.[60]

The "Agreement of the People" contained an odd assortment of objectives to present to the Prince de Conti. It called for a republican government by parliament, male suffrage for all over twenty-one who were neither servants nor recipients of alms, legal reforms to reduce special privilege, the right of all persons to trial by jury, and religious toleration.[61] The sum of these and other demands exceeded anything then in force in the Commonwealth. Not until the nineteenth century did England finally accept the program in most of its points, whereas, in the seventeenth century, Cromwell and other Commonwealth leaders fought against many of these demands as too radical. The Level-

---

[59] Condé to Lenet, March 10, 1653, "Mémoires de Lenet," *Nouvelle collection des mémoires,* XXIV, 599.

[60] Cosnac, *Souvenirs du règne de Louis XIV,* V, 256–262.

[61] *Ibid.,* V, 262–277.

ler party in England had slipped into steady decline after 1649, and Cromwell's government rearrested the Leveller leader, John Lilburne, in July, 1653. If Cromwell and others in England, considered in France to epitomize radicalism and revolution, rejected Leveller ideals, one can easily imagine the distaste with which the Princes' party in Bordeaux must have reacted, in private at least, to an abbreviated version of the Leveller program.

A second section of the document given to the Prince de Conti by the two English agents carried the title "Manifeste." This section, drafted for more specific application to Guyenne, suggests close collaboration with the Huguenot republicans of the Ormée. In it there was at least a mention of "our heroic Princes," although the manifesto was as republican as the "Agreement of the People." Some of the demands enunciated in the "Agreement of the People" were repeated, including an insistence upon government by a parliament, and an end to arbitrary taxation and to special privilege in fiscal matters. The manifesto sought to rally rural areas of Guyenne by requiring the abolition of servile status and by insisting that the peasant have the same rights in court as the lord. The manifesto bid for support from the urban middle class by demanding equal treatment for all persons of the country engaged in commerce. It called likewise for regular trade relations with England. To ease the sufferings of the very poor, the manifesto called on the state to make provisions for such persons. No more should the indigent be compelled to sleep—and to die—in the streets.

But above all, the manifesto appealed to the religious interest of the Huguenots. No person should be penalized because of his religious belief or practice. Every city, town, burg, and village ought to have designated places where Huguenots could perform their religious services without interference. A Huguenot ought to be able to hold any government office. Yet while the manifesto called for punishment of those who sought to provoke religious controversy, it envisaged that all, Catholics and Huguenots, should model their private lives according to a Puritan code of morality. Blasphemy, drunkenness, lechery, violation of the Sabbath ought to be dealt with "according to the laws of England" so that God might be pleased to restore peace.

Lenet obtained a copy of these two texts and forwarded them to the Prince de Condé. At the head of the document he scrawled an emphatic "I do not approve." [62] What comment Pierre Lenet or the Prince de Conti made to the English agents after reading the document, we do not know. Their response was probably vague and noncommittal. However, they did agree to let deputies from the city of Bordeaux go to London in quest of English help.

It was not a simple matter for the Princes to back the revolutionary faction of Huguenots in the Ormée and to let them negotiate with the English. Those in the Princes' party had lost none of their nervousness about the Huguenots and about English influence. Letters addressed to the Prince de Condé in June and July, 1652, at the time of the Ormée take-over in Bordeaux ought to have reminded the Prince of that. A "bourgeois" of Bordeaux had written to the Prince: "We fear the Huguenots. And . . . the English. . . . We are menaced by that Republic. We do not know where to take refuge. We have incurred the indignation of the King. And we cannot suffer heresy in the city . . . We here are in great despair. In the name of God, set things in order." [63] In July the same writer warned the Prince that "good Catholics will flee heresy, and the others persecution; . . . the republicans are attracting as many Huguenots as they can." [64]

---

[62] *Ibid.*, V, 277.

[63] "Un bourgeois de Bordeaux" to Condé, June 6, 1652, Chantilly, MS. série P, XIII, f. 269.

[64] "Un bourgeois de Bordeaux" to Condé, July 1, 1652, *ibid.*, série P, XIII, f. 301.

What Will England Do?

Propagandists for the Princes' party in 1651–1652 had even advertised their hostility to the Huguenots and to the English Puritans. In an agreement of union signed between the Princes and the Parlement and city of Bordeaux January 3, 1652, one of the articles stated unequivocally that the signatories would maintain and defend the Catholic religion to the last breath of life.[65] A brochure circulated in the Princes' behalf speculated darkly that "we will soon see the English at our gates." [66] Another suggested a landing by the English at La Rochelle, Blaye, and Bordeaux as one of the greatest dangers.[67] Yet another author concocted a completely fictitious story of a battle in which the Prince de Conti repulsed a landing attempted by the English at Bordeaux in May of 1652. The English, said the author, had come to establish a republic with the help of the Huguenots, but the heroic Prince de Conti had defeated them.[68]

Not all the Huguenots in Guyenne or in Bordeaux itself sided with Sexby. Far from it. A number of the more well-to-do Huguenots in Bordeaux refused to join, and in fact actively opposed the political designs of their radical coreligionists.[69] Although the Maréchal de La Force and his family had thrown in with the Frondeurs in 1652, most of the Huguenot population in the outlying districts continued to avoid committal for Condé, let alone support for the revolutionary program outlined in the documents of Sexby and Arundel. Many called to mind how the English Protestants had left them to defeat at La Rochelle

[65] *Concordat de l'union* (n.p., 1652), p. 5, Moreau No. 731.

[66] *La décadence visible* (n.p., 1652), pp. 15–16, Moreau No. 866.

[67] *Avertissement (second) à messieurs les prévost*, pp. 7–8, Moreau No. 446.

[68] *Lettre de monsieur le prince de Conti* (Paris, 1652), pp. 4–7, Moreau No. 2038. Condé's negotiations with England had caused him embarrassment in Paris. He went before the Parlement of Paris in August, 1652, and denied that Cugnac had gone to England on his orders. He also denied that he knew Monsieur de Barrière (*Journal de Jean Vallier*, IV, 35).

[69] Bishop of Tulle to Mazarin, August 4, 1653, *Archives historiques du département de la Gironde*, XV, 381.

almost twenty-five years before. They refused to build their hopes on English intervention a second time. Local synods of the Huguenots continued to exhort the faithful to remain loyal to the crown. A provincial synod in Saintonge recommended all pastors to urge their flocks not to depart from an "entire fidelity and obedience which are due the King." A synod in lower Guyenne expressed a wish "to live and die" loyal to the King.[70] Toward the end of May, 1653, Jean Daillé, preaching before the Huguenots of La Rochelle, explained that the spirit of God inspired the Huguenots with a resolution to remain loyal to their sovereign.[71]

The two principal leaders of the Ormée, Villars and Duretête, represented a Catholic, pro-Spanish viewpoint. Catholics in the Ormée gave an impressive show of strength in the fall of 1652 when they refused to allow trade between Bordeaux and the Huguenot towns of the upper Guyenne at a time when Bordeaux needed trade of any sort. Although the Princes approved trade with the Huguenots, the Ormée remained intransigent and would consent to a resumption of commerce only if the Huguenots agreed to return to the Catholic Church.[72]

Lenet and the other leaders of the Princes' party in Bordeaux had to find a way to convince their Catholic and politically conservative friends to collaborate with the radical Huguenots and to allow a deputation from the city to go to England. Lenet and his associates hand picked the deputies for England first, then submitted the names for general approval at the Hôtel de Ville. Originally they considered naming Monsieur de Labadie (probably the same who had worked with fellow Huguenots at La Rochelle and Montauban earlier), but they later scratched

[70] Frank Puaux, "L'évolution des théories politiques du Protestantisme français," *Bulletin—Société de l'histoire du Protestantisme français,* LXII (1913), 388.

[71] Galland, "Les pasteurs français," *ibid.,* LXXVII (1928), 232.

[72] Cosnac, *Souvenirs du règne de Louis XIV,* V, 56–57.

his name from the list.[73] Perhaps they decided he might be too radical. Of the three individuals actually named, the chief of the delegation was to be Trancas, a member of the Parlement of Bordeaux. Désert, a friend of Villars, the pro-Spanish leader of the Ormée, and an obscure goldsmith, Blarut, the only Huguenot of the three, were also named to the delegation. Written instructions, carefully setting forth the limits of negotiation, were drafted and submitted for approval at the Hôtel de Ville where they received the signatures of the *jurats* of the city, of Duretête and Villars, and of various other persons. The deputies received the most express order to confer and to act conjointly in London with the Prince de Condé's agent, Barrière, and with the Marquis de Cugnac.[74] As soon as Condé learned of the plan to send delegates to London, he wrote to Lenet several times emphasizing that the delegates must act in concert with Barrière.[75] Meanwhile, Condé summoned Barrière to confer with him in Brussels.

The written instructions for the Bordeaux deputies, the section termed public, authorized them to enter a league with the Parliament of England, to obtain ships, men, and financial help. Secret instructions went farther. The delegation could offer England a *lieu de sureté*, such as Royan, which the English might occupy in the same fashion that the Spaniards occupied Bourg, on the Dordogne. Or the deputies might offer La Rochelle, provided the English could capture it. But the deputies were told to avoid promises to make specific political or religious changes in Guyenne. They could imply that all the Huguenots of the region simply awaited the arrival of the Puritans to

[73] Lenet to Condé, March 24, 1653, Chantilly, MS. série P, XIII, f. 23; Lenet to Condé, March 31, 1653, *ibid.*, série P, XIII, f. 35; "Le royaliste de Bordeaux" to Mazarin, April, 1653, *Archives historiques du département de la Gironde*, VIII, 128.

[74] Cosnac, *Souvenirs du règne de Louis XIV*, VII, 3–7, 346.

[75] Condé to Lenet, April 26, 1653, B.N., MS. f.fr. 6714, ff. 296–297; Condé to Lenet, n.d., *ibid.*, 6714, ff. 12–13.

introduce political and religious innovations, but they must not make commitments.[76]

These preparations took some time. Not until April 8, 1653, had the instructions and the selection of the deputies for England received formal approval.[77] For reasons unclear, more than a month and a half elapsed before the delegation arrived in London, May 22, 1653.[78] In the intervening time, Cromwell had turned out the Rump Parliament, which the deputies learned only upon arrival in England. Their first act was to seek out Monsieur de Barrière, who had himself just returned from talks in Brussels with the Prince de Condé.[79] The Prince had evidently told Barrière the deputies had been carefully selected and could be trusted.[80]

Barrière, with relief, confirmed to the Prince that, on the basis of his first conversations, none of the three deputies gave sign of being republican. They admitted dissatisfaction with the government in Bordeaux, yes; but they were not republicans. They seemed firmly wedded, in fact, to the interests of the Princes. On the other hand, the delegation avoided the Spanish ambassador in London. Also Trancas, the delegation chief, and the Marquis de Cugnac bickered over precedence. However, in Barrière's opinion, the Prince need have no anxiety about the presence of the deputies in London.[81]

For several days before the arrival of the deputies, all London knew they were coming. It was widely assumed, however, that they had carte blanche to negotiate with the English govern-

---

[76] Cosnac, *Souvenirs du règne de Louis XIV*, VII, 346–354.

[77] *Ibid.*, VII, 354.

[78] Trancas to Condé, May 23, 1653, Chantilly, MS. série P, XIII, f. 119.

[79] Trancas to Condé, May 23, 1653, *ibid.*, série P, XIII, f. 119; Barrière to Condé, [May 23, 1653], *ibid.*, série P, XIII, ff. 116–117.

[80] Barrière to Condé, [May, 1653], *ibid.*, série P, XIII, f. 536.

[81] Barrière to Condé, [May, 1653, incorrectly given date August, 1653], *ibid.*, série P, XIII, f. 525.

ment.[82] Naturally, Trancas easily obtained immediate secret audiences with Cromwell.[83] However, the limited terms provided in the instructions from Bordeaux obviously fell short of what Cromwell expected.

Cromwell, who was then consolidating his position, realized the adverse reaction which his dissolution of Parliament had caused in some quarters of the English population. He realized, too, that many persons in England had strong misgivings about aiding the Frondeurs of Bordeaux. A number of merchants continued to urge an end to the sea war with France and the conclusion of a treaty with France.[84] The English press told readers about strong opposition to republicanism inside Bordeaux because of the agitation of the Catholic clergy.[85] These factors, combined with the poor terms brought by the Bordeaux deputies (poor terms from the Puritan viewpoint), provided Cromwell with little incentive to enter a pact with the Frondeurs. Evidently Sexby, in Bordeaux, had anticipated that the offer brought by the deputies might cause disappointment in England. Consequently he advised the government to receive the delegation warmly, even should England not then be ready to assist the Bordelais. Sexby was probably fairly certain that the revolutionary Huguenot group could gain the upper hand in Bordeaux. Sexby said when he returned to England that he

[82] Bordeaux to Brienne, May 15, 1653, P.R.O. transcript, 31/3/90, copied from B.N., MS. f.fr. 16008; intercepted letter of Sir Walter Vane, May 7, 1653 (O.S.?), *Thurloe Papers*, I, 240; Paulucci to Sagredo, May 17, 1653, *Calendar of State Papers . . . Venice*, XXIX, 71–73; Paulucci to Sagredo, May 23, 1653, *ibid.*, XXIX, 74–76.

[83] Paulucci to Sagredo, May 30, 1653, *ibid.*, XXIX, 79; Barrière to Condé, [May 23, 1653], Chantilly, MS. série P, XIII, 116–117.

[84] Bordeaux to Brienne, May 29, 1653, P.R.O. transcript, 31/3/90, copied from B.N., MS. f.fr. 16008.

[85] *French Occurrences*, No. 36, December 20/30–December 27/January 6, 1652/1653, p. 235; *Nouvelles ordinaires de Londres*, No. 150, May 5/15–12/22, 1653, p. 597; *The Weekly Intelligencer*, No. 117, May 3/13–10/20, 1653, pp. 836–837.

could explain why the deputation ought to be well received.[86]

At some point before Cromwell's meeting with Trancas, probably in the spring of 1653, the English government had proposed to the Spanish ambassador that England would send 6,000 troops to Bordeaux with naval support, if Spain paid for the operation.[87] This proposal had far exceeded the capability of the Spanish treasury, and the project was dropped. However, Cromwell decided now, in his conversations with Trancas, to try a similar offer on the citizens of Bordeaux. Cromwell told Trancas that he would send forty naval ships and 5,000 troops, but that he must have a *lieu de sureté*. The *lieu de sureté* he specified was Bordeaux itself.[88] Cromwell's offer of massive aid could entirely alter the military picture in Guyenne. But would the Bordelais accept English occupation?

Trancas transmitted the proposal in greatest secrecy to Bordeaux. He informed neither Barrière nor the Spanish ambassador. Though the Spanish ambassador learned enough to suspect that Trancas and the other deputies were up to something, Barrière refused to take his suspicions seriously.[89] The secret was so well kept that the French envoy, Monsieur de Bordeaux, had no inkling of it. Trancas probably informed the Prince de Condé of the offer, however, since the Prince wrote to Lenet on June 7, 1653, that chances of English help looked very promising.[90]

Trancas' letter conveying Cromwell's proposal reached the Frondeurs in Bordeaux at a moment of deepening crisis. The naval force of the Duc de Vendôme had by then moved to

[86] Letter of intelligence, May 15/25, 1653, *Thurloe Papers*, I, 245.

[87] Gardiner, *History of the Commonwealth*, III, 119–120.

[88] *Mémoires de Daniel de Cosnac*, I, 67–68; Theodorus to Conway, May 19/29, 1653, *Calendar of State Papers, Domestic Series, 1652–1653*, p. 340.

[89] Barrière to Condé, June 6, 1653, Chantilly, MS. série P, XIII, ff. 140·141.

[90] Condé to Lenet, June 7, 1653, B.N., MS. f.fr. 6715, f. 175.

within four or five leagues of Bordeaux, and a supporting army led by the Duc de Candale had seized the outlying territory before the city. Within Bordeaux, the populace began to panic before the specter of famine, and several popular assemblies threatened the Fronde leaders with violence if they did not unblock the river and ensure the arrival of supplies. The city was in such a ferment that the Frondeurs had to pull back troops needed to fight Candale and Vendôme, to maintain order inside Bordeaux. Although unknown to other Fronde leaders, the Prince de Conti had sunk into such discouragement that he was already in secret preliminary negotiations with the crown. Hence the receipt of Cromwell's offer struck like a bombshell.

The Prince de Conti greeted it warmly. Most of the other persons high in the counsels of the Princes' party in Bordeaux were enthusiastic, particularly the Comte de Marchin. Marchin, who commanded the Frondeur military force at Bordeaux, believed himself so compromised by the Fronde that he could never arrange an accommodation with the King.[91] Several assemblies at the end of May and beginning of June were already recommending the dispatch of new deputies to England with new conditions. Probably this agitation had begun even before Trancas' letters from England arrived. Cromwell's proposal was extremely well timed.[92]

On June 12, 1653, Pierre Lenet informed Condé that a solemn act calling for England's help was approved in the Hôtel de Ville and signed by the Prince de Conti, the Comte de Marchin, Lenet as representative of the Prince de Condé, and by all the other persons of importance in the city including the *jurats* and representatives of the Ormée. Certain documents to that effect

[91] *Mémoires de Daniel de Cosnac*, I, 66–69.

[92] *Le septième courrier bourdelois* (Paris, 1652), p. 5, Moreau No. 811; *Le véritable courrier général* (Paris, 1653), p. 3; letter of intelligence, June 18, 1653, *Thurloe Papers*, I, 276; Bishop of Tulle to Mazarin, May 17, 1653, *Archives historiques du département de la Gironde*, VIII, 153–155; Vendôme to Mazarin, June 6, 1653, *ibid.*, VIII, 440.

were sent to England.[93] Probably the document referred to by Lenet contained the "Agreement of the People" and the "Manifesto" which Sexby and Arundel had previously submitted. Furnished now with a preamble stating that the two Princes, Condé and Conti, the ministers, generals, magistrates, colonels, captains, officers, and people of Bordeaux and the country round about it "declare jointly and severally in the presence of God that they will not lay down their arms . . . until they have achieved the true aim of a free people, a republic modeled on those which have come nearest to justice and good government," the document reached Trancas in England. He presented it to the Council of State and made a speech in its behalf.[94]

Cromwell evidently expected Bordeaux to send additional deputies to ratify the conditions of the appeal for aid. Before this could be done, a reaction against the plan set in at Bordeaux. Despite all the efforts of the Princes' party to reassure their more conservative Catholic supporters, distrust of Huguenots and of republican England died hard. Many had suspected from the start that the deputies in England intended to ignore the written instructions. Cardinal Mazarin exploited these fears through his undercover agents in the city, who whispered that Trancas was dickering with the Puritans to establish a republic at Bordeaux under English auspices.[95] Now, it appeared, Trancas was trying to do just that.

[93] Lenet to Condé, June 12, 1653, B.N., MS. f.fr. 6715, ff. 180–181.

[94] Bordeaux to Brienne, November 9, 1653, P.R.O. transcript, 31/3/92, copied from B.N., MS. f.fr. 16008; Mazarin to Bordeaux, November 21, 1653, *ibid.*, 31/3/92, copied from A.E. Angleterre, LXI, f. 353; Bordeaux to Mazarin, December 14, 1653, *ibid.*, 31/3/92, copied from A.E. Angleterre, LXI, f. 364; Bordeaux to Mazarin, December 25, 1653, *ibid.*, 31/3/92, copied from A.E. Angleterre, LXI, f. 390; Bordeaux to Mazarin, January 5, 1654, *ibid.*, 31/3/92, copied from A.E. Angleterre, LXIII, f. 16. For information regarding Mazarin's copy, see Chéruel, *Histoire de France sous le ministère de Mazarin,* I, 57–60.

[95] "Le royaliste de Bordeaux" to Mazarin, April, 1653, *Archives historiques du département de la Gironde,* VIII, 127; Mazarin to Bishop of Tulle, June 2, 1653, *Lettres du cardinal Mazarin,* ed. Chéruel, V, 624.

What Will England Do?

The youthful and ambitious Abbé de Cosnac, one of the Prince de Conti's confidants, was among those unwilling to trust either the Huguenots or the English. The Abbé did all he could to implant doubts about the wisdom of accepting Cromwell's offer. He reminded the Prince de Conti that he derived his power from the city of Bordeaux. If he turned the city over to Cromwell, he would injure himself. The Abbé spoke of the shame Conti would bring upon him by allowing Catholic Bordeaux to fall under the sway of a heretic. Finally, he stressed that the Prince was tied to the interests of monarchy by his birth. As a Prince of the Blood, he might one day become King of France. Yet here he was, ready to countenance the surrender of Bordeaux to a tyrant who had killed his own king and might turn next against the Prince.[96]

The Abbé de Cosnac's arguments hit the mark. The Prince first hesitated, then rejected Cromwell's offer. The delay gave time to others to consider the matter more carefully and to ponder "the movements which seemed to be inseparable from so perilous a party." No new deputies left for England, and, as the "solemn act" calling for English help was pursued no farther, Cromwell's offer lapsed.[97]

However, revolution had seemed dangerously close. The Abbé de Cosnac believed that Cromwell would have followed through on his proposals if the Frondeurs had accepted.[98] Later Monsieur de Gentillot reported from Calais that the Bordelais could truly have obtained English military assistance had they accepted Cromwell's terms. Thank God they had not, he wrote.[99]

The refusal to send new deputies to Cromwell re-emphasized the miserable prospects of the Frondeurs in Bordeaux. The Prince de Conti admitted before June 6, 1653, that if the Garonne were not opened to traffic in a month's time, the Frondeurs

[96] *Mémoires de Daniel de Cosnac,* I, 66–69.   [97] *Ibid.,* I, 66–69.
[98] *Ibid.,* I, 69.
[99] Gentillot to Brienne, July 8, 1653, Cosnac, *Souvenirs du règne de Louis XIV,* VII, 430–433.

would have to sue for peace.[100] Actually the situation was not quite that bad, but a survey of the city's grain stocks on July 4, 1653, confirmed that the end was not far off.[101] Meanwhile, in London, Monsieur de Barrière tried to get provisions to Bordeaux and was bargaining in mid-June with English merchants for grain. He believed, if ships could be found, they might penetrate Vendôme's blockade. But first the ships had to be found and leased. The Prince de Condé sent an agent to London June 28, 1653, with funds to lease several ships, and counted on the Spaniards to stand as security in case the ships were lost. However, sailors to man the ships—400 were needed—lacked, and that shortage threatened to delay the sailing, even if the English approved all other arrangements.[102] The English government had drafted every available seaman for its own ships. It might take a month to round up crews for the Frondeurs. The Spanish ambassador tried to obtain the use of Dutch prisoners in English custody. But when Monsieur de Bordeaux heard of it, he quickly informed the Dutch envoys, then in London to negotiate peace with England, and their protests caused the English to refuse the Spanish request. The Spanish ambassador even toyed with the idea of bringing over sailors from Flanders. But Monsieur de Bordeaux succeeded meanwhile in buying off some of the English merchants involved in the Bordeaux project and persuaded them to withdraw two of the eight ships which the Frondeurs had planned to freight.[103]

[100] Bishop of Tulle to Mazarin, May 17, 1653, *Archives historiques du département de la Gironde*, VIII, 153–155.

[101] Marchin, etc., to Sainte-Croix, etc., July 1, 1653, *ibid.*, XV, 327.

[102] Paulucci to Sagredo, August 9, 1653, *Calendar of State Papers . . . Venice*, XXIX, 109; Barrière to Council of State, June 2, 1653 (O.S.?), *Thurloe Papers*, I, 250; Barrière to Condé, June 13, 1653, Chantilly, MS. série P, XIII, f. 163; Bordeaux to Brienne, June 16, 1653, P.R.O. transcript, 31/3/91, copied from B.N., MS. f.fr. 16008.

[103] Bordeaux to Brienne, July 17, 1653, Cosnac, *Souvenirs du règne de Louis XIV*, VII, 446–447; Bordeaux to Brienne, July 21, 1653, P.R.O. transcript, 31/3/91, copied from B.N., MS. f.fr. 16008; Bordeaux to

What Will England Do?

The repeated failures or postponements in obtaining help from England discouraged the Bordelais, but they were more immediately concerned by the collapse of their military position. This too was linked in a fashion to England. The Frondeurs at Bordeaux and their Spanish ally relied heavily on Irish mercenaries which the Puritans allowed them to recruit for a price. All through 1652 and early 1653, shipload after shipload of Irish troops disembarked in Guyenne. Four ships laden with twelve hundred Irish had arrived in late summer of 1652, and the supply seemed inexhaustible.[104] In May of 1653 two or three thousand more Irish were expected shortly, and in June, 1653, an agent from Spain was recruiting another four thousand Irish.[105] The Duc de Vendôme estimated in May, 1653, that, except for two hundred men serving under the Prince de Conti, all of the enemy infantry was Irish and increasing in number every day.[106] The Duke exaggerated, but certainly the Irish constituted an important part of the Spanish-Frondeur military force. A thousand men, half of whom were Irish, held the key Spanish base at Bourg. Pierre Lenet admitted that, of the troops defending the city of Bordeaux, only three or four hundred were French, while one thousand were Irish.[107]

By permitting the Irish to serve with the Frondeurs and the Spaniards in Guyenne, England seemed to have given the Frondeurs a decided military advantage. But the Frondeurs came

Brienne, July 24, 1653, Cosnac, *Souvenirs du règne de Louis XIV*, VII, 451–454; Bordeaux to Brienne, July 28, 1653, P.R.O. transcript, 31/3/91, copied from B.N., MS. f.fr. 16008; Bordeaux to Brienne, August 7, 1653, Cosnac, *Souvenirs du règne de Louis XIV*, VIII, 261–263.

[104] Candale to Mazarin, April 19, 1653, *Archives historiques du département de la Gironde*, VIII, 123.

[105] "Le royaliste de Bordeaux" to an unknown, May, 1653, *ibid.*, VIII, 166; Bordeaux to Brienne, June 23, 1653, P.R.O. transcript, 31/3/91, copied from BN., MS. f.fr. 16008.

[106] Vendôme to Mazarin, May 20, 1653, *Archives historiques du département de la Gironde*, VIII, 157.

[107] Marchin, etc., to Sainte-Croix, etc., July 1, 1653, *ibid.*, XV, 327.

to realize that their Irish troops were no bargain. According to some accounts, the Irish recruits were miserable wretches who had come to Guyenne lured by false promises of opportunity for enrichment. Their disappointment was keen, therefore, when upon disembarking they discovered the reality. They complained of ill treatment from the Spaniards; their officers grumbled at slights, real and imagined; and all complained because they did not receive their pay. The townspeople whom they had come to defend regarded them suspiciously, and incidents occurred which obliged the transfer of Irish soldiers elsewhere to appease the local inhabitants.[108] The Irish troops in Guyenne became so unhappy with their lot that in April, 1653, some of them drafted a manifesto of grievances.[109]

Agents of the French crown knew of the poor morale of the Irish. From London, Monsieur de Bordeaux regularly transmitted to his superiors proposals of persons involved in Irish recruitment, who said they could arrange for the Irish to come over to the side of the French king.[110] Inevitably the Irish already arrived in Guyenne became the targets of agents for the crown.[111] Several tactics were considered, including the use

[108] Memoir from Bordeaux (city) to Mazarin, March 10, 1653, *ibid.*, II, 89; Bishop of Tulle to Mazarin, March 20, 1653, *ibid.*, VII, 293; "Le royaliste de Bordeaux" to an unknown, May, 1653, *ibid.*, VIII, 166; Vivens to Mazarin, March 15, 1653, *ibid.*, VII, 282; intercepted letter from Paris, July 9, 1653, *Thurloe Papers*, I, 323; letter of intelligence from Paris, July 16, 1653, *ibid.*, I, 337.

[109] Memoir from Bordeaux (city) to Mazarin, March 10, 1653, *Archives historiques du département de la Gironde*, II, 89; "Le royaliste de Bordeaux" to Mazarin, April, 1653, *ibid.*, VIII, 128.

[110] Bordeaux to Brienne, January 2, 1653, P.R.O. transcript, 31/3/90, copied from B.N., MS. f.fr. 16008; Bordeaux to Mazarin, February 27, 1653, *ibid.*, 31/3/90, copied from B.N., MS. f.fr. 16008; Bordeaux to Brienne, March 20, 1653, Cosnac, *Souvenirs du règne de Louis XIV*, VI, 442–446.

[111] Bishop of Tulle to Mazarin, March 13, 1653, *Archives historiques du département de la Gironde*, VII, 280; Bishop of Tulle to Mazarin, February 4, 1653, *ibid.*, VII, 264; Bishop of Tulle to Mazarin, March 20, 1653, *ibid.*, VII, 293.

of English royalist pressure (to be examined in the following chapter), but, in the end, bribery seemed the safest and most effective approach. The Duc de Vendôme proved its great utility when he bought off the Irish garrison of the strategically important base at Lormont in May.[112] The baffled Frondeurs tried to prevent a recurrence by demanding hostages from their own Irish troops.[113] Even this was ineffective. In mid-July, the Irish at Bourg surrendered too.[114]

As one Irish garrison after another transferred its allegiance to the French crown, the crushing hopelessness of the Frondeurs' cause became apparent in Bordeaux. Lenet vainly tried to sustain the revolt by leaning on the revolutionary party in the city and by holding out promise of aid from England and Spain.[115] But this was not enough. The population, torn by faction and intrigue, had lost its will to continue the Fronde. The fighting at Bordeaux ceased August 3, 1653, and Sexby and his English assistants returned home.[116] Several weeks later, all resistance in the neighboring region of Périgueux ended too. The Fronde was over.

Cardinal Mazarin had won his race against the calendar in quelling the Frondeurs before the Puritans could intervene. Perhaps the French government had assumed a more alarmist view of England's intentions than the circumstances really warranted, but the danger had seemed grave. Representatives from Bordeaux, seeking peace, minimized their earlier appeals

---

[112] Bishop of Tulle to Mazarin, March 20, 1653, *ibid.*, VIII, 161; Gissard to Mazarin, May 30, 1653, *ibid.*, VIII, 177.

[113] Sagredo to Doge and Senate, June 10, 1653, *Calendar of State Papers . . . Venice*, XXIX, 84.

[114] Bishop of Tulle to Mazarin, August 11, 1653, *Archives historiques du département de la Gironde*, XV, 396.

[115] Sagredo to Doge and Senate, July 15, 1653, *Calendar of State Papers . . . Venice*, XXIX, 97.

[116] Edmund Ludlow tells the rather fanciful story that Sexby slipped over the city wall by night to make his escape, *The Memoirs of Edmund Ludlow*, ed. Charles H. Firth (Oxford, 1894), I, 415.

to England. They swore that the city had revoked the call for English help some months before.[117] However, when the court prescribed the terms of peace, it was evident that the Frondeur appeal to England had left a scar. The court bestowed a general amnesty but specifically excluded six persons because their conduct was adjudged too criminal for pardon. The six were: Villars and Duretête, the two leaders of the Ormée, Cleyrac, a bourgeois who had sought help in Spain, and Trancas, Désert, and Blarut, the delegates who had sought English help.[118] The Bishop of Tulle, Mazarin's principal liaison agent with the expedition against Bordeaux, wrote to the Cardinal just after Bordeaux's surrender, "If England had mixed in the Bordeaux revolt, it is not imaginable what profound roots the rebellion would have established in the province." [119] Surely, in reading that letter, Cardinal Mazarin must have breathed a fervent "Amen."

[117] *Archives historiques du département de la Gironde*, XV, 357.

[118] Memoir for Vendôme and Candale, July 28, 1653, *ibid.*, XV, 369; *Archives municipales de Bordeaux* (Bordeaux, 1878), II, 372–378.

[119] Bishop of Tulle to Mazarin, August 11, 1653, *Archives historiques du département de la Gironde*, XV, 396.

VIII

The English Exiles
and the Fronde

THE band of English royalist exiles in France who refused to
go home and compound with the Puritan régime after Charles
I's execution studied the shifting patterns of French attitude
toward England with intense interest. If it is anticlimax at this
point in the story to detail their quest for French assistance, their
activities do merit searching examination. The English exiles
in France had to plan their return to power in England in the
shadow of the Fronde. They could no more ignore the Fronde
than the French could ignore the English Civil War. Inevitably
the maneuvers of the English royalists became entangled in the
Fronde itself.

Naturally the English royalists wanted French aid. But, by
the time Charles II tried to pick up the pieces of the overturned
monarchy, some of the exiles doubted France would ever give
any substantial help. In these matters, as in others, the exiles
split into sharply opposed factions. With regard to France, the
two significant factions were the "Old Royalists" and the
"Louvre."

The "Old Royalists," men like Sir Edward Hyde, Chancellor
of the Exchequer, and Sir Edward Nicholas, Secretary of State,

placed little trust in the French. They could point out, correctly, that France had given minimal material help during the Civil War. Though the "Old Royalists" had occasional optimistic moments when they thought France might do something, in general they looked with skepticism on French promises. Sir Edward Nicholas could not forget the French crown's timidity after the condemnation of Charles I; its failure to expel forth-with the Parliamentary agent, René Augier; and its diffidence in asking the Scots to be less exacting in their terms to Charles II. Nicholas concluded that France was too weak a reed to support the English king.[1]

The "Old Royalists" understood well enough why France acted so timidly. Obviously, they thought, the Commonwealth inspired the Queen Regent and her government with dread;[2] obviously the war with Spain, and domestic strife inside France, left the French government "drawn so very low by war . . . and . . . so much impoverished by excessive taxes" that it could hardly cope with its own troubles.[3] Consequently the French "will not give themselves time to think of ours."[4] One spark of hope remained for the "Old Royalists." There was a possibility France might be drawn into a war with the Commonwealth. If that happened, nature would do the rest. The French would then see the advantage of helping the cause of the English royalists.[5]

If one did not turn to France, how might monarchy be restored in England? As time progressed, the answer to this

[1] Nicholas to Ormonde, March 4, 1649, Carte, *A Collection of Original Letters,* I, 223; Nicholas to Ormonde, March 30, 1649, *ibid.,* I, 227.

[2] Hyde to Nicholas, November 2, 1652 (O.S.?), *Clarendon State Papers,* III, 110.

[3] Nicholas to Ormonde, September 11, 1649, Carte, *A Collection of Original Letters,* I, 311.

[4] Byron to Ormonde, September 6/16, 1651, Historical Manuscripts Commission, *Calendar of the Manuscripts of the Marquess of Ormonde Preserved at Kilkenny Castle,* new ser., I (London, 1902), 207.

[5] Propositions of Clanricarde, November 29, 1651, *ibid.,* I, 239; Hyde to Nicholas, March 9, 1651/1652 (O.S.?), *Clarendon State Papers,* III, 53.

question became more difficult. One by one the exiles had to eliminate each possibility. Cromwell's victories in Ireland in 1649, and the mop-up continued there by his son-in-law, blocked an Irish route of return for the royalists. Cromwell's crushing defeat of Charles II at Worcester in 1651 closed the door from Scotland. Death, meanwhile, robbed the English royalists in 1650 of the Prince of Orange, their best friend on the Continent, and dashed prospects of Dutch intervention in their favor. When Spain rebuffed the royalists by officially recognizing the Commonwealth in 1651, France was virtually the only source of help left. Some, like Lord Byron, comforted themselves with the thought "that God will do this great work [the re-establishment of monarchy in England] without any foreign assistance." [6] Sir Edward Hyde liked to think some internal upheaval in the Commonwealth might provide the needed opportunity, if the help of other Christian princes proved to no avail.[7]

The "Louvre" faction, headed by the Queen Mother, Henriette-Marie, trusted less to internal fissures in the Commonwealth. The Queen Mother and her circle felt keenly the failure of France to give more help during the Civil War,[8] but as setback after setback struck down the chance of a royalist victory in England, the "Louvre" faction turned increasingly to France. Ways might be found—would have to be found—to bring the French more actively to their side.

The "Louvre" generally dominated Charles II in his thinking about France during the period of the Fronde. The "Old Royalists" grumbled that their effort to procure French help was useless, but this did not stop the "Louvre." Charles II, while

[6] Byron to Ormonde, September 6/16, 1651, *Calendar of Ormonde Manuscripts*, I, 207.

[7] Edward Hyde, 1st Earl of Clarendon, *The History of the Rebellion and Civil Wars in England*, ed. W. Dunn Macray (Oxford, 1888), V, 240.

[8] Nani to Doge and Senate, May 26, 1648, *Calendar of State Papers . . . Venice*, XXVIII, 59.

still Prince of Wales, had written imploringly to Anne of Austria and to Cardinal Mazarin shortly before his father's condemnation, saying "it is a concern to the security of all kings to oppose examples of such evil consequence and so prejudicial to their dignity." [9] Doubtless the exiles were heartened when officials of the French government and the Frondeurs all made similar statements. But to return to the plaint of the "Old Royalists," when would fair words produce tangible deeds? As long as France had to fight Spain and to quiet domestic quarrels, it could not do much for the English royalists. Might not the English royalists help themselves, therefore, by helping France to extricate herself from some of her distractions?

The first important essay came in the diplomatic field. Somewhat curiously, it came from the initiative of the "Old Royalist" faction. The immediate goal was a Franco-Spanish peace. Probably the Old Royalists were more interested in freeing Spain from war (and so obtaining Spanish aid) than in liberating France of its burden. The project gradually took shape as a consequence of the mission which Charles II sent to Madrid.

Charles, then at The Hague, decided in the spring of 1649 to send Lord Cottington and Sir Edward Hyde as ambassadors to the court of Philip IV in Madrid. The instructions covered a multitude of affairs but mentioned nothing about mediating the war between France and Spain. Yet, toward the end of June, the English royalist press speculated that Charles II might act as umpire between the two great warring powers. The report was premature, but obviously the English royalists were considering the possibility.[10]

When Hyde and Cottington passed through France that summer en route to Spain, they naturally halted at Paris. In a courtesy call on Cardinal Mazarin in September, the Cardinal

[9] Prince Charles to Mazarin, January 18, 1649, P.R.O. transcript, 31/3/89, copied from A.E. Angleterre, LX.
[10] *Mercurius Pragmaticus,* June 19/29–June 26/July 6, 1649, p. 80.

expressed a desire for "a peace between the two crowns [France and Spain], and said that he would give a pound of his blood to obtain it; and desired the ambassadors to tell Don Luis de Haro [Philip's principal minister] from him, that he would with all his heart meet him upon the frontiers, and that he was confident if they two were together but three hours, they should compose all differences." [11] Probably Mazarin reiterated the same assurances he had given Lord Jermyn the month before. He had told Jermyn that one of the greatest reasons why he wanted peace with Spain was for the sake of Charles II.[12]

Whether Cottington and Hyde gave much thought to mediating Franco-Spanish differences before, they now found the idea attractive. Upon arrival in Madrid, their first private interview with Philip IV convinced them that the Spanish monarch genuinely wanted peace. Truly excited, Cottington and Hyde concluded that if the Cardinal and Don Luis de Haro were to meet, "to which the last is marvellously inclined, or if commissioners were sent to the borders, a peace between France and Spain would undoubtedly ensue." [13]

Much encouraged, the English ambassadors returned their thoughts to France and begged Henriette-Marie in Paris to work on the French. They painted a glowing picture of the Spanish desire for peace to spur her on.[14] Meanwhile, the French government announced that if the Spaniards desired

[11] Basadonna to Doge and Senate, December 20, 1649, *Calendar of State Papers . . . Venice,* XXVIII, 129; Clarendon, *History of the Rebellion,* V, 68.

[12] Mazarin to Jermyn, August 29, 1649, P.R.O. transcript, 31/3/89, copied from A.E. Angleterre, LX, f. 131.

[13] Cottington and Hyde to Henriette-Marie, January 6, 1650, *Calendar of the Clarendon State Papers,* II, 37; Cottington to Jermyn, March 2, 1650, *ibid.,* II, 43.

[14] Hyde and Cottington to Henriette-Marie, November, 5, 1649, *ibid.,* II, 27; Cottington and Hyde to Henriette-Marie, December 15, 1649, *ibid.,* II, 33; Basadonna to Doge and Senate, December 20, 1649, *Calendar of State Papers . . . Venice,* XXVIII, 129.

peace, "nothing remains to be done but to settle the place and the time." [15] All the pieces seemed to be falling neatly into place, especially when Cottington and Hyde picked up a rumor in January, 1650, that the Puritans had joined with the Frondeurs. With a Franco-Spanish peace just around the corner, Hyde thought prospects for the exiles so good that he exulted, "I shall hope once more to see England." [16]

Unhappily for the exiles, this roseate promise vanished. The rumored alliance of the Puritans with the Frondeurs proved false. Furthermore, the peace talks, both on the part of France and of Spain, were largely stage play. While the Spaniards titillated the English ambassadors with encouragement, privately Don Luis de Haro confided to the Venetian ambassador that he had already proposed a peace congress in the Pyrenees the previous July. Cardinal Mazarin had not bothered to reply then. Why, the Spanish minister wondered, did Mazarin suddenly welcome the idea now and choose the two English royalists to be his messengers? [17] Philip IV thought he knew why. He believed that "the arrival of these diplomats and the tenor of their propositions are contrivances of the French to render Spain suspect to either Parliament or to Charles II." However, as Spain had not yet decided what to do about the Commonwealth, it had to be careful. Though it appeared that Mazarin's proposal for discussion "likely has no other reason than to show off pacific intentions," nevertheless, if the Cardinal "insists on having an interview with Luis de Haro, the King will give an order to this latter person to satify the desire." [18]

From all evidence, Philip IV and his ministers gauged Ma-

[15] Contarini to Basadonna, February 27, 1650, *ibid.*, XXVIII, 141.

[16] Hyde to Nicholas, January 6, 1649/1650 (O.S.?), *Clarendon State Papers*, III, 11.

[17] Basadonna to Doge and Senate, December 20, 1649, *Calendar of State Papers . . . Venice*, XXVIII, 129.

[18] Philip IV to Leopold William, January 3, 1650, *Correspondance de la cour d'Espagne*, IV, 160; Philip IV to Leopold William, January 17, 1650, *ibid.*, IV, 161.

zarin's motives more accurately than Hyde and Cottington. Mazarin certainly used the negotiations of Cottington and Hyde to embarrass the Spaniards. He suggested to the Puritans that Spain wanted peace with France to attack the Commonwealth.[19] Yet Mazarin never slackened preparations for renewed assaults against Spain in the spring of 1650.[20]

When at last the Spaniards decided to recognize the Commonwealth, they could abandon the pretense of preparing for peace with France. Cottington and Hyde, whom the Spanish government considered as Mazarin's spies, were told to leave. The comedy was over.[21] Yet the inglorious end of the English royalist mission to Madrid in December, 1650, did not altogether stop rumors that the English royalists might still engineer a Franco-Spanish peace. Occasionally the English royalist press represented Charles II in some new scheme to mediate the war, but the reports had no substance. If they were intended as trial balloons, they had little consequence.

One of the pamphlets distributed by the Frondeur publisher, Pierre Sévestre, suggested that Charles II and Queen Henriette-Marie ought to help the French settle their internal differences so that France could return the favor.[22] In spite of this and similar exhortations, the English royalists, of whatever faction, were at first disinclined to mix into the squabbles of the Fronde. The number of important friends which the exiles had in all camps made it awkward for them to take sides. Queen Henriette-Marie held a pension of 8,000 pistoles a year from the French crown; [23]

[19] Mazarin to Croullé, January 28, 1650, P.R.O. transcript, 31/3/90, copied from A.E. Angleterre, LX, ff. 230–231.

[20] See the correspondence of Mazarin in this period regarding the spring campaign to be undertaken against Spain in *Lettres du cardinal Mazarin,* ed. Chéruel, III.

[21] Basadonna to Doge and Senate, December 27, 1650, *Calendar of State Papers . . . Venice,* XXVIII, 163–164.

[22] *Lettre d'un seigneur françois* (Paris, 1649), pp. 4–5, Moreau No. 1897.

[23] Ormonde to Nicholas, May 4, 1651 (O.S.?), Carte, *A Collection of Original Letters,* I, 461–462.

the Duke of York received half that; [24] while Charles II was theoretically entitled to 6,000 livres a month toward the end of the Fronde.[25] Living quarters and other benefits, conferred by the Queen Regent, increased the assistance. Cardinal Mazarin asserted in May, 1651, that he had loaned Henriette-Marie 300,000 livres from his own account.[26] The French agent in Scotland had been directed in 1649 to send 3,000 écus to Charles II at The Hague.[27]

On the other hand, persons who were, or who would become, enemies of the Queen Regent also showed generosity to the exiles. The English Queen and her sons received a gift of 2,000 crowns from the Prince de Condé's mother,[28] and perhaps another 100,000 livres from the Condé family before the end of the Fronde.[29] The Prince de Condé in March, 1649, "expressed a particular sense against the rebels in England for their high sin against God, their sovereign, and monarchy itself, and openly protested that he will assist His Majesty, that now is, cordially, when peace shall be made in France." [30] This statement was pronounced before Condé's break with the Queen Regent, but he continued on warm personal terms with the English royalists much of the time, even when seeking help from the English republicans. The Duc d'Orléans, who eventually joined

[24] Ormonde to Nicholas, May 4, 1651 (O.S.?), *ibid.*, I, 461–462.

[25] Ormonde to Nicholas, May 4, 1651 (O.S.?), *ibid.*, I, 461; see also *Calendar of the Clarendon State Papers*, II, 158.

[26] Mazarin to Lionne, May 26, 1651, *Lettres du cardinal Mazarin*, ed. Chéruel, IV, 221. Mazarin also ordered Colbert to pay 20,000 florins in interest due on the jewels Henriette-Marie had pawned earlier (Mazarin to Colbert, May 6, 1653, *ibid.*, V, 608).

[27] Graymond to Brasset and d'Estrades, June 17, 1649, Cosnac, *Souvenirs du règne de Louis XIV*, V, 420–421.

[28] Hatton to Nicholas, December 24, 1649, *The Nicholas Papers*, XL, 160.

[29] *Mémoires de Mlle de Montpensier*, ed. Pierre-Adolphe Chéruel, II (Paris, 1868), 84.

[30] Nicholas to Ormonde, March 20/30, 1648/1649, Carte, *A Collection of Original Letters*, I, 227.

the Fronde, was Henriette-Marie's brother. He drove out from Paris in his carriage to welcome Charles II back to the French capital in October, 1651, after the battle of Worcester.[31] The Duke's daughter, the Grande Mademoiselle, was often mentioned as a marriage partner for Charles.[32] Another Frondeur, the Coadjutor of Paris (later Cardinal de Retz), appeared even to the jaundiced eye of Sir Edward Hyde to be the best friend Charles II had in France. He frequently bestowed gifts upon the English royal family during the Fronde.[33] It would be possible to catalogue other examples of largess extended to the exiles by the Frondeurs, as well as offers of hospitality and sympathy.

When the Fronde began in January, 1649, Charles II's presence in Holland allowed his mother to dominate the exile colony in Paris. The youth and inexperience of the Duke of York, who was living in Paris, presented no challenge to Henriette's leadership. Instead of fleeing Paris at the outbreak of the Fronde, Henriette-Marie and her entourage, including the Duke of York, elected to remain in Paris, Frondeur headquarters. Yet when the Parlement of Paris voted to confer upon Henriette a pension of 20,000 livres, she politely refused it, despite her desperate lack of funds.[34]

As time passed, the exiles found it harder to preserve their neutrality in the Fronde. It seemed so obviously to their advantage to have the Fronde ended, and there were so many

[31] Morosini to Doge and Senate, November 7, 1651, *Calendar of State Papers . . . Venice*, XXVIII, 202.

[32] *Mémoires de Mlle de Montpensier*, I (Paris, 1858), 102, 324.

[33] *Oeuvres du cardinal de Retz*, II, 197–198, and note no. 4, p. 197; Hyde to Nicholas, December 20, 1652 (O.S.?), *Clarendon State Papers*, III, 128; Gerard to Nicholas, November 4, [1651], *Nicholas Papers*, XL, 280; "Mémoires de Jacques II," *Collection des mémoires relatifs à la révolution d'Angleterre*, ed. François P. G. Guizot, XXII, Part I (Paris, 1827), 74.

[34] *Journal de Jean Vallier*, I, 159–160; *Oeuvres du cardinal de Retz*, II, 197–198 and note 4, p. 197; "Mémoires de Omer Talon," *Nouvelle collection des mémoires*, XXVIII, 322.

alluring temptations for them to help end it, that at last the "Louvre" party began to yield to them. But if they were to interfere, which side ought they assist? None of the exiles felt any great love for Cardinal Mazarin. The "Old Royalists" hated him with a passion which the failure of the peace talks with Spain doubtless increased. He was, to Sir Edward Nicholas, that "accursed Cardinal." Nicholas believed the "juggling Cardinal will not suffer the King of France to do any good for the King; and I may tell you I very much apprehend that the design of that Cardinal is (and I pray God some in the Louvre do not concur in it) to keep the King still a pensioner of France." [35] His friend Hyde believed that not even Henriette-Marie and Lord Jermyn looked upon the Cardinal as one who had either helped or expected to help them but rather as "one who can do them more hurt and may do them some good, and so must not be unnecessarily provoked." [36] Charles II's brief visit in France in 1649, before setting out for Scotland, left him greatly annoyed with the French government, convinced that he was the victim of its deceit; or, to put it more specifically, the victim of Mazarin's deceit.[37]

Despite Cardinal Mazarin's lack of popularity, the English royalists, including the "Old Royalists," were troubled by an uneasy conviction that the Queen Regent had the better cause. Lord Inchiquin might protest that he did not think it a concern of his conscience "to fight rather to continue the government of a child in the hands of the Queen and Cardinal than to bring it

[35] Nicholas to Hatton, December 7, [1650], *Nicholas Papers*, XL, 204; Nicholas to Hyde, October 7/17, [1652], *ibid.*, XL, 312. Sir Richard Browne had written to Nicholas that he believed the Cardinal to be a pensioner of the English Commonwealth (January 1, 1649/1650 (O.S.?), B.M., Additional MS. 12186, III, f. 107).

[36] Hyde to Nicholas, October 26, 1652 (O.S.?), *Clarendon State Papers*, III, 108.

[37] Morosini to Doge and Senate, September 28, 1649, *Calendar of State Papers . . . Venice*, XXVIII, 119–120.

into others," but he confessed that in spite of that, and in spite of his friendship with the Duc d'Orléans and the Parisian Frondeurs, he would rather be engaged on the Queen Regent's side.[38] The Marquess of Ormonde was prepared in 1651 to secure men for the service of the rebellious Prince de Condé if he could, but only after he made several offers first to the Queen Regent.[39] Not even Sir Edward Nicholas' dislike of Mazarin could change his opinion, written after the Peace of Rueil, that those who opposed the King of France and the Queen Regent would have cause to repent of their rebellion.[40] The Duke of York, who eventually enrolled in the French king's army to fight the Frondeurs in 1652, summed up his own feelings when he said that the Frondeurs were going down the path trod by all revolutionaries when they claimed to direct their fire against the minister and not the King.[41]

The first significant partisan act did not occur until the end of 1650 and beginning of 1651. It happened at that stage of the Fronde when the friends of the Princes were striving to secure their release from prison at Le Havre. It will be recalled that the Duc d'Orléans was being urged by the conspirators to join their cabal, and that Mazarin sensed the Duke might join the opposition. Among the Cardinal's several countermoves was a plan to use Henriette-Marie to keep her brother, the Duke, in line.[42] Henriette was reluctant to forsake her neutrality, but the Cardinal won her over. What inducements he used we cannot be sure. Some said Henriette wanted permission for the Duke of York to return to France after his departure for Brussels in

[38] Inchiquin to Ormonde, 1651, *Calendar of Ormonde Manuscripts,* I, 248.

[39] Ormonde to Muskerry, September, 1651, *ibid.,* I, 215.

[40] Nicholas to Ormonde, May 3, 1649, Carte, *A Collection of Original Letters,* I, 272.

[41] *The Memoirs of James II,* trans. A. Lytton Sells (Bloomington, 1962), p. 59.

[42] Nicholas to Hatton, March 1, [1651], *Nicholas Papers,* XL, 222.

1650. The Marquess of Ormonde denied it.[43] In any case, Henriette repeatedly begged her brother to stay out of the party of the Princes. As she left the Duke's residence after such a visit, several persons who had gathered on the entrance steps insolently cried, "A la Mazarine." Henriette, furious, turned on her heels, went back into the room where she had left her brother, and angrily declared that he would never see her again if she could not be assured of proper respect during her visits.[44] Obviously, though, Henriette was no match for Retz and the Frondeurs, whose skillful blandishments, coupled with Mazarin's tactical error in comparing the Frondeurs to the English rebels, drew the Duke into the conspiracy.

The Cardinal's resulting disgrace and exile naturally left Queen Henriette-Marie in a predicament. Accounts of what she had done found their way even to the London press.[45] The "Old Royalists" angrily attacked her for having compromised them all, and were still more incensed at reports she had offered the Cardinal a haven for his exile on the Isle of Jersey, one of the few remaining bits of soil then under royalist control. The "Old Royalists" were not at all surprised when the Prince de Condé refused to call on Henriette-Marie for more than a fortnight after his return to Paris. The "Old Royalists" derived some meager comfort that the incident had not been worse.[46] Fortunately Charles II and the Duke of York, being then outside France, were not included in their mother's disgrace; and the "Old Royalists" learned that the two brothers had sent congratulatory letters to the Princes to undo Henriette's blunder. With relief, they noted that Lord Digby still enjoyed the good graces of the Prince de Condé and had received a larger pension, with

[43] Ormonde to Nicholas, March 30, 1651 (O.S.?), Carte, *A Collection of Original Letters*, I, 429.

[44] "Mémoires de la duchesse de Nemours," *Nouvelle collection des mémoires*, XXI, 637.

[45] Carte, *A Collection of Original Letters*, I, 422.

[46] Ormonde to Nicholas, March 30, 1651 (O.S.?), *ibid.*, I, 429.

appointment to command French troops in Normandy and promise of better things to come.[47]

It was some time before the English royalists meddled again in the Fronde. For the while, Scotland drew their attention, anyway—not France. Charles II sailed from Holland in June, 1650, to head the Scots' army against the Commonwealth. For more than a year, the King's unsteady relationship with the Scots, and his plans to meet and defeat Cromwell on the field of battle, occupied the thoughts of the exiles. But the final sad chapter of that episode was written in September, 1651, with the King's defeat at Worcester—some seven months after Cardinal Mazarin had gone into exile. When Charles made his way back to France in October, 1651, France again began to figure in the calculations of at least some of the exiles.

The possibility that Charles might contract an advantageous French marriage had frequently occurred to the English royalists. As early as 1645 Henriette-Marie had tried to interest the very wealthy Grande Mademoiselle, daughter of the Duc d'Orléans, in a marriage with Charles. Though the project failed, it was revived in the summer of 1649. The proposed marriage seemed to have the blessing of the French court; but Charles's tepid courtship, his refusal to pronounce the *douceurs* which the Grande Mademoiselle expected from him, cooled the lady's interest in the match. Now, in 1651, talk of marriage alliances resumed. This time the plan was more ambitious. Charles II would marry the Grande Mademoiselle, and his brother James would marry Mademoiselle de Longueville, daughter of the Duc de Longueville by his first wife.

Evidently the entourage of the Duke of York initiated the marriage project in the fall of 1651, with Henriette's help.

---

[47] Nicholas to Ormonde, March 1, 1651 (O.S.?), *ibid.*, I, 413; Nicholas to Hatton, March 12/22, [1650/1651], *Nicholas Papers*, XL, 228; Nicholas to Hatton, March 19/29, [1650/1651], *ibid.*, XL, 230–231; Nicholas to Hatton, May 21/31, [1651], *ibid.*, XL, 254.

Mademoiselle de Longueville expressed eagerness for the marriage, and the Duke of York was favorably disposed. Then, when Charles II returned to France, the campaign to obtain the Grande Mademoiselle's hand for him began. After Worcester, Charles was far more conscious of what the Grande Mademoiselle's wealth could mean to him than when he had last courted the lady in the summer of 1649. Charles needed no urging this time to employ all of his charm (which was considerable when he took the trouble). He besieged the Grande Mademoiselle with a romantic ardor she had always craved. Charles's remarkable improvement impressed and flattered her. From the wings, Queen Henriette-Marie played her familiar Cupid's role.[48]

Despite hopeful beginnings, both marriage projects soon foundered. Some of the exiles scorned Mademoiselle de Longueville's fortune as too small.[49] Besides, the Grande Mademoiselle disliked her prospective sister-in-law. It was feared that insistence on the Duke of York's marriage might jeopardize the more important one of his brother. The French court administered the kiss of death by letting word get back that it could not approve the Duke of York's marriage with Mademoiselle de Longueville, ostensibly because she was not of sufficiently elevated rank for the Duke.[50] Actually the court probably balked because of the enhanced prestige which the Duc de Longueville would receive from the marriage of his daughter to one next in succession to the English throne. Considering the Duke's past record in the Fronde, the moment seemed a poor one to inflate him with illusions of grandeur.

[48] *Mémoires de Mlle de Montpensier*, I, 102, 126–128, 137–140, 217–224, 319–322; "Mémoires de Jacques II," *Collection des mémoires relatifs à la révolution d'Angleterre*, XXII, Part I, 74–75; Clarendon, *The History of the Rebellion*, V, 247–251.

[49] Nicholas to Seymour, December 13, [1651], *Nicholas Papers*, XL, 281; Hyde to Nicholas, January 6, 1652, *Calendar of the Clarendon State Papers*, II, 114.

[50] "Mémoires de Jacques II," *Collection des mémoires relatifs à la révolution d'Angleterre*, XXII, Part I, 75–76.

Almost simultaneously, Charles's hope for marriage with the Grande Mademoiselle encountered resistance. Some of the English royalists, "Old Royalists" in particular, disapproved of the match because of the religious overtones—even if Charles repulsed the efforts of the Grande Mademoiselle's friends to convert him to Catholicism. The French court raised no objection to the marriage, but its very acquiescence aroused the Grande Mademoiselle's suspicions. She was soon persuaded that the court wanted to see her fortune dissipated in fruitless endeavors for Charles II, rather than to see it used in assisting the Frondeurs. One of her father's close advisers argued this point very ably with her. The Princess Guémenée delivered the final blow by encouraging the Grande Mademoiselle to set her cap for a more brilliant marriage—with her cousin, Louis XIV. Under the spell of that enchanting vision, Mademoiselle lost interest in Charles. She suggested pointedly to him that he should see less of her in the future.[51]

Impartial observers agreed that both marriages were doomed in December, 1651.[52] Gloom enveloped the exiles. Charles consoled himself with the favors of Madame de Châtillon, a wealthy widow whose charms were savored more or less simultaneously by some of the most distinguished members of the French and English aristocracy. Though Charles reportedly wanted to marry the captivating widow, the marriage was impossible. Both Henriette-Marie and Anne of Austria disapproved.[53] No other suitable marriage partners remained in France for Charles or his brother.

Meanwhile, the finances of the exiles, always precarious, had become deplorable. The French court could not honor its recent grant of 6,000 livres per month to Charles II, because of the

[51] *Mémoires de Mlle Montpensier,* I, 324–332.

[52] Morosini to Doge and Senate, December 19, 1651, *Calendar of State Papers . . . Venice,* XXVIII, 207.

[53] Hester W. Chapman, *The Tragedy of Charles II in the Years 1630–1660* (London, 1964), p. 236.

Fronde.[54] Something had to be done. The first to react was the Duke of York, who in April of 1652 announced his intention of enlisting in the army of the King of France. On April 21, 1652, the Duke rode out of Paris to join the forces commanded by the Vicomte de Turenne. He recommended to his fellow exiles that they follow him to battle against the Frondeurs. This was the first public breach of neutrality in the Fronde by a member of the English royal family.[55]

Charles greeted his brother's decision with something less than enthusiasm. Both Charles and his mother believed that more could be gained by acting the role of peacemaker in the Fronde than by taking sides. But though the English king had toyed with the idea of mediating the Fronde in November, 1651,[56] not until April, 1652, did he find a suitable occasion. By April, the Fronde had achieved no decisive result since the latest outbreak of the summer before. Mazarin was by then back at the side of Anne of Austria and Louis XIV in the neighborhood of Paris, though not in the city itself. The Prince de Condé, after having spent the winter months in Guyenne, arrived in Paris April 11, 1652, after having inflicted a relatively unimportant defeat on the army of the King at Bléneau. These many months of comparative stalemate, along with the inconsequential result of the battle of Bléneau, suggested to many persons that the Fronde had settled back into the familiar pattern. Cracks in Frondeur unity widened as the friends of the Princes, the faction led by the Parlement of Paris, and the various strata of the general population of Paris consulted their respective interests. The climate seemed right for negotiations.

When the Prince de Condé entered Paris, one of those on whom he called was Charles II. On the advice of his Council,

[54] Clarendon, *The History of the Rebellion*, V, 232.

[55] *French Occurrences*, No. 1, May 10/17–17/27, 1652, p. 172; Loret, *La muze historique*, I, 235.

[56] Hyde to Nicholas, November 8, 1651 (O.S.?), *Clarendon State Papers*, III, 37; *The Memoirs of James II*, p. 57.

Charles did not return the courtesy for fear of angering the French court; but apparently his talk with Condé, and his conversations with others in the French capital, convinced him that he could play a starring role in arranging a domestic peace in France. In this sentiment, he had the backing of Henriette-Marie and the "Louvre."

On April 23, 1652, Charles and his mother journeyed to Corbeil, where, joined by the Duke of York, they appeared before Louis XIV and his court. Charles discoursed on his plan to end the Fronde. The project received the sympathetic attention of the court. Heartened, the English king and his mother promptly rode back to Paris to sound out the Duc d'Orléans and to persuade him to accept the plan. The Duke seemed agreeable and went before the Parlement of Paris on April 26, 1652, to explain Charles's proposal. Present were the Prince de Condé and his friends. All publicly supported Charles's proposed peace negotiations.[57] The Frondeur chiefs reached public agreement on this point by tortuous paths, however. Many felt that the peace talks might be just another adroit maneuver of the French court to confuse them and to cause them to fall out with one another over the peace terms, as had happened before. Yet popular insistence on peace was so strong that none of the Frondeur leaders dared risk public wrath by refusing to negotiate. After the Duc d'Orléans had given his consent, the other Frondeurs had no choice but to allow the peace talks to go forward.[58]

With much fanfare, the Prince de Condé and the Duc d'Orléans appointed three representatives to accompany those of Charles II and Henriette-Marie on April 28, 1652, for discussion with the French court. The following day, Charles and his

[57] Hyde to Nicholas, April 20, 1652 (O.S.?), *Clarendon State Papers,* III, 63; Loret, *La muze historique,* I, 237–238; *Journal de Jean Vallier,* III, 211; *Calendar of State Papers . . . Venice,* XXVIII, 223.

[58] "Mémoires de Guy Joly," *Nouvelle collection des mémoires,* XXIV, 72.

mother arrived on the scene to give added push to the confer-
ences.[59] The English king and his mother enjoyed great popularity in Paris as the populace cheered their initiative for peace.

The negotiations broke down almost immediately because
Cardinal Mazarin insisted on being present. With the greatest
reluctance the deputies of the Frondeurs agreed to meet with
him. But when word reached Paris that the deputies were conferring with Cardinal Mazarin, the Parlement of Paris was
thrown into pandemonium. Peace or no, the members of Parlement refused to hear of discussions with the hated Mazarin,
whose dismissal they considered indispensable. The angry jurists selected deputies of their own to go forthwith to remon-
strate with the King for having permitted the Cardinal to at-
tend the peace talks. Before all the shouting quieted, the peace
project of Charles and Henriette-Marie was clearly dead.[60]

Inevitably the prestige of the English king and his mother
sank. The Frondeurs let it be known that the negotiations had all
been a plot of Cardinal Mazarin to set the Frondeurs to quarreling among themselves. Certainly the negotiations had accentuated Frondeur differences. However, the Frondeurs pinned the
blame for failure of the talks on the English royalists. Henriette-
Marie, they said, had urged Anne of Austria not to dismiss
Mazarin, which made solution of the Fronde impossible.[61] These
stories acquired greater plausibility as Charles and Henriette
reacted to the failure by assuming a more partisan role in favor
of the French court. No doubt skillful persuasion by the Cardinal, occasioned by the arrival on the scene of a new person-

---

[59] *Gazette de France*, No. 55, May 4, 1652, p. 443; "Mémoires de
Valentin Conrart," *Nouvelle collection des mémoires*, XVIII, 543–544; *Le
courier de la paix* (Paris, 1652), p. 3, Moreau No. 823; *Lettre d'un
bourgeois de Paris* (Paris, 1652), p. 4, Moreau No. 1854.

[60] "Mémoires de Valentin Conrart," *Nouvelle collection des mémoires*,
XVIII, 543–544; Hyde to Nicholas, May 3, 1652 (O.S.?), *Clarendon
State Papers*, III, 66.

[61] "Mémoires de Valentin Conrart," *Nouvelle collection des mémoires*,
XVIII, 545.

ality in early May—Duc Charles IV de Lorraine—made it difficult for them to do otherwise.

The Duc de Lorraine had fought a series of running battles with Louis XIII and Richelieu, from which he emerged in 1643 dispossessed of his lands, though still in command of an army. Becoming a *condottiere,* the Duke cheerfully hired himself and his troops to the highest bidders and found long-term employment in Spanish service. Many years before, his sister, Marguerite, had married the Duc d'Orléans (one of the reasons why Duc Charles's relations with Richelieu had soured). Because of that marriage, he was in close contact with the Duc d'Orléans. What with the push of the Spaniards and the pull of the Frondeurs, Duc Charles and his army entered France. Leisurely, he crossed through Champagne, headed toward Paris.

The Duke and his army caused excited comment in France. Conceivably he might shift the balance of military power in favor of the Frondeurs and set in train a psychological reaction against Anne of Austria and the government. On the other hand, should the Duke quietly depart from France, the Frondeurs would be demoralized and easy prey for the army of Turenne. Mazarin set about to secure the Duke's withdrawal; but the Frondeurs, equally industrious, sought to obtain from him a commitment of support. Masking his intentions in gay but enigmatic banter, Charles IV obligingly gathered in the propositions of both sides. Quite rightly, contemporaries considered him to be the most unpredictable person imaginable.

The English royalists knew the Duc de Lorraine. They had tried to enlist his help for Charles I.[62] Ever since, they continued to negotiate with him. As late as the spring of 1652, Charles II had proposed a marriage of the Duke's daughter with the Duke of York.[63] The proposal came to nothing, but the dialogue of

[62] Nani to Doge and Senate, February 25, 1648, *Calendar of State Papers . . . Venice,* XXVIII, 44.

[63] Charles II to Norwich, February 15, 1652, *Calendar of the Clarendon*

the English royalists and the Duke continued. Thus, when Cardinal Mazarin cast about for appropriate negotiators to approach the Duc de Lorraine, he naturally thought of the English royalists.

The English king was willing to help Mazarin, but he expected something in return. In an obvious *quid pro quo* arrangement, Charles asked that supplies be sent to Ireland, sufficient to allow his Lord Deputy to stand off Puritan attacks for the summer. Charles evoked the probability of Commonwealth attack against France, tactfully omitting mention of the Duc de Lorraine.[64] In these same weeks, the French government was also considering an alliance with Cromwell and haggling over the price, Dunkirk. But this Charles did not know, and obviously the French government did not volunteer the information. On the contrary, Charles must have believed that his request for aid to Ireland had a real chance, for almost immediately in early May, Lord Wilmot and Lord Jermyn began talks to get the Duc de Lorraine out of France. Charles II, accompanied by various English and French nobles, called on the Duke on June 3, 1652. Henriette followed her son's visit with one of her own two days later.[65]

Cardinal Mazarin had gained too much experience in cutting his way through the jungles of intrigue in France to place himself solely at the mercy of the English royalists in negotiating with Duc Charles. The Cardinal also occupied the Duke with proposals sent through his agent Brégy, through Madame de Chevreuse, and through the Princess Guémenée. Given the available evidence, it is difficult to determine precisely who was

---

State Papers, II, 119; Charles II to Norwich, March 16, 1652, *ibid.,* II, 126; letter of April, 1652, *ibid.,* II, 129.

[64] Hyde to Nicholas, January 11, 1652/1653 (O.S.?), *Clarendon State Papers,* III, 133.

[65] *Gazette de France,* No. 64, May 25, 1652, p. 516; *ibid.,* No. 70, June 8, 1652, pp. 563–564.

most important in these negotiations at any one moment.[66]

However, on June 6, 1652, the French succeeded in obtaining an agreement from the Duke that he would lead his troops out of France. He in turn received a promise from the French crown that if the Frondeur stronghold, Etampes, were not captured by June 10, Turenne would automatically lift the siege. In this way, Duc Charles evidently hoped to mollify his Frondeur friends, when the treaty should become public. Meanwhile, however, the Frondeurs suspected nothing.[67]

Turenne failed to crack the defenses of Etampes within the stipulated time. By terms of the treaty, he ought to have marched his army away. But Turenne doubted that Duc Charles intended to fulfill his part of the bargain because the Duke had made no preparations to lead his army out of France. Therefore Turenne maneuvered his troops into a position to force the Duke's exit. The situation became tense. The Duke countered by calling for reinforcements from the Frondeurs and received a detachment commanded by the Duc de Beaufort. Though Turenne felt confident he could win in open battle, the French court was less inclined to risk everything to the fortunes of war.[68]

On June 14, 1652, Charles II in Paris received a message signed by Louis XIV. It appealed to him to use his influence with the Duc de Lorraine to avoid a battle, and to induce the Duke to accompany him to Melun for conversations at court.[69] Charles discussed the appeal with his mother. She advised

[66] Mazarin to Brégy, May 2, 1652, *Lettres du cardinal Mazarin,* ed. Chéruel, V, 672; Mazarin to Duchesse de Chevreuse, June 5, 1652, *ibid.,* V, 674.

[67] Jean Jacquart, "La Fronde des Princes dans la région parisienne et ses conséquences matérielles," *Revue d'histoire moderne et contemporaine,* VII (1960), 259–262.

[68] *Ibid.,* pp. 259–262.

[69] The Duke of York said the Duc de Lorraine asked Charles to come. See *The Memoirs of James II,* p. 78; Hyde to Nicholas, June 22, 1652 (O.S.?), *Clarendon State Papers,* III, 77–78.

against entanglement with the Duc de Lorraine, whose violation of the treaty of June 6 had apparently disillusioned her. But her son had already committed himself so far in trying to be the peacemaker of the Fronde, and was probably so carried away by prospects of French aid if he succeeded, that he preferred to disregard his mother's counsel. Besides, Charles worried that a refusal to co-operate with the French government might leave him open to reproach for letting slip an opportunity to bring peace to France, so necessary, it seemed, for the advancement of his own affairs. Charles set out at once to confer with the Duke.[70]

No sooner had Charles arrived in the Duke's camp and begun to discuss the situation with him than he regretted his rashness. The Duke welcomed the English king but announced firmly that he had no intention of accompanying him to Melun to meet Louis XIV and his court. The Duke expected to use Charles's presence to delay and to confuse the battle plans of the Vicomte de Turenne. Charles found himself trapped. If the two armies came to blows, what was he to do? To remain with the Duke was tantamount to a public commitment for the Frondeurs against the court, which had given him asylum and which was his sole means of support. To abandon Duc Charles was to turn his back on a friend who wanted help, one whom the English royalists looked to for aid eventually in recovering their estates. Nor could the King, with honor, flee the field at a moment of approaching battle.[71]

Trying to find some acceptable way out of the dilemma, Charles II, assisted by Jermyn and the Abbé Montaigu, who had accompanied him to the Duke's camp, sought to mediate between the two commanders. The Duke of York, serving with

[70] Hyde to Nicholas, May 11, 1652 (O.S.?), *Clarendon State Papers*, III, 67; Hyde to Nicholas, June 22, 1652 (O.S.?), *ibid.*, III, 77; *The Memoirs of James II*, pp. 78–79.

[71] *The Memoirs of James II*, p. 79.

Turenne's army, was sent for and brought through the lines to consult with his brother. But the Duke of York kept his sympathy for Turenne and offered his brother little comfort, saying only that Turenne could not be swayed from his decision to attack unless the Duc de Lorraine agreed to march out of France. Meanwhile, Jermyn and the Abbé Montaigu raced back and forth between the two armies in fruitless mediation.[72]

Just as Turenne's troops made final preparations for the attack, Turenne consented to offer the Duc de Lorraine one last chance to adhere to the conditions of the treaty of June 6, 1652, and to depart from France within fifteen days. Upon receiving the message, the Duke pretended to reject the offer and ordered his artillery to commence firing. However, the Duke had privately passed word that his order was to be disregarded. With a show of dismay at the "disobedience" of his men, the Duke then accepted Turenne's offer, excusing himself because his troops would not fight. The contingent of Frondeurs, headed by the Duc de Beaufort, left Duc Charles's army in haste and soon announced the shocking news of Lorraine's defection to the Paris populace.[73]

The removal of the Duc de Lorraine and his army from the Frondeur camp dealt a severe blow to the Frondeurs. Within a few days the royal army under Turenne pushed the force of the Frondeurs to the very walls of Paris. Because of the divisions among the Frondeurs and the desire for peace, the municipal authorities of the city refused entry to the troops. With their backs literally to the wall, Condé and his soldiers faced utter defeat. Only in the nick of time did the Grande Mademoiselle save the day by ordering the Paris gates opened to Condé and his men, and so robbed Turenne of his prey.

However, the relief of the Frondeurs was only temporary.

[72] *Ibid.*, pp. 79–81.
[73] *Ibid.*, p. 81. See also the account given by the Marquis de Montglat in "Mémoires," *Nouvelle collection des mémoires,* XXVII, 269–270.

Dissension increased now that the Parisians had to contend with the actual presence of the Princes' army within their city. The highhanded behavior of the soldiers, the shocking riots against the Hôtel de Ville on July 4, 1652, which Condé was accused of having inspired, drove the wedge farther. To re-establish unity, the Princes and their friends hunted for a scapegoat upon whom to vent the general frustration. The English royalists were almost ideal for the purpose. The Duc de Beaufort, as we have said, had blamed Charles II and the English royalists for the Duc de Lorraine's withdrawal. The public accepted the charge as fact.[74] Persons of differing factions also shared the view. The Frondeur Guy Joly was convinced of Charles II's complicity,[75] just as was the Comte de Brienne.[76] Some, like the Grande Mademoiselle, believed that somebody else, perhaps the Princess Guémenée, had been the real mover for Mazarin, with Charles an unwitting pawn. Nonetheless, the Grande Mademoiselle, her father, and the Prince de Condé were incensed that Charles II had lent himself to such an intrigue in view of all the monetary aid and encouragement they had given him. The Grande Mademoiselle, in particular, had many harsh things to say. She even exclaimed that the King of England ought to be sent to Cromwell! [77]

The anger of the Princes was small, however, compared to that whipped up in the general populace. Charles, his mother, and their friends dared not step out of the Louvre for fear the mob outside would do them harm. There were shouts of, "They want

[74] *The Memoirs of James II*, pp. 82–83; *La honteuse sortie des Mazarins* (Paris, 1652), p. 5, Moreau No. 1664; *L'illusion publique* (n.p., 1652), p. 8, Moreau No. 1676; *Les intrigues de la paix* (n.p., 1652), p. 7, Moreau No. 1725; *Harangue de M. le chancelier* (Pontoise, 1652), p. 9, Moreau No. 1552; *La trahison du duc Charles* (Paris, 1652), p. 7, Moreau No. 3792.

[75] "Mémoires de Guy Joly," *Nouvelle collection des mémoires*, XXIV, 73.

[76] "Mémoires du comte de Brienne," *ibid.*, XXV, 142.

[77] *Journal de Jean Vallier*, III, 269; *Mémoires de Mlle de Montpensier*, II, 82–84.

to make us as miserable as they are, and they are doing every-thing possible to ruin France as they did England." [78] From having been the popular hero, Charles II had now become the public villain.

The sudden fall from popularity of the English royalists helped set the stage for a new propaganda drive by the Fron-deurs to rally the populace against the French court. Cardinal Mazarin had often been held up to public scorn because he was a foreigner. Now, in the summer of 1652, the Frondeurs began to find foreigners everywhere in the government of Louis XIV and Anne of Austria. There was Prince Thomas de Savoie, who sat in the Council of the King. They cited the mysterious Italian, Ondedei, the detested creature of Mazarin, as another undesira-ble foreigner. Then there were all the English royalists: Lord Jermyn, the Abbé Montaigu, Lord Digby, said to have become a part of the governing council too. Aliens were taking over the country, the propagandists warned.[79]

Pamphleteers spelled out in detail the danger of having the English exiles close to the King. The English were men who in their own country had traditionally been enemies of France. Did not Charles II lay claim to the throne of France, as had his predecessors? One could be sure that the English royalists, along with the other foreigners, were quite unconcerned about French defeats, especially as they might actually profit from the defeats. Charles II, for example, might patch up his differences with the Commonwealth and sell out to Cromwell. Surely it was ob-vious that he wanted to reduce France to the same miserable level as his own country.[80] They accused Charles and his sub-

[78] *Mémoires de Mlle de Montpensier,* II, 82; *Le mercure de la cour* (Paris, 1652), p. 18, Moreau No. 2452.

[79] *Instruction faite au peuple de Paris* (n.p., n.d.), pp. 4–5; *Réponse du roi servant de réplique* (n.p., 1652), pp. 19–20, 26, Moreau No. 3441; *La vérité prononçant ses oracles* (n.p., 1652), Part II, pp. 33–35, Moreau No. 3998.

[80] *De la nature et qualité du parlement de Paris* (Paris, 1652), p. 57, Moreau No. 857.

jects, Lord Jermyn, Abbé Montaigu, and Lord Digby, of tendering the worst possible counsel to Louis XIV and his government. It was the same kind of advice, it now appeared, which had doomed Charles's father.[81] That the English knew nothing of French law was bad enough,[82] but they worsened the fault, it was said, by plotting the murder of the Frondeur Duc de Beaufort, and by urging the court to seize Paris on the premise that Charles I's failure to control London had cost him crown and life.[83] These Englishmen, these foreigners, knew that they could never be secure until the Parisians were stripped of power. They would never advise the King of France to make peace with the Frondeurs, except for lack of wherewithal to continue the fight.[84] The Frondeurs explained that Queen Anne and the Cardinal had packed the government with foreigners because good Frenchmen, as they well knew, could never have condoned their odious policies. As it was now, the few Frenchmen on the King's Council feared to speak out in the presence of so many foreigners. With these and similar charges, the propagandists played on national sentiment by insisting that Mazarin's defeat would mean the defeat of the foreigners in France.[85]

The propaganda campaign enflamed public feeling against the exiles to such a degree that Charles II, his mother, and their entourage decided finally to leave Paris to avoid further incidents and to retire to St. Germain, where the French court had made provision for them to stay. When they departed the city in July, the Prince de Condé and the Duc d'Orléans were

[81] *Avis pressant et nécessaire* (Paris, 1652), p. 13, Moreau No. 531; *Réponse au manifeste* (Paris, 1652), p. 14, Moreau No. 3380; *La vérité prononçant ses oracles,* Part II, pp. 33–35, Moreau No. 3998.

[82] *De la nature et qualité du parlement de Paris,* p. 57, Moreau No. 857.

[83] *Avis pressant et nécessaire,* pp. 13–14, Moreau No. 531; *Le serpent britannique* (Paris, 1652), p. 7, Moreau No. 3665.

[84] *L'aveuglement des Parisiens,* p. 7, Moreau No. 467.

[85] *Le dépositaire des secrets de l'Etat* (n.p., n.d.), pp. 9–10, Moreau No. 1006.

both on hand to supervise the arrangements for their safe passage. They exchanged adieux, politely enough, all things considered.[86]

Charles and his friends had only a brief time to wait until the gates of Paris opened to them again. When Louis XIV and Queen Anne staged their festive re-entry in the capital in October, 1652, they allotted Charles II a prominent place in the procession. They also extended thanks to the English royalists for their efforts to restore domestic peace in France. But the thanks were perfunctory.[87] Too many others claimed credit for the return to peace in Paris. However much the English royalists may have contributed to the withdrawal of the Duc de Lorraine in June, it was forgotten in the excitement of more recent events.

The exiles felt the more disappointed when Admiral Blake's attack on the French relief squadron for Dunkirk failed to precipitate war between France and England.[88] Yet, though their spirits were low, they were still quite unprepared for the shock of learning that France planned to send an ambassador to London in December, 1652. Charles and his mother protested the decision in person. Afterward, Charles had his Council debate and prepare a formal note of protest which Jermyn delivered. Apparently these tactics caused a small delay in Monsieur de Bordeaux's departure, but they failed to get the mission cancelled. Mazarin proffered unctuous assurance that the mission was only for the purpose of recovering the ships captured by Blake, but the English royalists suspected otherwise. Sir

[86] Sagredo to Doge and Senate, August 13, 1652, *Calendar of State Papers . . . Venice*, XXVIII, 269; Hyde to Nicholas, July 19, 1652 (O.S.?), *Clarendon State Papers*, III, 83. The propagandists for the Prince de Condé still continued their attacks on Charles, however. See Victor Cousin, *Madame de Longueville pendant la Fronde* (Paris, 1872), p. 440.

[87] *Le journal contenant ce qui se passe*, pp. 18–25, October, 1652, Moreau No. 1740.

[88] Hyde to Nicholas, October 12, 1652 (O.S.?) *Clarendon State Papers*, III, 105–106.

Edward Hyde believed the dispatch of Monsieur de Bordeaux to London would be "of unspeakable disadvantage to our poor master," [89] and, for once, Henriette-Marie agreed with Hyde. Indeed, she admitted that not since the death of her husband had anything affected her so much.[90]

When nothing very dramatic followed French recognition of the Commonwealth, the spirits of the exiles in Paris revived slightly. Perhaps they might still find a way to obtain French help. The English royalists realized the anxiety of French officials that the Puritans might intercede for the Frondeurs at Bordeaux. As late as July of 1653, when the Fronde was almost played out, Hyde commented on "the terrible apprehension they [the French government] have the English will relieve Bordeaux; which gives them great pain." [91] Perhaps, then, the exiles could help bring the revolt to an end more quickly, and perhaps this time the French government would reward them.

The Irish mercenaries, relied on so extensively by the Spaniards and the Frondeurs for the defense of Guyenne, seemed likely to furnish the exiles with their opportunity. We have indicated in the previous chapter the unhappiness of the Irish troops with the conditions of their service in Guyenne, and we have discussed the various attempts of the French government to obtain their surrender by bribery. However, it occurred to many, and not just to the English royalists, that Charles II and those in his following might be able to hasten matters. Monsieur de Bordeaux wrote from London in early April, 1653, that according to reports he had received, a Colonel Preston had

[89] Hyde to Taylor, December 7, 1652, *Calendar of the Clarendon State Papers,* II, 160; Hyde to Nicholas, December 28, 1652 (O.S.?), *Clarendon State Papers,* III, 129–130.

[90] Henriette-Marie to Duke of York, December 15, 1652 (O.S.?), Baillon, *Henriette-Marie de France,* p. 561.

[91] Hyde to Nicholas, July 4, 1653 (O.S.?), *Clarendon State Papers,* III, 176.

several agents at work in Languedoc to persuade the Irish to change sides. This was the same Thomas Preston who had fought against Ireton in Ireland and had but recently crossed to France. However, the French ambassador believed Preston could accomplish little unless he received a direct order from the King of England telling the Irish to shift their allegiance to the French crown. The order was required, the ambassador thought, because the Irish did not wish to stain their honor by betrayal; but, considering themselves subjects of Charles II, they could use his order to excuse their surrender.[92] The same thought occurred to one of Mazarin's spies in the city of Bordeaux. In late April or early May, he advised the Cardinal to employ the King of England, Colonel Preston, or someone else of the English royalist following, to bring about the surrender of the Irish.[93] The Bishop of Tulle, who represented the Cardinal with the military forces moving against Bordeaux, was also much taken by the possibility. On May 20, 1652, he suggested that the Marquess of Ormonde, who had departed Ireland in 1650 after his army crumbled before Cromwell's attacks, might be a good choice; or, failing him, some other English royalist.[94]

Those at the court of Charles II actively supported some such scheme by late April or early May. Several of them proposed the Marquess of Ormonde as the right person to co-ordinate the subversion of the Irish. He could then lead them when they agreed to support the French crown. Lord Jermyn argued the plan before Cardinal Mazarin at Fontainebleau, and the Cardinal expressed interest. He requested a written memorandum

[92] Bordeaux to Brienne, April 3, 1653, P.R.O. transcript, 31/3/90, copied from B.N., MS. f.fr. 16008.

[93] "Le royaliste de Bordeaux" to Mazarin, April, 1653, *Archives historiques du département de la Gironde*, VIII, 127–130; "Le royaliste de Bordeaux" to unknown person, May 1, 1653, *ibid.*, VIII, 132–136.

[94] Bishop of Tulle to Mazarin, May 20, 1653, *ibid.*, VIII, 161.

on the subject. The memorandum was in due course drafted and presented to him, obviously with the approval of Charles II and Henriette-Marie.[95]

The Frondeurs suspected that the Irish might yield to pressure from the English royalists. Pierre Lenet took alarm in April about reports that the Irish were already exposed to the cajolery of Charles and his suite. The situation prompted Lenet to suggest that the Spaniards bring in troops of some other nationality: Spanish, Walloon, German, or Neapolitan. It seemed pure folly to Lenet to make the defense of Bordeaux almost wholly dependent on Irish troops whose King assisted Cardinal Mazarin.[96] Had the Spaniards been disposed to follow Lenet's advice, it could have cost them dearly to import troops of other nationalities. Certainly it would have required considerable time for the transfer. Unfortunately, the Frondeurs lacked both time and money.

Toward the end of May, 1653, as the forces of the French crown advanced closer to Lormont, a strategic bastion of the Frondeurs on the Gironde, guarding the approaches to Bordeaux, Admiral Vendôme, seconded by the Bishop of Tulle, negotiated secretly with the Irish commander at Lormont, Colonel James Dillon. On his own, Vendôme concluded a treaty with Dillon on May 24, 1653, calling for the surrender of the Irish there and the admission of the forces of Louis XIV into Lormont. To the consternation of the Frondeurs, the surrender occurred on May 26, 1653. However, to get the surrender, Vendôme promised Colonel Dillon that all the Irish troops could serve under the command of the Duke of York; that as

---

[95] "Mémoires touchant les Irlandois," July, 1653, P.R.O. transcript, 31/3/91, copied from A.E. Angleterre, LXI, ff. 255–256.

[96] Lenet to Condé, March 3, 1653, Chantilly, MS. série P, XIII, f. 8; Lenet to Saint-Agoulin, after May 8, 1653, Cosnac, *Souvenirs du règne de Louis XIV*, VII, 114–115.

soon as the Fronde was terminated, the Irish could go immediately against England, Scotland, or Ireland, if they wished,
in the service of Charles II.[97]

In spite of previous recommendations, when Monsieur de
Bordeaux learned of the secret treaty in London, he wrote home
immediately warning of the bad effect it would produce if it
became generally known in England. The ambassador suggested
that the King of France disavow the treaty publicly to head
off trouble with Cromwell.[98] Mazarin had had almost the same
reaction even before he read Monsieur de Bordeaux's letter.
Fear of Cromwell had already caused the Cardinal to drop the
earlier proposal to use the Marquess of Ormonde in negotiations
with the Irish.[99] The same consideration had also caused the
rejection of plans, talked of at the French court, to shift the
Duke of York into Guyenne.[100] Thus, when Mazarin learned
of the treaty with Dillon, he replied in haste. The King of
France could not ratify such a treaty, he said.[101] Though the
Bishop of Tulle believed the treaty could be kept a secret from
Cromwell,[102] Mazarin was equally certain it could not. News
would leak to the Frondeurs in Bordeaux, he said, and from
there it was sure to be passed on to London. This could ruin
the negotiations of Monsieur de Bordeaux, because it implied

[97] Articles of Agreement, May 24, 1653, *Calendar of the Clarendon State
Papers,* II, 207.

[98] Bordeaux to Brienne, June 12, 1653, P.R.O. transcript, 31/3/91, copied
from B.N., MS. f.fr. 16008.

[99] "Mémoires touchant les Irlandois," July, 1653, *ibid.,* 31/3/91, copied
from A.E. Angleterre, LXI, ff. 255–256.

[100] Sagredo to Doge and Senate, June 3, 1653, *Calendar of State Papers
. . . Venice,* XXIX, 80.

[101] Mazarin to Bishop of Tulle, June 2, 1653, *Lettres du cardinal Mazarin,* ed. Chéruel, V, 625; Mazarin to Vendôme, June 29, 1653, *ibid.,* V,
718.

[102] Bishop of Tulle to Mazarin, June 7, 1653, *Archives historiques du département de la Gironde,* VIII, 443.

military support for Charles II and assistance to him for a future attack against England.[103]

The disavowal of the treaty with Colonel Dillon had no effect on the surrender of Lormont. The surrender was already an accomplished fact and could not be undone, even had the Irish wished it. But it was soon evident that the Irish were not much bothered by the consideration of "honor" after all. The judicious payment of bribes and promises of favors easily overcame their scruples. The Irish officers rationalized their surrender without need of orders from the King of England. The surrenders continued, but not in such a way as to compromise the French government with Cromwell. For, as Mazarin had rightly foreseen, it was impossible to keep the Puritans in ignorance about the conditions of the surrender. If the French government did later send Lord Digby into Guyenne, as Pierre Lenet suspected, it did not employ him to draw over the Irish defenders of Bordeaux.[104]

Mazarin's reluctance to call on the English royalists for help in this instance was yet another disappointment for the exiles. All the more so since they received blame for it anyway. The Spaniards refused to admit that shabby treatment of their Irish troops could have caused the massive surrenders. Instead they either believed, or affected to believe, that the King of England had acted as the evil genius. When 4,000 more Irish troops deserted to the French in Catalonia in August, 1653, the Spaniards similarly attributed it to the machinations of Charles II. These charges exasperated the English royalists. Sir Edward Hyde wrote several letters to correspondents in Madrid attempting to clear the English monarch of any complicity. The King was entirely innocent, he wrote. In fact, Hyde confided, Charles

[103] Mazarin to Bishop of Tulle, June 2, 1653, *Lettres du cardinal Mazarin,* ed. Chéruel, V, 625.

[104] *Nouvelles ordinaires de Londres,* No. 154, June 2/12–9/19, 1653, p. 614; intercepted letter, July 9, 1653, *Thurloe Papers,* I, 323; Lenet to Condé, June 26, 1652, Cosnac, *Souvenirs du règne de Louis XIV,* VII, 224.

had forbidden the Duke of York to serve in Guyenne or in Catalonia to prevent defections of the Irish to him. Rather plaintively, Hyde complained that the Spaniards blamed Charles II for something he had not done; but then, ambiguously, Hyde added that the French were not as grateful to Charles for what he had done as they ought to be.[105]

Each of the policies pursued by the English royalists during the period of the Fronde terminated in failure. The efforts of Hyde and Cottington to end the Franco-Spanish war had produced nothing. Attempts to remain neutral during the Fronde gained nothing. Attempts to arrange marriage alliances in France had also failed. Nor had mediation between the Frondeurs and the French crown brought the exiles any profit. Still less successful had been the decision to assist the French crown against the Frondeurs in the last months of the Fronde. The lack of real influence enjoyed by the English royalists in the closing weeks of the Fronde was revealed at the arrival of Prince Rupert's bedraggled squadron at Nantes, after a cruise to the West Indies. French authorities allowed him to put into Nantes; but they held up sale of the few prizes he brought with him, notwithstanding forceful representations at court by the English royalists. The French government had no intention of provoking Cromwell into a final hour rescue of the Frondeurs at Bordeaux for the sake of the English royalists.[106]

---

[105] Querini to Doge and Senate, August 20, 1653, *Calendar of State Papers . . . Venice*, XXIX, 113–114; Hyde to Bellings, September 12, 1653, *Calendar of the Clarendon State Papers*, II, 250; Hyde to Wright, September 13, 1653, *ibid.*, II, 251–252.

[106] Eva Scott, *The King in Exile* (London, 1905), pp. 484–487.

IX

The Partnership of
Mazarin and Cromwell

WITHIN a few weeks of the surrender of the Bordeaux Frondeurs in August, 1653, the *Gazette de France* described for its readers an idyllic picture of the kingdom. Readers were asked to look about them at the calm which had settled over the country; then, by way of contrast, to let their thoughts run back to the confusion which had prevailed only the year before. Then, recalled the *Gazette*, Frenchmen had lived in dread of general upheaval, exposed to the whims of evil men. Then, their lives, their liberty, and their property had been threatened. But now, continued the *Gazette*, men could taste the fruits of an agreeable liberty—a liberty secured by the legitimate authority of their sovereign working through the regulated obedience of his subjects. Only a memory now, the souvenir of the Fronde might serve to render the populace of France more constant in its duty and wiser for the future, the *Gazette* concluded.[1]

Many of the memoirists who wrote of this period concurred with the judgment of the *Gazette*. Among them was Jean Vallier, Maitre d'Hôtel for the King, who was reminded of the contrast between France and England at the close of 1653. "In France," he confided in his journal, "things had turned out quite differ-

[1] *Gazette de France*, No. 123, October 4, 1653, p. 995.

248

ently [from those in England]; one could see here [in France] royal authority at its highest point, and the people breathed only obedience; internal disorders were entirely calmed." [2] Though we shall have more to say about this "return to order," it is true that the French government was better able to combat domestic trouble than before. It is also true that a revolt on the scale of the Fronde did not occur again in France until the Revolution of 1789, more than a century and a quarter later.

But how did the conclusion of the Fronde affect the conduct of affairs with the English? Cromwell's agents in France insisted all through the summer of 1653 that, once the French crown subdued the Frondeurs, it would drop negotiations with the Puritan régime and would apply itself to the re-establishment of Charles II.[3] Though Mazarin had consistently denied such intentions, he had also privately assured the English royalists in December, 1652, and upon other occasions that present necessity dictated French *rapprochement* with the Puritan government, which did not signify a permanent desertion of the royalists.[4] What then were the Cardinal's real intentions?

The full story of Anglo-French relations in the immediate post-Fronde period is exceedingly complex. Since the scope of this study is limited primarily to the period of the Fronde itself, we cannot trace in detail the twists and turns of that later relationship. However, the later policies of Cromwell and Mazarin provide insight into earlier behavior, and for this reason a brief résumé may be helpful for a fuller understanding of the impact of the English Civil War and Revolution on the Fronde.[5]

[2] *Journal de Jean Vallier*, IV, 399–400.
[3] Letter of intelligence, July 2, 1653, *Thurloe Papers*, I, 312; letter to Thurloe, n.d., *ibid.*, I, 333; letter of intelligence, July 19, 1653, *ibid.*, I, 344–345.
[4] Sagredo to Doge and Senate, December 10, 1652, *Calendar of State Papers . . . Venice*, XXVIII, 317.
[5] Charles P. Korr is preparing a dissertation under the direction of Pro-

Contrary to the expectations of many, French policy toward England immediately after the Fronde remained little changed. No declaration came forth from Paris in behalf of Charles II, as the English royalists had hoped and as the Puritans had feared. But neither were relations with Cromwellian England more harmonious than before. Several times between 1653 and 1655 England and France edged back to the brink of open war. The initiative in this elaborate diplomatic ballet, which involved as principals not only England and France but Spain and Holland too, lay chiefly with Cromwell. Especially after England and Holland patched over their differences and terminated the first Anglo-Dutch war in early 1654, Cromwell, by now "Protector" of England, was freer to try his hand in other adventures. But he could not decide whether France or Spain offered the better target.

Would it be more profitable to trade with Spain, or would it be better to raid and pluck away some of the Spanish colonial possessions? Would Protestants in France gain or lose if England went to war with France? How could the present régime in England best safeguard itself from the machinations of the English royalists? Did friendship with France or with Spain offer the better chance to increase English national power and prestige? These were some of the considerations to debate and to decide.

Cardinal Mazarin felt sure that Cromwell was encouraging the French and the Spaniards to bid against one another for his favor. But the Cardinal determined to win that favor for France if the price were reasonable. Despite the breathtaking dips which Anglo-French relations entered from time to time, the French were ready to negotiate with Cromwell as long as the faintest glimmer of hope remained.

The sea war hampered the bargaining with Cromwell, how-

---

fessor Andrew Lossky at U.C.L.A. which will explore in detail Anglo-French relations from 1653 to 1658.

ever. The number of captures at sea and confiscations on land remained high as ever in the two years following the Fronde. "Pirates" sailing under commission of Charles II sailed in and out of French ports with the same relative impunity. Officially, the French government, as before, opposed this activity, and Mazarin and Monsieur de Bordeaux righteously denied recurrent reports in England that wholesale confiscations of English property in France had been ordered.[6] But though the admiralty court which the exiles maintained in Brest was shut down,[7] the fact remained that the trade and sea war continued unchecked.

Perhaps the French government failed to adopt effective measures because it doubted the English would halt their attacks against French shipping. Or perhaps the French government could not enforce its directives to the port areas. Hugh Morel, representative of the English merchants in Paris, whom we have met on previous occasions, wrote home that the French government was actually afraid to apply an effective check to this activity. The port governors, he said, were so many "petty kings."[8] Undeniably, just as during the Fronde, port authorities acted independently of Paris. The French government frankly admitted, in a draft treaty prepared in 1654, that the governors of "Nantes, Toulon, Calais, Brest, and other French places are accustomed not to accord to the orders of their sovereign the obedience they owe him" when it involved treatment of the English.[9]

As before, local officials and local shipping and merchant groups could not reach a consensus on what to do. In October, 1653, representatives of merchants from Normandy and Brittany journeyed to Paris to ask for a halt of all freebooter attacks

[6] *The Clarke Papers*, ed. Charles H. Firth, III (London, 1899), 29, 30–31, 32–33, 34–35.
[7] Bernhard to Horne, October 25/November 4, 1653, *Thurloe Papers*, I, 554.
[8] Morel to Thurloe, May 27, 1655, *ibid.*, III, 444.
[9] Guizot, *History of Oliver Cromwell*, II, 465, article 13.

against the Puritans and for a call-in of all commissions issued by Charles II.[10] Some of the local inhabitants of the port towns turned against the "pirates" working for the English royalists and obliged several of them to surrender their commissions because their activity offended the Puritans.[11] But as before, many others evidently preferred a more aggressive response and subjected the English to constant harassment in France. Sentiment in the coastal areas of France became increasingly unfriendly toward the Puritans. In April, 1653, report had it that every day commissioners from Normandy, Poitou, and the Biscay region solicited the French court for permission to arm against the English. They wanted war.[12]

Knowing how sensitive the Puritans were to the presence of Charles II and the other exiles in France, Mazarin admitted in early 1654 that perhaps the time had come to sacrifice Charles. If expelling Charles from France might dissuade the Protector from war with France, the Cardinal informed Monsieur de Bordeaux, then the government would not shrink from it.[13] As it happened, Mazarin escaped the unpleasantness of a formal order of expulsion. So uncongenial had become the official French attitude that Charles II was quite ready—indeed eager—to leave of his own accord. The French hastened his departure plans by advancing him funds for traveling expenses. To soften the resentment of the exiles as much as possible, the government doled out sums for his upkeep long after he left.[14] When Charles headed for Cologne in the summer of 1654, the event occasioned silent relief among officials of the French government and public expressions of satisfaction from the Puritans.

[10] Letter of intelligence to Augier, November 19/29, 1653, *Thurloe Papers*, I, 609.

[11] Letter of intelligence, October 15/25, 1653, *ibid.*, I, 545.

[12] Bordeaux (father) to Bordeaux (son), April 14, 1655, *ibid.*, III, 343.

[13] Mazarin to Bordeaux, June 22, 1654, *Lettres du cardinal Mazarin*, ed. Chéruel, VI, 183.

[14] Mazarin to Bishop of Dromone [sic], September 3, 1656, *ibid.*, VII, 669–670.

The Cardinal continued after the Fronde to interpose his influence in behalf of the Huguenots and to protect them in some measure from the Catholic *dévots*. Typical was his letter to the Comte d'Estrades, regarding a Huguenot synod to be held in the upper Guyenne in the fall of 1654. He remarked, "Having seen in all the past disturbances that those of the said Religion have maintained an unshakeable loyalty for the service of His Majesty, I will render them all the offices which are in my personal power, in order to maintain them in the enjoyment of privileges accorded to them by the Edicts." [15] The Cardinal's protection of the Huguenots was not bestowed exclusively out of respect for Cromwell, but the Cardinal naturally ensured that the Protector learned of it.[16] Monsieur Augier, who had represented the English Parliament in Paris during the Fronde, was bribed to provide the Protector with the desired kind of information.[17] When Cromwell protested later about the brutal treatment of the non-Catholic Vaudois in 1655 by forces of the Catholic Duc de Savoie, the French crown disclaimed any part of it. But, to placate the Puritans, the French exerted all their influence to bring the persecutions to an end. The Protector was officially informed of the government's action.[18] Again, to make sure Cromwell received appropriate information, Monsieur de Bordeaux bribed Stouppe, one of Cromwell's emissaries among the Huguenots in France, to praise the French action.[19]

[15] Mazarin to d'Estrades, September 7, 1654, *Archives historiques du département de la Gironde,* VIII, 477.

[16] Mazarin to Bordeaux, July 20, 1654, *Lettres du cardinal Mazarin,* ed. Chéruel, VI, 227.

[17] Bordeaux to Brienne, May 7, 1654, P.R.O. transcript, 31/3/94, copied from B.N., MS. f.fr. 16009, f. 139.

[18] Louis XIV to Cromwell, June 12, 1655, *ibid.,* 31/3/98, copied from A.E. Angleterre, LXVI, ff. 631–632.

[19] Bordeaux to Brienne, July 1, 1655, *ibid.,* 31/3/98, copied from B.N., MS. f.fr. 16010; Bordeaux to Brienne, July 8, 1655, *ibid.,* 31/3/98, copied from B.N., MS. f.fr. 16010. For a discussion of this affair and for additional background regarding the alliance see Jacob N. Bowman, *The*

England and the Fronde

When Cromwell allowed a squadron of ships to attack the Spanish West Indies in 1655, to which the Spaniards angrily retaliated by imposing an embargo on English trade, French persistence won its reward. Cromwell was ready to come to an understanding with France. On November 3, 1655, Monsieur de Bordeaux affixed his signature to the Treaty of Westminster —a treaty which in various forms he had labored over for almost three years.

The Treaty of Westminster was limited in its provisions, but it eliminated a number of irritations. The trade war from which England and France both suffered was declared at an end. The embargoes which had prevented French wines and textiles from moving into England, and English textiles from entering France, were abolished. The unofficial sea war and the harassment of merchants and shippers ashore was also terminated. Each side solemnly agreed further not to harbor any persons who wished to harm the trade of the other—a provision aimed at the privateers sailing under commission of Charles II. A joint committee would study the reparations claimed on both sides. This latter provision became a dead letter. Nonetheless the treaty had the desired effect in restoring normal economic relations.[20]

The treaty also carried a secret provision of greatest importance. Under its terms each country promised not to shelter the domestic enemies of the other. In practical language, this meant that England must expel the agents of the Prince de Condé and the representatives of the city of Bordeaux who had either lingered on in England after the Fronde or had arrived since then. For its part, France pledged that Charles II could not return to France and agreed that the Duke of York and members of Charles's Privy Council must stay outside French territory. Queen Henriette-Marie could continue her residence in France because of her French birth. Other English royalists were also

Protestant Interest in Cromwell's Foreign Relations (Heidelberg, 1900), pp. 33–45.

[20] A.E. Angleterre, LXVI, ff. 136–137.

authorized to stay with her. But the treaty denied French haven to those considered most dangerous by the Puritans.[21]

Reaction in France to the improvement in relations with the Puritans was mixed. Cardinal Mazarin and the shipping and merchant interests considered the treaty a triumph. Doubtless those engaged in textile manufacture accorded it a less enthusiastic reception. For much of the French population, saturated in the propaganda which had flooded France during the Fronde, a treaty with the heretical "regicides" was unwelcome news. The government, as provided in the agreement with England, ordered public announcement of the treaty by heralds and ordered bonfires lit in the streets and bells rung to celebrate.[22] Yet one of the famous preachers of the day dared inveigh against the treaty in the hearing of Louis XIV and his mother.[23] While the treaty was still being negotiated in the summer of 1655, pictures of Cromwell were sold, with verses attached, describing him as the enemy of the Church and of all monarchies.[24] Another picture offered for sale showed Cromwell seated on a closestool "at his business and the King of Spain on the one side and the King of France on the other, offering him paper to wipe his breech" [25]—a crude but graphic demonstration of how deeply some persons in France resented the treaty. An agent of the Puritan government in Paris confirmed that Cromwell received affront everywhere.[26]

Though Cardinal Mazarin might congratulate himself on the conclusion of the Treaty of Westminster,[27] whatever others in France might think of it, his nervousness about England con-

[21] *Ibid.*, LXVI, ff. 136–137.
[22] Bordeaux to Brienne, July 8, 1655, P.R.O. transcript, 31/3/98, copied from B.N., MS. f.fr. 16010; *Gazette de France*, No. 152, November 13, 1655, pp. 1271–1272.
[23] Radcliffe to Traps, December 15, 1655, *Thurloe Papers*, IV, 284.
[24] Letter of intelligence, June 12, 1655, *ibid.*, III, 501–502.
[25] Letter of intelligence, July 28, 1655, *ibid.*, III, 658.
[26] Letter of intelligence, June 12, 1655, *ibid.*, III, 501–502.
[27] Mazarin to Bordeaux, December 8, 1655, *Lettres du cardinal Mazarin,* ed. Chéruel, VII, 594.

tinued. The treaty was one of friendship, not alliance. If the Spaniards could arrange an alliance with England, they might in effect supersede the Treaty of Westminster. To no one's surprise, the Spaniards presently tried to do just that. Not in the least abashed by a secret treaty they had concluded with Charles II in 1656, the Spaniards offered to help Cromwell take Calais from the French.[28] Mazarin labored just as determinedly to obtain an alliance of his own with Cromwell to reinforce the Treaty of Westminster.

As the Cardinal had gotten nowhere in his most recent peace talks with Spain, he was all the more anxious for an English alliance. Eventually Cromwell decided that Mazarin's bid was the more attractive and the Cardinal walked off with the prize —a one-year defensive and offensive alliance directed against Spain. The Cardinal had held out Dunkirk to the English. He had in fact offered it in 1654, but it was in 1657 that Cromwell accepted the offer. In return for English sovereignty over Dunkirk, a French pledge of 20,000 troops to help capture it, and a French promise to pay half the expenses of the English force, Cromwell agreed to throw 6,000 English soldiers into the battle and to furnish the requisite naval support.[29]

In the first year of the alliance, the allies took only Mardike from Spain. The town was transferred to Cromwell, provisionally, until Dunkirk's turn came. The treaty of alliance was then renewed in 1658 for another year. On June 14, 1658, the combined Anglo-French forces badly defeated the Spaniards at the Battle of the Dunes, making possible the capture of Dunkirk a few days later. As stipulated by the Anglo-French treaty,

[28] Guizot, *History of Oliver Cromwell*, II, 542–548.

[29] *Ibid.*, II, 562–568; *Recueil des instructions données aux ambassadeurs, XI, Espagne*, ed. A. Morel (Paris, 1894), I, xi–xii, 98–99. For more information about the alliance and the campaigns to capture Dunkirk see Charles H. Firth, *The Last Years of the Protectorate, 1656–1658* (London, 1909), I, 268–301; II, 177–222. Also useful is Jules Bourelly, *Cromwell et Mazarin—deux campagnes de Turenne en Flandre* (Paris, 1886).

Dunkirk immediately came under English sovereignty. The summer fighting ended after the fall of Gravelines to the French in August.

Spain emerged from the campaign badly mauled, its resolve to continue the war shaken. The losses sustained from the joint Anglo-French attack caused the Spaniards to listen more receptively to the peace terms which Cardinal Mazarin again held out to them. The Treaty of the Pyrenees, signed in 1659, which terminated the long-drawn-out Franco-Spanish war and which provided for the marriage of Louis XIV and the Infanta, was thus partially an outgrowth of the brilliant successes scored because of Mazarin's alliance with Cromwell.

But what a strange assortment of bedfellows the *rapprochement* of England and France had produced. On the one hand the Spaniards, Charles II and the English royalists, and the Frondeur Prince de Condé; on the other, Mazarin and Cromwell. The strangeness of these combinations, in view of all that had gone before, was apparent to French contemporaries; but it was especially the union of Mazarin and Cromwell which stirred emotions. Opinion in France about the Puritan régime had scarcely improved since the signing of the Treaty of Westminster. Many of the *gens de bien* adjudged the alliance with the Puritans and the promised transfer of Dunkirk to "a heretic and a usurper" as nothing short of odious.[30] The Puritan ambassador, Lockhart, spoke of the "exceeding high and universal" discontents in Paris, due in large part to the English alliance with France, and of complaints that France should be ready to deliver Dunkirk into the hands of "their old and most dangerous

---

[30] *Mémoires de Mme de Motteville,* IV, 109; *Histoire du ministère du Cardinal sous le règne de Louis XIV* (n.p., 1668), p. 540. Boileau's "Ode sur un bruit qui courut, en 1656, que Cromwell et les Anglois alloient faire la guerre à la France," *Oeuvres de Boileau,* ed. Georges Mongrédien (Paris, 1961), pp. 234–235, indicates the climate of hostility in France which preceded the alliance: "Arme-toi, France; prends la foudre:/C'est à toi de répandre en poudre/Ces sanglans ennemis des lois."

enemies, which, they say, is not only against the interest of France in particular, but against the whole Catholic interest in general." [31] London heard of the distaste of "the better sort of bourgeois" in Paris for the English alliance and of their preference for the "Catholic religion before the enlarging of their dominion and the weakening of their enemies." [32]

Those formerly associated with the Fronde did their best to capitalize on the unpopularity of the alliance and to pose as defenders of monarchy and Catholicism. The Cardinal de Retz, whom the crown had imprisoned in late 1652 and who escaped in 1654 and made his way circuitously to Rome, grasped at the opportunity to hit back at Mazarin. Exercising his very considerable literary talent, Retz composed a masterful presentation of arguments against the English alliance, and hence against Mazarin, the architect of the alliance. The pamphlet did not appear under Retz's name, but its authorship was quickly suspected. Printed in Holland and smuggled into France in late 1657 or early 1658, the pamphlet evidently circulated widely in France.[33]

Retz skillfully revived a theme which the Frondeurs had so often employed, namely that Cardinal Mazarin and Cromwell were brother tyrants. As in the past, Retz carefully avoided attacking the King but aimed his shafts at Mazarin for having sought an alliance with those in England responsible "for the most furious rebellion which has ever shattered a crown and for the most abandoned heresy which has ever sought to dishonor Christianity." Mazarin had compelled the unfortunate Charles II to leave France, Retz explained, to please Cromwell, "that murderer of kings," and had obliged Queen Henriette-Marie to live in squalid poverty. All the while Cromwell was

---

[31] Lockhart to Thurloe, April 5/15, 1658, *Thurloe Papers*, VII, 51–52.
[32] Letter of intelligence, August 20, 1658, *ibid.*, VII, 322.
[33] "Très-humble et très-importante remonstrance au roi sur la remise des places maritimes de Flandres entre les mains des Anglois," *Oeuvres du cardinal de Retz*, V, 291–327. See also the editor's note, *ibid.*, V, 275–291.

dreaming of revolts in Guyenne and Normandy, was lining up his friends in France, and was enflaming the Huguenots. Because of it, there was reason to believe France might fall victim to a terrible religious and political civil war. Furthermore, by allying with Cromwell and the Independents, clearly the enemies of every crown and of every religion, France was bound to repel all her friends. Should Cromwell later fall from power and the King of Great Britain recover his throne with Spanish help, France would surely feel the lash of Charles's anger.[34]

Cardinal Mazarin was stung by the attack. Though undeterred from the alliance with Cromwell, he directed Secretary of State Hugues de Lionne to draft, under his coaching, a response to Retz's pamphlet. The reply, complete with supporting documents, is most curious for its omissions. The government built its defense around the premise that the Spaniards had sought for an alliance of their own with Cromwell, which, had they succeeded, could have had disastrous consequence for France. Lionne demonstrated the care with which the government had safeguarded Catholic rights in Dunkirk. However, he offered no defense for alliance with a "parricide"; he took no direct notice of the charge that Cromwell, under cover of the alliance, might incite revolts inside France. Only a veiled statement that His Majesty had taken precautions in this respect, "secrets which ought not to be divulged," referred very obliquely to the matter. Otherwise, the pamphlet served up for French consumption arguments similar to those which Monsieur de Bordeaux had used in England. As Lionne expressed it here, "It does not belong to us to control the secrets of Providence nor to examine too curiously why It permits the changes which occur among our neighbors in religion or in the state; we are not obliged, because of them, to break off the commerce, association, and friendship which proximity requires us to maintain." [35] The

[34] *Ibid.,* V, 291–327.
[35] Hugues de Lionne, *Remarques sur la reddition de Dunkerque entre les mains des anglois* (Paris, 1658), pp. 7–8, 11, 14.

great significance of this statement is evident! It served clear notice on the French public that their government rejected any notion of waging ideological war against England. In modern parlance, Mazarin declared through Lionne that neither a "hot war" nor a "cold war" with the revolutionary government of England could serve the best interests of the French monarchy or the French state.

But how to explain the reasoning by which Mazarin justified his alliance with Cromwell? Had he decided that the Fronde was a quarrel of the past, that he need now concern himself solely with the defeat of Spain? Had he decided that an alliance with the revolutionary government of England was necessary to accomplish Spanish defeat, that hence an English alliance had all the justification it needed? Certainly the military advantage of having Cromwell as an ally against Spain weighed heavily with the Cardinal. But could the alliance with the Puritans be reduced to terms so simple? If so, then Mazarin's behavior toward England in the past, and especially during the Fronde, is most puzzling.

If Cardinal Mazarin had been motivated uniquely by considerations of international power politics and by his desire to strike a crippling blow at the Spaniards, why had he waited so long to come to terms with the revolutionaries in England? Perhaps, as Monsieur de Grignon had written from London just after Charles I's execution, there was then still some faint hope for an eventual royalist victory in England. But surely after the defeats at Dunbar in 1650, and at Worcester in 1651, only the wildest optimist would have placed his bet on the English king. The wary Spaniards, no lovers either of republicanism or of Puritanism, had nonetheless dismissed the English royalists from their calculations in 1650–1651 and tried to achieve friendship with the Commonwealth. Yet Cardinal Mazarin and the French crown had continued to balk. This was a policy which had cost France dearly, at a time when the gov-

ernment could ill afford it. Refusal to jettison the English royalists had left France embroiled in a sea war with one of the
greatest naval powers of the age and helped whip up a trade
war which paralyzed French commerce overseas. Great numbers
of people in France lived on so narrow an economic margin
that the slightest diminution in their income could spell ruin.
What, then, must have been the effect of the progressive stran-
gulation of external trade which France bore as a result of its
government's distrust of the revolutionary régime in England?
At the same time, the French court had knowingly risked a
Spanish alliance with England and the threat of hostile intervention by the English revolutionaries in the Fronde.

Only with the greatest reluctance, and after most painful
deliberation, had Mazarin and his associates in the government
slowly and hesitantly begun to reshape their policies toward
the Puritans. Not until Admiral Blake dramatically pointed up
the vulnerability of France to English sea power in 1652 did
the French government extend so much as an unconditional
recognition to the Commonwealth. Even then, though a prey to
anxious moments that England might stage a last-minute rescue
of the Frondeurs in Bordeaux, the French court was strikingly
restrained in its bargaining with England.

Perhaps it will be said that conditions vis-à-vis the Puritans
which confronted Mazarin during and after the Fronde were
of different kinds—that naturally the Cardinal hesitated to
recognize the revolutionary government in England while the
memory of Charles I's death was still so fresh and while civil
war raged in France; but that later, as time dulled memories,
and as the Fronde drew its last gasp, Mazarin need no longer
concern himself with questions of revolution and with the
safety of the French monarchy when dealing with the Puritans.
Yet we have stressed Cardinal Mazarin's intimate familiarity
with the English Civil War, and his alarm before and during
the Fronde that a similar revolutionary outbreak might shatter

the French monarchy. Was it possible for the same man who had applied so many lessons and parallels from England, and who felt so strongly about revolution, to erase all this so easily from his thoughts? If bystanders like Madame de La Fayette, Madame de Motteville, and the great majority of French memoirists still shuddered in recalling the revolution in England years afterward, was it likely that Cardinal Mazarin could forget? Certainly the Cardinal's pupil, Louis XIV, had not forgotten the "terrible agitations" of his childhood. Still shaken, fifteen years after the Fronde, he ordered all records of the Parlement of Paris relating to the Fronde destroyed, as if to blot out history.[36] Years later, those who preached funeral sermons over individuals prominent in the era of the Fronde often skipped quickly over that period. As the Bishop of Amiens remarked in his oration for Anne of Austria, "I do not want to enter into the shadows of those times of confusion and of disorders nor to recall them to your memory. . . . It is better to draw a veil over these occurrences in our history." [37]

More to the point, was Cardinal Mazarin really so confident of his hold on the country after the surrender of Bordeaux in 1653 that he could dismiss apprehension about a lingering revolutionary peril? Despite the boasts of the *Gazette de France*, and the comments of some contemporaries about the outward serenity of conditions inside France at the close of 1653, internal dangers remained. Much about the immediate post-Fronde years was reminiscent of the stirring in France shortly after Anne of Austria had become Regent. Had Louis XIV really uttered the famous "L'état, c'est moi" to the Paris Parlement in

[36] *Actes du Parlement de Paris,* ed. Edgard Boutaric, I (Paris, 1863), ccliv–cclvi; *Mémoires et lettres de Louis XIV* (Paris, 1942), pp. 3–5.

[37] François Faure, *Oraison funèbre de la Reyne mère du Roy . . . le 12 février de l'année 1666* (Paris, 1666), p. 24. See also the funeral sermons of Bossuet, especially those for the Prince de Condé and the Princess Palatine, *Oraisons funèbres,* ed. Jacques Truchet (Paris, 1961), pp. 255–291; 353–410.

1655, as tradition long held, the statement would have to be considered more as a prophecy than as a political reality then. The closer we examine France in these years, the more fragile the internal peace appears to have been.

Criticism—violent criticism—of the government persisted in spite of watchful censorship. The government seized quantities of subversive publications in December of 1653 in several parts of Paris, the work of persons unknown.[38] But confiscation and harsh punishments, when the offenders could be found, could not silence the critics. In 1656 Mazarin had to admit that manuscript news sheets circulated each week despite their prohibition on penalty of death.[39] He acknowledged that he had even less control over what people said to one another about the government. As he observed in July, 1657, "If it were in my power to repress this license which the French take of decrying everything, I would prevent them firstly from talking against the persons of their Majesties, against the state, and then against my friends; but it is a liberty that they have always had, which has been made greater in the disorders of the last civil wars." [40]

On almost every level of French society, trouble of a serious nature persisted. The Prince de Condé, though outside France, battled on alongside his Spanish allies against the army of the French crown and maintained secret contacts with his confederates inside France. When the Cardinal de Retz escaped from his prison at Nantes in 1654 and eventually reached Rome, he and his circle of friends in France were constantly suspected of plotting against the government. High-ranking members of the French aristocracy, like the Comte d'Harcourt, the Maréchal

---

[38] Letter of intelligence, December 13, 1653, *Thurloe Papers*, I, 622–623.

[39] Mazarin to Caracène, December 28, 1656, *Lettres du cardinal Mazarin*, ed. Chéruel, VII, 437–438.

[40] Mazarin to Fouquet, July 2, 1657, *ibid.*, VIII, 4.

d'Hocquincourt, and others defected or threatened to defect to Condé and the Spaniards.[41]

The Parlement of Paris and several of the parlements in the provinces rejected the docile role which the government tried to thrust upon them. Repeatedly, they resorted to obstructionist tactics, greatly embarrassed the government, and aroused suspicion at court about their motives. As in the days before the Fronde, the government resorted to force, a potentially dangerous expedient, and arrested a number of members of the Parlement of Paris and the Parlement of Rouen.[42] Challenge to royal authority came at many other levels. At Poitiers, the citizenry rioted against the arrival of a new intendant charged with overseeing the collection of new taxes and ran him out of town.[43] At Toulouse, a similarly hostile reception was reserved for the newly arrived intendant there by jealous local officials, supported by the Parlement of Toulouse.[44] In Angers, riots swept over the city because of attempts by the crown to levy new imposts. Several of the magistrates were beaten up and some of the lesser officials killed before troops could quell the disorders.[45] Bordeaux was a hotbed of intrigues, notwithstanding the defeat of 1653.[46] Peasant unrest remained evident, as at Coutras, where a peasantry in arms opposed collection of the taille. One thousand troops were required to restore order, and even then the peasants did not give up but retreated into the forest, hopeful that peasants from Saintonge and Périgueux

[41] Alphonse Feillet, *La misère au temps de la Fronde* (Paris, 1886), pp. 486–487; 489–490.

[42] Letter of intelligence, April 29, 1656, *Thurloe Papers*, IV, 715–716.

[43] Letter of intelligence, October 8/18, 1653, *ibid.*, I, 533.

[44] Letter of intelligence, October 15/25, 1653, *ibid.*, I, 544.

[45] Letter to Bordeaux, October 15, 1656, *ibid.*, V, 476; Letter of Colonel Bampfield, November 15, 1656, *ibid.*, V, 560–561; Letter of Colonel Bampfield, December 23, 1656, *ibid.*, V, 704–705.

[46] Mazarin to Surintendants, July 24, 1654, *Lettres du cardinal Mazarin*, ed. Chéruel, VI, 594.

would join in their revolt.[47] The crown faced the ill will of much of the clergy, resentful of the government's protection of the Huguenots.[48] On the other hand, some Huguenots, particularly those from Languedoc, were angered at the crown for failing to give them enough protection against Catholic persecution.[49]

Innumerable examples of lingering unrest in France after the Fronde could be added to these. But, granted their existence, how serious were they, and of what practical consequence were they to the internal stability of the state? Reports sent back to England from agents in the field gave sharply conflicting impressions. In October, 1653, one of the English agents predicted that "the troubles and dangers of this state are not yet ended." [50] Yet at virtually the same moment Joachim Hane, a German military expert touring France for Cromwell on a spy mission, reported everything calm.[51] In April, 1654, Secretary Thurloe, who succeeded Thomas Scot as head of the English intelligence service, read a report that there had never been as much discontent in France as there was at that moment; [52] but he had to balance this with a report in the summer that "the government is firm and settled; there are only some *reliques de la Fronde qui grondent.*" [53] In October, 1656 (after the Treaty of Westminster,

[47] Letter of intelligence, April 29, 1656, *Thurloe Papers,* IV, 715–716.
[48] Blet, *Le clergé de France et la monarchie,* II, 352–361.
[49] Letter of intelligence, October 15/25, 1653, *Thurloe Papers,* I, 544; letter of intelligence, November 25, 1653, *ibid.,* I, 587; letter of intelligence, November 26, 1653, *ibid.,* I, 590; letter of intelligence, November 23/December 3, 1653, *ibid.,* I, 608–609; letter of intelligence, March 1/11, 1653/1654, *ibid.,* II, 127–128. A somewhat overdrawn picture of Huguenot restlessness is presented by Augustin Cochin, "Les églises Calvinistes du Midi: Le cardinal Mazarin et Cromwell," *Revue des questions historiques,* LXXVI (1904), 109–156.
[50] Letter of intelligence, October 5/15, 1653, I, 525.
[51] *The Journal of Joachim Hane,* ed. Charles H. Firth (Oxford, 1896), pp. xxii–xxix.
[52] Letter of intelligence, April 1, 1654, *Thurloe Papers,* II, 184.
[53] Letter of intelligence, August 7, 1654, *ibid.,* II, 491.

but before the English alliance), the Puritan ambassador, Lockhart, remarked that the discontent in Paris was considerable. Involved, he said, were "the Parliament [sic], the assembly of clergy, the Prince's party, and that of the Cardinal de Retz, which begins now to be talked of." [54] A few weeks later Colonel Bampfield, another agent for the English in Paris, wrote to Secretary Thurloe that "without the spirit of prophecy, one may with great assurances foresee and foretell a civil war here within eight months if a general peace prevents it not." [55] Again, these reports had to be read beside others which indicated nothing amiss.

The English were most interested in the disposition of the Huguenots to revolt, but reports about them were contradictory. Some of the letters arriving in London indicated that a spark could set them all on fire, that the Huguenots looked upon the English as the "instrument of their delivery." [56] Others stressed the unwillingness of the Huguenots to risk a revolt and reported that the wisest of the Huguenots hoped for Anglo-French agreement, as promising greater advantage than an Anglo-French war.[57] When Cromwell sent emissaries to France to cut through the confusion, he received back more contradictions. The Genevan minister, Stouppe, whom he had sent over on several missions, was one of those who provided differing appraisals.[58]

Cardinal Mazarin was keenly aware of the pockets of discontent in France. In his often cited letter to Anne of Austria in November, 1655, he wrote of his fear of subversion and re-

[54] Lockhart to Thurloe, October 8, 1656, *ibid.*, V, 450–451.
[55] Bampfield to Thurloe, November 29, 1656, *ibid.*, V, 610–611.
[56] Letter of intelligence, February 3, 1654, *ibid.*, II, 48.
[57] Petit to Augier, May 5/15, 1654, *ibid.*, II, 262.
[58] For some of his varying appraisals see: Bordeaux to Mazarin, April 27, 1654, P.R.O. transcript, 31/3/94, copied from A.E. Angleterre, LXIII, f. 339; Mazarin to Bordeaux, June 17, 1654, *ibid.*, 31/3/95, copied from A.E. Angleterre, LXIII, ff. 455–457; Bordeaux to Brienne, June 24, 1655, *ibid.*, 31/3/98, copied from B.N., MS. f.fr. 16010. Other letters of Bordeaux to Brienne in July and August also discuss Stouppe.

marked that, as he had often told the Queen, the veritable enemies of France were the French themselves.[59] In his dispute with the Paris Parlement over a coinage decree, Mazarin grimly noted the activity of "firebrands who had sowed a panicky terror in the majority of the populace by publishing that the disputes that we had with the Parlement on the subject of the coinage were threatening us with a new revolution." [60] He observed how quickly his political enemies reacted to the slightest military setback suffered by the armies of the crown. After the failure to capture Valenciennes from the Prince de Condé in 1656, the Cardinal assumed his enemies had assured the Cardinal de Retz that this defeat "had placed our affairs in a position where they could not quickly be raised again; that we dared not repress the enterprises of the parlements; that the people of Paris were ready to embark upon the greatest follies as in the past; and that the Prince de Condé was all ready to enter France with a great army." [61] In each case Mazarin minimized the danger and expressed confidence that the government could quell the dissidence—but so he had done in almost identical language on the eve of the Fronde.

It is in this uncertainty about the seriousness of the opposition to the crown in France that the relationship of France with England must be regarded following the Fronde. The Prince de Condé, though less hopeful now of aid from England, nevertheless had kept his agents in London industriously occupied. Monsieur de Conan, who had approached Cromwell with a proposal to attack La Rochelle in 1651, again conferred in London in the fall of 1653.[62] Several leaders of the Princes' party in Bordeaux stopped off in London for consultations after the

---

[59] Mazarin to Queen Anne of Austria, November 5, 1655, *Lettres du cardinal Mazarin,* ed. Chéruel, VII, 121.

[60] Mazarin to Castelnau, May 5, 1656, *ibid.,* VII, 209.

[61] Mazarin to Colbert, September 13, 1656, *ibid.,* VII, 356–357.

[62] Longchamps to Lenet, October 23, 1653, B.N., MS. f.fr. 6716, f. 127.

surrender of Bordeaux, including Lenet and Marchin.[63] Various other representatives from the Prince constantly came and went. Colonel Sexby and his associate, Arundel, upon their return to England from Bordeaux, continued to work closely with the Prince's chief agent in England, Monsieur de Barrière, all through the winter of 1653–1654 and into the summer.[64] Trancas and his two fellow deputies from the city of Bordeaux stayed on in London.[65]

Through Monsieur de Bordeaux and other sources, Cardinal Mazarin knew of all this activity. He knew how hard the agents of the Prince de Condé strove to obtain English intervention at Bordeaux, La Rochelle, and elsewhere. Time and again rumors of imminent English attack were relayed to him.[66] Basically, the Cardinal did not believe Cromwell would go to war against France. He was satisfied with the statement of Huguenot leaders who told him that only a few individual Huguenots had gone to Cromwell for help, that the Huguenot Church remained loyal to Louis XIV.[67] But could he be sure? Could he be absolutely certain he was right about England and so many others were wrong? Having just received in January, 1654, a copy of the "Agreement of the People" and the "Manifesto" drawn up earlier by Sexby and Arundel, which he learned Trancas had presented to the Council of State,[68] it was hardly

[63] Baas to Mazarin, January 18, 1654, P.R.O. transcript, 31/3/92, copied from A.E. Angleterre, LXIII, f. 44.

[64] Barrière to Condé, April 3, 1654, Chantilly, MS. série P, XIV f. 56; Barrière to Condé, July 17, 1654, *ibid.*, MS. série P, XIV, f. 230.

[65] Baas to Mazarin, June 25, 1654, P.R.O. transcript, 31/3/95, copied from A.E. Angleterre, LXIV, f. 110. For Thurloe's résumé of English foreign policy in this period see Bischoffshausen, *Die Politik des Protectors Oliver Cromwell,* p. 191.

[66] Bordeaux to Brienne, March 19, 1654, P.R.O. transcript, 31/3/93, copied from A.E. Angleterre, LXIII, f. 149.

[67] Letter of intelligence, April 15, 1654, *Thurloe Papers,* II, 210.

[68] Mazarin to Bordeaux, November 21, 1653, P.R.O. transcript, 31/3/92, copied from A.E. Angleterre, LXI, f. 353; Bordeaux to Mazarin, January 5, 1654, *ibid.*, 31/3/92, copied from A.E. Angleterre, LXIII, f. 179.

reassuring to know that Sexby was working hand-in-glove with Condé's agents in London.[69] The Cardinal knew Bordeaux was again a theatre of numerous intrigues. The Cardinal believed there were "as many factious persons there as ever." [70] Doubtless he received reports that several Ormistes from Bordeaux had arrived in London in February, 1654.[71]

In spite of the Cardinal's confidence in the Huguenots, he worried that Cromwell's agents could cause mischief among them. He was sufficiently troubled to ask the French ambassador to send descriptions of these agents, so he could have them arrested.[72] Letters of some of these persons who conferred with the Huguenots (Stouppe, for example) were intercepted. Mazarin could read that Stouppe found the Huguenots ready for revolt as soon as the English should arrive in France.[73]

What did the Cardinal think of an English landing on the coast of Brittany in May, 1654, supported by a force of eighteen English ships and 1,200 men? The English withdrew, with the loss of two ships, and Cromwell promptly disavowed the unsuccessful attack.[74] But could it have taken place without the Protector's approval? When a short time later the personal representative whom Mazarin had sent to London to back up Monsieur de Bordeaux in his negotiations was implicated with great hullabaloo in an assassination plot against the Protector, the Cardinal surmised that the charges were trumped up, as a

[69] Baas to Mazarin, March 23, 1654, *ibid.*, 31/3/93, copied from A.E. Angleterre, LXIII, f. 179.

[70] Mazarin to Pontac, July 30, 1654, B.N., MSS. mélanges de Colbert, LI, f. 58v.

[71] Letter of February 4, 1654, B.N., MS. f.fr. 5844, f. 220.

[72] Mazarin to Bordeaux, December 2, 1653, P.R.O. transcript, 31/3/92, copied from A.E. Angleterre, LXI, f. 368v.

[73] Mazarin to Bordeaux, June 17, 1654, *ibid.*, 31/3/95, copied from A.E. Angleterre, LXIII, ff. 455–457.

[74] Brienne to Bordeaux, May 23, 1654, *ibid.*, 31/3/94, copied from A.E. Angleterre, LXIII, f. 426; Bordeaux to Mazarin, June 1, 1654, *ibid.*, 31/3/94, copied from A.E. Angleterre, LXIV, f. 60.

prelude to conflict with France.[75] When several bourgeois from Bordeaux arrived in London in mid-June carrying a new proposal to Cromwell, assuring him the city would revolt if he sent aid,[76] and when it appeared the Spaniards were concluding a treaty with England, we can understand why the Cardinal momentarily panicked and thought war with England was inescapable.[77] Even after officials broke up the plot at Bordeaux, and after it seemed that Cromwell had decided against immediate war with France, the situation remained tense. New reports told that Trancas had been seen in the Bordeaux area and had then gone to San Sebastián to confer with the just escaped Cardinal de Retz and with Spanish officials before returning again to England.[78]

For almost a year after the Fronde, the Cardinal kept a reported 10,000 troops tied down in Guyenne—far more than needed to police the local population—for the express purpose of warding off English attack.[79] After the crisis of June–July, 1654, cooled off, the Cardinal ordered most of these troops withdrawn, some to go into Saintonge, others to Picardy and to the Catalonian area.[80] No sooner had they left than the Duc de Vendôme worried the Cardinal with his estimate that Calais could not hold out against an English attack,[81] while Monsieur de Bordeaux told the Cardinal that the citizens of Bordeaux

[75] Servien to Mazarin, July 1, 1654, *ibid.*, 31/3/95, copied from A.E. Angleterre, LXIII, ff. 478–482.

[76] Brienne to Bordeaux, June 19, 1654, *ibid.*, 31/3/95, copied from A.E. Angleterre, LXIV, f. 110.

[77] Mazarin to Bordeaux, June 18, 1654, *ibid.*, 31/3/95, copied from A.E. Angleterre, f. 461.

[78] Mazarin to Saint-Simon, July 29, 1654, Archives Nationales, KK 1221, f. 507; Mazarin to Bordeaux, November 6, 1654, P.R.O. transcript, 31/3/96, copied from A.E. Angleterre, LXIII, ff. 631–632.

[79] Vendôme to Mazarin, September 22, 1653, *Archives historiques du département de la Gironde*, XV, 443.

[80] Mazarin to d'Estrades, July 30, 1654, *ibid.*, II, 102.

[81] Charles de La Roncière, *Histoire de la marine française*, V (Paris, 1920), 207.

had made fresh overtures to the Prince de Condé.[87] In December, 1654, the Cardinal betrayed his anxiety by directing close co-ordination between the Maréchal de La Meilleraye in Brittany and the Comte d'Estrades in Guyenne for mutual assistance in case either were attacked by the English.[83] The Cardinal admitted now that he did not know what the Protector might do.[84]

In Mazarin's estimation, almost anything was preferable to war with England. When, in the summer of 1654, war had seemed so near, the Cardinal wrote to Monsieur de Bordeaux that France would bear almost anything from England rather than go to war. Under no circumstances, he emphasized, ought France make a move which could precipitate open conflict. If this required patient endurance of stepped-up attacks at sea from the Puritans, then France must accept that burden. As the Cardinal analyzed the situation, one of the great dangers lay in the probability that Frenchmen of "evil intent" would use it as an excuse to "spit their venom," and to act more boldly and insolently than before.[85] Even a simple rupture between France and England, he thought, might encourage the troublemakers.[86] In other words Mazarin feared a reawakening of the Fronde.

The father of the French ambassador in London, himself a habitué of the court, experienced the same fear when he urged his son to hasten the settlement with England. "It would be a means to prevent much mischief here at home, if any should be plotted at any time." [87] Hugh Morel was similarly

[82] Bordeaux to Brienne, September 7, 1654, P.R.O. transcript, 31/3/96, copied from B.N., MS. f.fr. 16009.

[83] Mazarin to d'Estrades, December 12, 1654, Archives Nationales, KK 1221, f. 588v.

[84] Mazarin to d'Estrades, December 30, 1654, *ibid.*, KK 1221, f. 599.

[85] Mazarin to Servien, July 3, 1654, *Lettres du cardinal Mazarin,* ed. Chéruel, VI, 201.

[86] Servien to Mazarin, July 1, 1654, P.R.O. transcript, 31/3/95, copied from A.E. Angleterre, LXIII, ff. 478–482.

[87] Bordeaux (father) to Bordeaux (son), [September 4, 1654], *Thurloe Papers,* II, 564.

convinced that the French government could only be secure with English friendship. "However they name their king absolute, unless we be his friends, they find it is but titular," he wrote.[88]

Because of these considerations, Mazarin had insisted strongly on the inclusion in the Treaty of Westminster of the secret clause whereby England and France renounced assistance or haven to the domestic enemies of the other. The Cardinal's obstinate refusal to give ground on this provision held up the signing of the treaty for months after both sides had reached understanding on the other issues. The Puritans feared the provision would tie their hands should the Huguenots need their help later. But Mazarin was adamant. Over and over he instructed Monsieur de Bordeaux that the secret clause was the "fundamental point of the whole treaty." [89] Mazarin obviously valued the Treaty of Westminster more for its check on subversion than for the relief it gave the merchants.[90]

The Cardinal's subsequent alliance with England was in a sense an extension of the same reasoning. He realized that France must make a choice. Unless she had Cromwell as an ally, she would probably have him as an enemy. France stood to lose far more by fighting to vanquish revolution in England than she did by accepting the régime there and working with it. France by then had little hope of putting Charles II on the throne of England. A revolutionary government seemed likely to remain there. All France would accomplish by a war with Cromwell would be revolt inside France, whose political and religious course the English might influence profoundly. Dam-

---

[88] Morel to Thurloe, May 27, 1655, *ibid.*, III, 444.

[89] Mazarin to Bordeaux, March 31, 1655, P.R.O. transcript, 31/3/97, copied from A.E. Angleterre, LXVI, f. 42; Bordeaux to Brienne, April 5, 1655, *ibid.*, 31/3/97, copied from B.N., MS. f.fr. 16010; Mazarin to Bordeaux, February 24, 1655, *Lettres du cardinal Mazarin*, ed. Chéruel, VI, 438; Mazarin to Bordeaux, February 27, 1655, *ibid.*, VI, 442.

[90] Letter of March 7, 1654, B.N., MS. f.fr. 5844, f. 232v.

age to the French economy from the maritime war with England would continue, and French capacity to fight the Spaniards would be weakened. Therefore an alliance with a "Puritan regicide" actually seemed the best way to safeguard the French monarchy and the Catholic Church, as well as to defeat the Spaniards.

Thus Mazarin's willingness to brave hostile public opinion in France over his agreements with England cannot be explained either as a convenient lapse of memory, a disregard of the dangers of revolution, or as singleminded concentration on war against Spain. Rather, alliance with the English "regicides" represented, in part at least, a changing conception of the nature of the threat posed by revolutionary England. At the opening of the Fronde, when the Commonwealth had been preoccupied in settling her own domestic disorders, Mazarin worried principally about the lessons of English experience and about the subversive force of the English example on the French population. Although the Cardinal doubtless retained a vivid recollection of the English Revolution for the rest of his life, he must have realized by 1652 that the Frondeurs were not exploiting the example of the Puritan Revolution in the manner he had anticipated. With few exceptions, the Frondeurs, though thoroughly familiar with the details of the English Revolution, had carefully avoided public praise of the English model. In fact, the "excesses" of the English Civil War were so widely condemned in France that, as we have tried to show, the net effect of the English example restrained rather than encouraged extremist republican talk among the Frondeurs, and, by reaction, caused them to stress the legitimacy of their demands. England's unpopularity made it unwise, even had there been much desire, to advocate constitutional novelties.

The clique of Huguenot republicans in the city of Bordeaux was an exception. However, it was not the simple attractive force of the English example which had aroused them. It was, as Mazarin well knew, the arrival of aggressive English agents like Sexby and Arundel, who stirred them up, and whose promises of English help sustained them. The mere existence of a revolutionary government in England did not of itself constitute a great danger to the security of the French monarchy—unless that powerful government intervened or threatened to intervene in the internal affairs of France. The only way to prevent that danger was to neutralize it by allying with Cromwell.

Mazarin's change of tactics, though tardy, paid handsome dividends. The English alliance, as we have remarked before, delivered the *coup de grâce* to Spain. French trade profited enormously, and by 1662 France had become the most important supplier to England.[91] Indeed, Englishmen began to worry about the imbalance of their trade with France and to bemoan a situation "whereby their nation becomes enriched and ours impoverished." [92] The *rapprochement* with England also dampened the rebellious zeal of the malcontents in France, because it eliminated the inflammatory activities of English agents in France and the possibility of English support for the rebellion; and, after the Treaty of the Pyrenees, Spain also ceased to befriend the rebels in France. Domestic flare-ups still occurred, but they were potentially less dangerous than before.[93]

True, the Cardinal de Retz had correctly predicted that France might be backing the wrong side in England. For when

[91] Manna Prestwich, "Diplomacy and Trade in the Protectorate," *The Journal of Modern History,* XXII (1950), 103–121. See also Maurice P. Ashley, *Financial and Commercial Policy under the Cromwellian Protectorate* (Oxford, 1962), pp. 138–139. The coming of Charles II to power did not therefore affect the pattern of Anglo-French trade which had developed after the Treaty of Westminster. See comment from 1659 below.

[92] *The Marchants Humble Petition and Remonstrance* (London, 1659), p. 3.

[93] For a study of the problem see Leon Bernard, "French Society and Popular Uprisings under Louis XIV," *French Historical Studies,* III (1964), 454–474.

Oliver Cromwell died in late 1658, his son and successor, Richard Cromwell, was unequal to heading the government; and the powerful régime fashioned by his father quickly fell apart. Parliament thrust Richard aside in 1659, at which time the possibility of a royalist restoration in England was the common talk of Europe. When it came to pass in 1660, it did not represent the calamity for France which Retz had prophesied. Cardinal Mazarin had quietly set to work, even while recognizing the short-lived English republic of 1659, to collaborate with Queen Henriette-Marie in planning for the restoration. Charles recovered his throne quite independently of anything Mazarin or Henriette-Marie accomplished, and so he owed them nothing. Still, Mazarin's behind-the-scenes activity had removed some of the curse of his alliance with Cromwell.[94] The Cardinal gave Charles a timely reminder of the considerable financial aid he had received over the years and graciously offered to consider it a gift.[95] In any event, Mazarin knew that Charles would not jeopardize his newly recovered throne by plunging into a war of revenge against France, especially with the French freed of the Spanish war.

Thus France weathered the transition back to royal government in England with minimum disturbance. Though, unhappily, Cardinal Mazarin did not live to see the day, Louis XIV purchased Dunkirk from Charles II in 1662. Eight years later Charles concluded a secret treaty of alliance with France and agreed among other things to announce publicly at some future time his conversion to Roman Catholicism. The Cardinal would surely have considered these events additional vindication of his much criticized *rapprochement* with England.

---

[94] F. J. Routledge, *England and the Treaty of the Pyrenees* (Liverpool, 1953), pp. 76–118.

[95] Colbert to Mazarin, March 2, 1660, *Lettres, instructions, et mémoires de Colbert*, I, 423; Mazarin's marginalia to above letter of Colbert, *ibid.*, I, 423.

Chronological Table

FRANCE	ENGLAND
	Charles I leads an army against the Scots Presbyterians, 1639
	Short Parliament assembled, April 23, 1640
	Long Parliament assembled, November 13, 1640
Louis XIII forbids Parlement to interfere in state policy, January 21, 1641	
	Earl of Strafford executed by Parliament, May 22, 1641
	Irish rebellion begins, November 1, 1641
	Grand Remonstrance presented by Parliament to the King, December 11, 1641
Mazarin elevated to rank of Cardinal, December 16, 1641	
	Charles I unsuccessfully attempts to arrest five members of Commons, January 14, 1642
Cinq Mars executed after discovery of his plot against the government, September 12, 1642	
	Battle of Edge Hill, November 2, 1642—first battle of the Civil War

FRANCE	ENGLAND
Richelieu's death, December 4, 1642	
Mazarin appointed by Louis XIII to replace Richelieu on the Council, December 5, 1642	
Louis XIII's death, May 14, 1643 — succeeded by four-year-old Louis XIV	
Condé (then Duc d'Enghien) defeats the Spaniards at Rocroi, May 19, 1643	
Queen Regent crushes Cabale des Importants, September, 1643	
	One-year cessation of hostilities agreed to in Ireland, September 25, 1643
	House of Commons accepts the Solemn League and Covenant, October 5, 1643
Disturbances over enforcement of Edict of the Toisé, January 27, 1644	
	Battle of Marston Moor—defeat of Prince Rupert by Cromwell and Fairfax, July 12, 1644
	Queen Henriette-Marie sails for France, July 24, 1644
	Archbishop Laud executed by Parliament, January 20, 1645
Two members of Parlement of Paris punished for opposition, March 27, 1645	
	Battle of Naseby, a Parliament victory, ends the First Civil War, June 24, 1645

Chronological Table

FRANCE	ENGLAND
Louis XIV appears before Parlement in lit de justice, September 7, 1645	
	Charles I flees to the Scots, May, 1646
	Prince of Wales leaves Isle of Jersey for France, July 6, 1646
Dunkirk taken from Spain by France, October 11, 1646	
	Charles I left by Scots in hands of English commissioners, February 9, 1647
	The Army takes Charles I into custody, June 14, 1647
	The Army occupies London, August 16, 1647
Louis XIV appears before Parlement in lit de justice, January 15, 1648	
Sovereign Courts of Paris resolve on union, May 13, 1648	
	Renewal of Civil War, summer, 1648
Condé defeats Spaniards at Lens, August 20, 1648	
Queen Regent attempts to arrest certain members of Parlement of Paris—riots ensue, August 26, 1648	
Queen Regent accepts demands of Parlement of Paris, October 22, 1648	

Chronological Table

FRANCE	ENGLAND
Peace of Westphalia signed ending Thirty Years' War, October 24, 1648	
	Purge of Long Parliament by Colonel Pride, December 16, 1648
Withdrawal of Queen Regent from Paris and beginning of the Fronde, January 6, 1649	
	Execution of Charles I, February 9, 1649
	Abolition of Kingly office, March 27, 1649
Peace of Rueil temporarily ends hostilities at Paris, April 1, 1649	
	Cromwell accepts command of an army to subdue Ireland, April 9, 1649
Queen Regent arrests the Princes, January 18, 1650	
Princess de Condé and entourage given protection in the city of Bordeaux, June 1, 1650, by Parlement of Bordeaux	
	Charles II lands in Scotland, July 3, 1650
	Cromwell defeats the Scots at Dunbar, September 13, 1650
City of Bordeaux and Queen Regent agree to peace, October 1, 1650	

Chronological Table

FRANCE	ENGLAND
Princes liberated February 13, 1651, and Mazarin soon after begins his 1st exile	
Louis XIV celebrates his majority, September 7, 1651	
	Cromwell defeats Charles II at Worcester, September 13, 1651
Condé organizing rebellion against the government, September, 1651	
	Navigation Act passed, October 19, 1651
Condé obtains treaty of assistance with Spain, November 6, 1651	
Mazarin returns to France, December 24, 1651	
Condé and the Duc d'Orléans unite, January 24, 1652	
	First Anglo-Dutch War begins, May, 1652
Duc de Lorraine arrives in Paris, June, 1652	
Mazarin enters 2d exile, August 19, 1652	
Dunkirk lost to Spain because of English fleet action, September 16, 1652	
Louis XIV enters Paris in triumph, Fronde at Paris crushed, October 21, 1652	

Chronological Table

FRANCE	ENGLAND
France officially recognizes the Commonwealth, December 31, 1652	
Mazarin returns to Paris, February 3, 1653	
Bordeaux surrenders, August 3, 1653	
	Cromwell expells Rump of Long Parliament, April 30, 1653
	Cromwell installed as Protector, December 26, 1653
	End of First Anglo-Dutch War, April 15, 1654
	English fleet attacks Spanish colony, Santo Domingo, April 23, 1655
Anglo-French friendship—Treaty of Westminster, November 3, 1655	
Anglo-French Alliance, March 23, 1657	
Defeat of Spaniards at Battle of the Dunes, June 14, 1658	
Fall of Dunkirk, June 25, 1658	
	Cromwell's death, September 13, 1658
	Richard Cromwell's retirement to private life, June 4, 1659
Franco-Spanish Treaty of the Pyrenees, November 7, 1659	
	Charles II lands in England, June 5, 1660
Mazarin's death, March 9, 1661	

282

Bibliography of Materials Cited in the Text*

PRIMARY SOURCES

Manuscripts

Chantilly. Musée Condé. MSS. série P. Vols. XIII–XIV.
Claydon House MSS. Verney Family Papers.
London. British Museum. Additional MSS. 12184–12186. Original Drafts or Copies of the Dispatches of Sir Richard Browne.
——. Public Record Office. Transcripts of Paris Archives. Nos. 31/3/74–31/3/98.
Paris. Archives du Ministère des Affaires Etrangères. Correspondance politique. Angleterre. Vols. L–LXIV.
——. Archives Nationales. Série KK 1221, U 336.
——. Bibliothèque Nationale. MSS. fonds français 4138, 5844, 6715, 15996–15997, 16008–16010, 18324, 18592, 25025; MSS. mélanges de Colbert. Vol. LI.

Published Source Material

Amyraut, Moïse. *Discours de la souveraineté des roys.* N.p., 1650.
Archives historiques du département de la Gironde. Vols. II, III, IV, VII, VIII, XIII, XV. Bordeaux, 1860–1874.

* A complete bibliography of works useful in the preparation of this study would be too extensive to list here. Bibliographical suggestions are provided in chapter I.

Bibliography of Materials Cited in the Text

Archives municipales de Bordeaux. Vol. II. Bordeaux, 1878.

Bates, George. *Les vraies causes des derniers troubles d'Angleterre*. Trans. Samuel Sorbière. Orange, 1653.

Bayle, Pierre. *Dictionnaire historique et critique*. 4th ed., Vol. III. Amsterdam, 1730.

Berthod, Père François. "Mémoires," in *Nouvelle collection des mémoires pour servir à l'histoire de France*. Ed. Joseph F. Michaud and Jean F. Poujoulat. Vol. XXII. Paris, 1838. Volume numbers of this collection conform to those given by the Library of Congress. Add two for the Bibliothèque Nationale.

Bochart, Samuel. *Omnia opera*. Vol. I. Leiden, 1712.

Boileau-Despréaux, Nicolas. *Oeuvres*. Ed. Georges Mongrédien. Paris, 1961.

Bossuet, Jacques-Bénigne. *Oraisons funèbres*. Ed. Jacques Truchet. Paris, 1961.

Brienne, Henri-Auguste de Loménie de. "Mémoires," in *Nouvelle collection des mémoires pour servir à l'histoire de France*. Vol. XXV.

Calendar of State Papers, Domestic Series. Vols. for years 1648–1655.

Calendar of State Papers . . . Venice. Ed. Allen B. Hinds. Vols. XXVII–XXIX. London, 1926–1929.

Carte, Thomas. *A Collection of Original Letters and Papers, Concerning the Affairs of England from the Year 1641 to 1660*. Vol. I. London, 1739.

Cary, Henry. *Memorials of the Great Civil War in England from 1646 to 1652*. Vol. II. London, 1842.

Clarke, William. *The Clarke Papers*. Ed. Charles H. Firth. Vol. III. London, 1899.

Colbert, Jean-Baptiste. *Lettres, instructions et mémoires de Colbert*. Ed. Pierre Clément. Vol. I. Paris, 1861.

Colletet, Guillaume. *Epigrammes du sieur Colletet*. Paris, 1653.

Conrart, Valentin. "Mémoires," in *Nouvelle collection des mémoires pour servir à l'histoire de France*. Vol. XXVI.

Correspondance de la cour d'Espagne sur les affaires des Pays-Bas au XVIIᵉ siècle. Ed. Henri Lonchay, continued by Joseph Cuvelier. Vol. IV. Brussels, 1933.

Bibliography of Materials Cited in the Text

Cosnac, Daniel de. *Mémoires.* Ed. Jules de Cosnac. Société de l'histoire de France. Vol. I. Paris, 1852.

Cosnac, Jules de. *Souvenirs du règne de Louis XIV.* 8 vols. Paris, 1866–1882.

Du Moulin, Peter. *Regii sanguinis clamor ad coelum adversus parricidas Anglicanos.* The Hague, 1652.

Eikon Basilike. Ed. Philip A. Knachel. Ithaca, 1966.

——. Ed. Edward J. L. Scott. London, 1880.

Eon, Jean. *Le commerce honorable, ou considérations politiques.* Nantes, 1646.

Estrades, Comte d'. *Relation inédite de la défense de Dunkerque (1651–1652).* Ed. Philippe Tamizey de Larroque. Collection méridionale, Vol. III. Paris, 1872.

Estrées, Maréchal d'. *Mémoires.* Ed. Paul Bonnefon. Société de l'histoire de France. Paris, 1910.

Evelyn, John. *Diary.* Ed. E. S. de Beer. Vol. II. Oxford, 1955.

Faure, François. *Oraison funèbre de la Reyne mère du Roy . . . le 12 février de l'année 1666.* Paris, 1666.

French Intelligencer.

French Occurrences.

Gazette de France.

Goulas, Nicolas. *Mémoires.* Ed. Charles Constant. Société de l'histoire de France. Vol. II. Paris, 1879.

Hane, Joachim. *Journal.* Ed. Charles H. Firth. Oxford, 1896.

Histoire du ministère du Cardinal sous le règne de Louis XIV. N.p., 1668.

Hobbes, Thomas. *Elémens philosophiques du citoyen, traicté politique.* Trans. Samuel Sorbière. Amsterdam, 1649.

Hyde, Edward, Earl of Clarendon. *A Brief View and Survey of the Dangerous and Pernicious Errors to Church and State, in Mr. Hobbes's Book, Entitled "Leviathan."* Oxford, 1676.

——. *Calendar of the Clarendon State Papers.* Ed. W. Dunn Macray and F. J. Routledge. Vols. II–IV. Oxford, 1889–1932.

——. *The History of the Rebellion and Civil Wars in England.* Ed. W. Dunn Macray. Vol. V. Oxford, 1888.

——. *State Papers Collected by Edward Earl of Clarendon.* Vol. III. Oxford, 1786.

Bibliography of Materials Cited in the Text

James II. "Mémoires," in *Collection des mémoires relatifs à la révolution d'Angleterre*. Ed. François P. G. Guizot. Vol. XXII. Paris, 1827.

——. *Memoirs*. Trans. A. Lytton Sells. Bloomington, 1962.

Joly, Guy. "Mémoires," in *Nouvelle collection des mémoires pour servir à l'histoire de France*. Vol. XXIV.

Journals of the House of Commons. Vol. VI. [London], n.d.

La Fayette, Marie-Madeline de. "Mémoires," in *Nouvelle collection des mémoires pour servir à l'histoire de France*. Vol. XXX.

Lefèvre d'Ormesson, Olivier. *Journal*. Ed. Pierre-Adolphe Chéruel. Collection de documents inédits sur l'histoire de France. Vol. I. Paris, 1860.

Lenet, Pierre. "Mémoires," in *Nouvelle collection des mémoires pour servir à l'histoire de France*. Vol. XXIV.

Letters and Papers Relating to the First Dutch War, 1652–1654. Ed. Samuel R. Gardiner and C. T. Atkinson. Navy Records Society. Vols. XXX, XXXVII. London, 1906–1910.

Lionne, Hugues de. *Remarques sur la reddition de Dunkerque entre les mains des Anglois*. Paris, 1658.

Loret, Jean. *La muze historique, ou recueil des lettres en vers*. Ed. J. Ravenel and Ed. de la Pelouze. Vol. I. Paris, 1857.

Louis XIV. *Mémoires et lettres*. Paris, 1942.

Ludlow, Edmund. *Memoirs*. Ed. Charles H. Firth. Vol. I. Oxford, 1894.

The Marchants Humble Petition and Remonstrance. London, 1659.

Marsys, Sieur de. *Histoire de la persécution présente des catholiques en Angleterre*. N.p., 1646.

Mazarin, Jules, Cardinal. *Lettres du cardinal Mazarin pendant son ministère*. Ed. Pierre-Adolphe Chéruel. 9 vols. Paris, 1872–1906.

——. *Lettres du cardinal Mazarin à la reine, à la princesse palatine . . . écrites pendant sa retraite hors de France, en 1651 et 1652*. Ed. J. Ravenel. Paris, 1836.

Mentet de Salmonet, Robert. *Histoire des troubles de la Grande-Bretagne*. Paris, 1661.

Le mercure anglois.

Mercurius Pragmaticus.

Bibliography of Materials Cited in the Text

Milton, John. *The Life Records of John Milton.* Ed. J. Milton French. 5 vols. New Brunswick, 1949–1958.

——. *Works.* Ed. Frank A. Patterson. Vols. V, VII. New York, 1932.

Molé, Mathieu. *Mémoires.* Ed. Aimé Champollion-Figeac. Société de l'histoire de France. Vol. IV. Paris, 1857.

Montereul, Jean de. *The Diplomatic Correspondence of Jean de Montereul and the Brothers de Bellièvre, French Ambassadors in England and Scotland, 1645–1648.* Ed. J. G. Fotheringham. Publications of the Scottish History Society. 2 vols. Edinburgh, 1898.

Montglat, François de. "Mémoires," in *Nouvelle collection des mémoires pour servir à l'histoire de France.* Vol. XXVII.

Montpensier, Anne-Marie d'Orléans. *Mémoires.* Ed. Pierre-Adolphe Chéruel. 4 vols. Paris, 1858–1859.

Motteville, Françoise de. *Mémoires.* Ed. F. Riaux. 4 vols. Paris, 1869.

Nemours, Marie d'Orléans-Longueville de. "Mémoires," in *Nouvelle collection des mémoires pour servir à l'histoire de France.* Vol. XXI.

Nicholas, Edward. *The Nicholas Papers. Correspondence of Sir Edward Nicholas.* Ed. George F. Warner. Camden Society. New Series, Vol. XL. London, 1886.

Nouvelles ordinaires de Londres.

Ormonde, Marquess of. Historical Manuscripts Commission. *Calendar of the Manuscripts of the Marquess of Ormonde Preserved at Kilkenny Castle.* New Series, Vol. I. London, 1902.

Patin, Guy. *Lettres du temps de la Fronde.* Ed. André Thérive. Collection des chefs d'oeuvre méconnus. Paris, 1921.

Portland, Duke of. Historical Manuscripts Commission. *The Manuscripts of His Grace the Duke of Portland.* Vol. I. London, 1891.

Recueil des instructions données aux ambassadeurs et ministres de France depuis les traités de Westphalie jusqu'à la révolution française, XXIV, Angleterre. Ed. J. J. Jusserand. Vol. I. Paris, 1929.

——. *XI, Espagne.* Ed. A. Morel. Paris, 1894.

Retz, Jean François Paul de Gondi, Cardinal de. *Oeuvres.* Ed. Alphonse Feillet. Les grands écrivains de la France, Vols. I–V. Paris, 1870–1886.

Saint-Amant, Marc Antoine Gérard de. "Albion," in *Oeuvres complètes.* Ed. Charles L. Livet. Vol. II. Paris, 1855.

Sarrau, Claude. *Marquardi Gudii et doctorum virorum ad eum epistolae . . . et Claudii Sarravii senatoris Parisiensis epistolae.* Utrecht, 1697.

Saumaise, Claude de. *Apologie royale pour Charles I.* Paris, 1650.

———. *Defensio regia pro Carolo I.* N.p., 1649.

Séguier, Pierre. *Lettres et mémoires adressés au chancelier Séguier.* (1633–1649). Ed. Roland Mousnier. Publication de la Faculté des Lettres et Sciences Humaines de Paris. Série "Textes et Documents," Vol. VII, Fascicule 2. Paris, 1964.

Talon, Omer. "Mémoires," in *Nouvelle collection des mémoires pour servir à l'histoire de France.* Vol. XXVIII.

Tavannes, J. de Saulx de. *Mémoires.* Ed. Célestin Moreau. Paris, 1858.

Thurloe, John. *A Collection of the State Papers of John Thurloe.* 7 vols. London, 1742.

Vallier, Jean. *Journal.* Ed. Henri Courteault and Pierre de Vaissière. Société de l'histoire de France. Vol. II. Paris, 1912.

Verney Family. *Memoirs of the Verney Family during the Civil War.* Ed. Frances P. Verney. Vol. II. London, 1892.

A Vindication of K. Charles the Martyr. London, 1711.

Voltaire, François-Marie Arouet. *Lettres philosophiques.* Rouen, 1734.

The Weekly Intelligencer.

Mazarinades

L'accord passé entre les quatre empereurs. Paris, 1649. Moreau No. 18.

Almanach politique. N.p., n.d. Moreau No. 62.

Ambassade de la bonne paix générale. N.p., n.d. Moreau No. 68.

L'âne rouge. Paris, 1652. Moreau No. 85.

Apologie de messieurs du parlement. Paris, 1652. Moreau No. 105.

Apologie pour monseigneur le cardinal Mazarin. Paris, 1649. Moreau No. 127.

Apparition merveilleuse de l'Ange gardien. Paris, 1649. Moreau No. 142.

Articles de l'union de l'Ormée. Paris [1652]. Moreau No. 408.

Bibliography of Materials Cited in the Text

Les articles des crimes capitaux. Paris, 1652. Moreau No. 418.

Articles proposées et arrestées en la chambre S. Louis par les deputez des quatre compagnies. Paris, 1648.

Avertissement (second) à messieurs les prévost. Paris, 1652. Moreau No. 446.

Avertissements aux rois et aux princes. Paris, 1649. Moreau No. 453.

Aveuglement de la France. N.p., n.d., Moreau No. 465.

L'aveuglement des Parisiens. N.p., n.d. Moreau No. 467.

Avis à la reine d'Angleterre. N.p., 1650. Moreau No. 471.

Les avis héroïques et importants. Paris, 1649. Moreau No. 514.

Avis pressant et nécessaire. Paris, 1652. Moreau No. 531.

La balance d'état. N.p., n.d. Moreau No. 559.

"Bandeau levé de dessus les yeux des Parisiens," Paris, 1649, in Célestin Moreau, *Choix de Mazarinades.* Société de l'histoire de France. Paris, 1853. I, 228–246.

Le caducée d'état. Paris, 1652. Moreau No. 617.

Les calomnies du cardinal Mazarin. Paris, 1649. Moreau No. 618.

Les cautèles de la paix. N.p., n.d. Moreau No. 659.

Le chevalier chrétien. Paris, 1649. Moreau No. 696.

Le comète royal. N.p., 1652. Moreau No. 716.

Concordat de l'union. N.p., 1652. Moreau No. 731.

La conférence de Mazarin avec la Fortune. Paris, 1649. Moreau No. 738.

La conférence des députés de Son Altesse royale. Paris, 1652. Moreau No. 741.

Consolations tirées du tableau de la passion de Nostre Sauveur. Paris, 1649. Moreau No. 776.

Le courrier bourdelois. Paris, 1649. Moreau No. 811.

Le courrier de l'armée. Paris, 1652. Moreau No. 819.

Le courrier de la Guyenne. Paris, 1652. Moreau No. 822.

Le courier de la paix. Paris, 1652. Moreau No. 823.

Le courrier françois. Paris, 1649. Moreau No. 830.

De la nature et qualité du parlement de Paris. Paris, 1652. Moreau No. 857.

La décadence visible. N.p., 1652. Moreau No. 866.

"Décision de la question du temps," Paris, 1649, in Moreau, *Choix de Mazarinades.* I, 246–262.

Bibliography of Materials Cited in the Text

Déclaration du duc Charles. Paris, 1649. Moreau No. 897.

Déclaration du parlement d'Angleterre. London [Paris], 1649. Moreau No. 899.

Déclaration du roy portant reglement sur le fait de la navigation . . . extrait, greffe de l'admirauté de Toulon. N.p. [1650].

La déplorable mort de Charles Ier. Saint-Germain-en-Laye, 1649. Moreau No. 1005.

Le dépositaire des secrets de l'Etat. N.p., n.d. Moreau No. 1006.

Le déréglement de l'Etat. N.p., 1651. Moreau No. 1009.

Les dernières paroles du roi d'Angleterre. Paris, 1649. Moreau No. 1037.

Dialogue de Rome et de Paris au sujet de Mazarin. N.p., 1649. Moreau No. 1083.

Discours d'un théologien. Paris, 1649. Moreau No. 1111.

L'esprit du feu roi Louis XIII. Paris, 1652. Moreau No. 1287.

Exorcisme du D. Mazarin. N.p., 1649. Moreau No. 1331.

Factum pour messieurs les princes. N.p., 1650. Moreau No. 1367.

Factum pour Messire Henry d'Anglure de Bourlemont. N.p., n.d.

Le franc bourgeois de Paris. Paris, 1652. Moreau No. 1408.

Les généreux conseils d'un gentilhomme françois. Paris, 1649. Moreau No. 1485.

Harangue de M. le chancelier. Pontoise, 1652. Moreau No. 1552.

La harangue des provinciaux. Paris, 1649. Moreau No. 1557.

La harangue du roi de la Grande-Bretagne. Paris, 1652. Moreau No. 1560.

L'heureuse captivité. Paris, 1651. Moreau No. 1629.

Histoire du temps. Rouen, 1649. Moreau No. 1644.

La honteuse sortie des Mazarins. Paris, 1652. Moreau No. 1664.

L'illusion publique. N.p., 1652. Moreau No. 1676.

Instruction faite au peuple de Paris. N.p., n.d.

Les intérêts et motifs. Paris, 1649. Moreau No. 1719.

Les intrigues de la paix. N.p., 1652. Moreau No. 1725.

Journal contenant ce qui se passe de plus remarquable. Paris, 1652. Moreau No. 1740.

Journal de l'assemblée de la noblesse. N.p., 1651. Moreau No. 1750.

Journal de la Lettre de (madame)la princesse douairière de Condé. N.p., 1650. Moreau No. 1751.

Bibliography of Materials Cited in the Text

Journal des délibérations. N.p., 1650. Moreau No. 1759.

Les justes soupirs. Paris, 1649. Moreau No. 1790.

Les larmes et complaintes de la reine d'Angleterre. Paris, 1649. Moreau No. 1805.

Lettre d'un bourgeois de Paris. Paris, 1652. Moreau No. 1854.

Lettre d'un gentilhomme à la reine. Paris, 1649. Moreau No. 1866.

Lettre d'un marquillier de Paris à son curé. Paris, 1651. Moreau No. 1885.

Lettre d'un milord d'Angleterre. Paris [1649]. Moreau No. 1886.

Lettre d'un seigneur françois. Paris, 1649. Moreau No. 1897.

Lettre de consolation à la reine d'Angleterre. Paris, 1649. Moreau No. 1916.

Lettre de la reyne d'Angleterre à la reyne régente. Paris, 1649. Moreau No. 1943.

Lettre de Monsieur le duc d'Epernon à un de messieurs du Parlement de Paris, N.p., 1650.

Lettre de monsieur le prince de Conti. Paris, 1652. Moreau No. 2038.

Lettre des milords d'Angleterre. Paris, 1649. Moreau No. 2074.

Lettre du prince de Galles. Paris, 1649. Moreau No. 2129.

Lettre véritable du Prince de Galles. Paris, 1649. Moreau No. 2258.

Liste des empereurs et des rois. Paris, 1649. Moreau No. 2311.

Manifeste du roi de la Grand' Bretagne. Paris, 1649. Moreau No. 2394.

"Manuel du bon citoyen," n.p., 1649, in Moreau, *Choix de Mazarinades.* I, 437–469.

"La Mazarinade" [Paris], 1651, in Moreau, *Choix de Mazarinades.* II, 241–253.

Mémoire pour les marchands de Paris, Rouen, S. Malo, Nantes, Morlay, Le Havre, & Dieppe, traffiquans en mer. N.p., n.d.

Le mercure de la cour. Paris, 1652. Moreau No. 2452.

Les nations barbares. Paris, 1649. Moreau No. 2526.

Observations véritables et désintéressées. Paris, 1652. Moreau No. 2574.

L'ombre du roi d'Angleterre. N.p., n.d. Moreau No. 2597.

Le parallèle politique chrétien du Jansénisme. N.p., 1651. Moreau No. 2681.

Le philosophe et casuiste de ce temps. Paris, 1649. Moreau No. 2753.

Plainte publique sur l'interruption du commerce. Paris [1650]. Moreau No. 2784.

Le politique chrétien de Saint-Germain à la reine. Paris, 1649. Moreau No. 2811.

Prédiction òu se voit comme le Roy Charles II . . . doit estre remis au royaume d'Angleterre. Rouen, 1650.

Les préparatifs de la descente du cardinal Mazarin. Paris, 1652. Moreau No. 2857.

Le procès . . . du roi d'Angleterre. Paris, 1649. Moreau No. 2888.

Les quarante-cinq faits criminels. N.p., 1650. Moreau No. 2931.

Question: si la voix du peuple est la voix de Dieu. N.p., 1649. Moreau No. 2951.

Raisonnement sur les affaires présentes. Paris, 1649. Moreau No. 2970.

Récit véritable de tout ce qui s'est fait au procès du roi. N.p., 1649. Moreau No. 3016.

La relation extraordinaire contenant le traité de Mazarin. Paris, 1651. Moreau No. 3167.

Relation véritable contenant tout ce qui s'est fait et passé à Bordeaux. N.p., 1652.

Relation véritable de la mort barbare. Paris, 1649. Moreau No. 3241.

Remède aux malheurs de l'Etat de France. Paris, 1649. Moreau No. 3270.

Remontrance de Fairfax. Paris, 1649. Moreau No. 3301.

Remontrance très-humble au sérénissime prince Charles II. Paris, 1652. Moreau No. 3333.

Réponse au (Véritable) bandeau de Thémis. Paris, 1649. Moreau No. 3374.

Réponse au manifeste. Paris, 1652. Moreau No. 3380.

Réponse de la reine d'Angleterre. Paris, 1649. Moreau No. 3395.

La réponse de messieurs les princes. Paris, 1652. Moreau No. 3400.

Réponse du nouveau roi d'Angleterre. Paris, 1649. Moreau No. 3430.

Réponse du roi servant de réplique. N.p., 1652. Moreau No. 3441.

Requête présentée à monseigneur le Prince. Paris, 1649. Moreau No. 3501.

Bibliography of Materials Cited in the Text

Les sanglots pitoyables. Paris, 1649. Moreau No. 3585.

Le secret, ou les Véritables causes. N. p., 1651. Moreau No. 3634.

Les sentiments d'un fidèle sujet du roi. N.p., 1652. Moreau No. 3648.

Les sentiments des François. N.p., 1650. Moreau No. 3653.

Le serpent britannique. Paris, 1652. Moreau No. 3665.

"Sommaire de la doctrine curieuse du Cardinal Mazarin," Paris, 1649, in Moreau, *Choix de Mazarinades.* I, 314–348.

Sommaire de tout ce qui s'est passé. Paris, 1650. Moreau No. 3684.

"Les souhaits de la France," n.p., 1649, in Moreau, *Choix de Mazarinades.* I, 82–87.

Sujet de la farce représentée par Mazarin. Paris, 1649. Moreau No. 3729.

Le TI ΘEION de la maladie de l'Etat. Paris, 1649. Moreau No. 3775.

La trahison du duc Charles. Paris, 1652. Moreau No. 3792.

Très-humble remontrance des bons bourgeois de Paris. Paris, 1652. Moreau No. 3813.

Le véritable courrier général. Paris, 1653.

La vérité prononçant ses oracles. N.p., 1652. Moreau No. 3998.

"La vérité toute nue, ou avis sincère," Paris, 1652, in Moreau, *Choix de Mazarinades.* II, 406–438.

Secondary Materials

Anger, Rolf. *Die Flugschriftenpublizistik zur Zeit der Pariser Fronde, 1648–1652.* Dissertation; Münster, 1957.

Artsikliovsky, A. V. and D. I. Nadtocheev. "Teaching of the Social Sciences in the Higher Educational Establishments of the USSR," *International Social Science Journal,* UNESCO. Vol. XI, No. 2, 187–201.

Ascoli, Georges. *La Grande-Bretagne devant l'opinion française au XVIIᵉ siècle.* 2 vols. Paris, 1930.

Ashley, Maurice P. *Financial and Commercial Policy under the Cromwellian Protectorate.* Oxford, 1962.

Baillon, Charles de. *Henriette-Marie de France, reine d'Angleterre.* Paris, 1877.

Bastide, Charles. *The Anglo-French Entente in the XVII Century.* London, 1914.

Bibliography of Materials Cited in the Text

Battifol, Louis. "Les idées de la révolution sous Louis XIV," *Revue de Paris*, March, 1928, pp. 97–120.

Bernard, Leon. "French Society and Popular Uprisings under Louis XIV," *French Historical Studies*, III (1964), 454–474.

Bertrand, Louis. *La vie de Messire Henry de Béthune, archevêque de Bordeaux (1604–1680)*. Vol. I. Paris, 1902.

Bigby, Dorothy A. *Anglo-French Relations, 1641 to 1649*. London, 1933.

Bischoffshausen, Sigismund von. *Die Politik des Protectors Oliver Cromwell in der Auffassung und Thätigkeit seines Ministers, des Staatssecretärs John Thurloe*. Innsbruck, 1899.

Blet, Pierre. *Le clergé de France et la monarchie*. 2 vols. Rome, 1959.

Bourelly, Jules. *Cromwell et Mazarin: deux campagnes de Turenne en Flandre*. Paris, 1886.

Boutaric, Edgard. "Introduction," in *Actes du Parlement de Paris*. Vol. I. Paris, 1863.

Bowman, Jacob N. *The Protestant Interest in Cromwell's Foreign Relations*. Heidelberg, 1900.

Brailsford, H. N. *The Levellers and the English Revolution*. London, 1961.

Chapman, Hester W. *The Tragedy of Charles II in the Years 1630–1660*. London, 1964.

Chéruel, Pierre-Adolphe. *Histoire de France pendant la minorité de Louis XIV*. 4 vols. Paris, 1879–1880.

——. *Histoire de France sous le ministère de Mazarin*. 3 vols. Paris, 1882.

Cochin, Augustin. "Les églises Calvinistes du Midi: Le cardinal Mazarin et Cromwell," *Revue des questions historiques*, LXXVI (1904), 109–156.

Cosnac, Jules de. *Souvenirs du règne de Louis XIV*. 8 vols. Paris, 1866–1882.

Cousin, Victor. "Des carnets autographes du cardinal Mazarin conservés à la Bibliothèque Imperiale," *Journal des savants* (1854–1856), *passim*.

——. *Madame de Longueville pendant la Fronde*. Paris, 1872.

Crémieux, Adolphe. *Marseille et la royauté*. Paris, 1917.

Bibliography of Materials Cited in the Text

Crisis in Europe, 1560–1660. Ed. Trevor Aston. London, 1965.

Cubells, Madame. "Le parlement de Paris pendant la Fronde," *Dix-septième siècle,* No. 35 (1957), 171–201.

Dahl, Folke, and Fanny Petibon, and Marguerite Boulet. "Les débuts de la presse française: nouveaux aperçus," *Acta bibliothecae Gotoburgensis.* Vol. IV (1951).

Deyon, Pierre. "A propos des rapports entre la noblesse française et la monarchie absolue pendant la première moitié du XVIIe siècle," *Revue historique,* CCXXXI (1964), 341–356.

Dickmann, Fritz. *Der Westfälische Frieden.* Münster, 1959.

Doolin, Paul. *The Fronde.* Cambridge, Mass., 1935.

Durand-Lapie, Paul. *Un académicien du XVIIe siècle, Saint-Amant, son temps, sa vie, ses poésies, 1594–1661.* Paris, 1898.

Farnell, J. E. "The Navigation Act of 1651, the First Dutch War, and the London Merchant Community," *Economic History Review,* 2d ser., XVI (1964), 439–454.

Feillet, Alphonse. *La misère au temps de la Fronde.* Paris, 1886.

Firth, Charles H. *The Last Years of the Protectorate, 1656–1658.* 2 vols. London, 1909.

———. "Thomas Scot's Account of His Activities as Intelligencer during the Commonwealth," *English Historical Review,* XII (1897), 116–126.

———, and S. C. Lomas, *Notes on the Diplomatic Relations of England and France 1603–1688.* Oxford, 1906.

Frank, Joseph. *The Beginnings of the English Newspaper, 1620–1660.* Cambridge, Mass., 1961.

Franklin, Alfred. *Histoire de la Bibliothèque Mazarine et du Palais de l'Institut.* Paris, 1901.

French, J. Milton. "The Burning of Milton's *Defensio* in France," *Modern Language Notes,* LVI (1941), 275–277.

Galland, A. "Les pasteurs français Amyraut, Bochart . . . et le royauté de droit divin de l'édit d'Alais à la Révocation (1629–1685)," *Bulletin—Société de l'histoire du Protestantisme français,* LXXVII (1928), 14–20, 105–134, 225–241, 413–423.

Gardiner, Samuel R. "Cromwell and Mazarin in 1652," *English Historical Review,* XI (1896), 476–509.

——. *History of the Commonwealth and Protectorate, 1649–1656.* 4 vols. London, 1903.

——. *History of the Great Civil War, 1642–1649.* 4 vols. London, 1898–1901.

Gilles de la Tourette, G. *Théophraste Renaudot.* Paris, 1884.

Grose, Clyde L. "England and Dunkirk," *American Historical Review,* XXIX (1933), 1–27.

Guizot, François P. G. *History of Oliver Cromwell and the English Commonwealth,* trans. Andreas R. Scoble. 2 vols. London, 1854.

——. *History of the English Revolution of 1640,* trans. William Hazlitt. London, 1846.

Hardacre, Paul H. "The Royalists in Exile during the Puritan Revolution, 1642–1660," *Huntington Library Quarterly,* XVI (1953), 353–370.

Hatin, Louis E. *Bibliographie historique et critique de la presse périodique française.* Paris, 1866.

Hill, Christopher. "The English Revolution and the Brotherhood of Man," in *Puritanism and Revolution.* London, 1958. Pp. 123–152.

——. "Recent Interpretations of the Civil War," *History,* new ser., XLI (1956), 67–87.

Hobsbawm, E. J. "The General Crisis of the European Economy in the 17th Century," *Past and Present,* No. 5 (1954), 33–53, and No. 6 (1954), 44–65.

Hoskins, S. Elliot. *Charles the Second in the Channel Islands.* 2 vols. London, 1854.

Jacquart, Jean. "La Fronde des Princes dans la région parisienne et ses conséquences matérielles," *Revue d'histoire moderne et contemporaine,* VII (1960), 257–290.

Jusserand, J. J. "Le maréchal d'Estrades et ses critiques," *Revue historique,* CLVIII (1928), 225–254.

Kerviler, René de, and Ed. de Barthélemy. *Valentin Conrart, sa vie et sa correspondance.* Paris, 1881.

Kossmann, Ernst H. *La Fronde.* Leiden, 1954.

Lacour-Gayet, Georges. *L'éducation politique de Louis XIV.* Paris, 1898.

La Roncière, Charles de. *Histoire de la marine française.* Vol. V. Paris, 1920.

Bibliography of Materials Cited in the Text

Logié, Paul. *La Fronde en Normandie.* 3 vols. Amiens, 1951–1952.

Lorris, Pierre-Georges. *La Fronde.* Paris, 1961.

Lutaud, Olivier. "Le parti politique 'Niveleur' et la première Révolution anglaise" (Essai d'historiographie), *Revue historique,* CCXXVII (1962), 377–414.

MacDonald, Hugh, and Mary Hargreaves. *Thomas Hobbes—A Bibliography.* London, 1952.

McDougall, Dorothy. *Madeleine de Scudéry.* London, 1938.

McNeil, W. "Milton and Salmasius, 1649," *English Historical Review,* LXXX (1965), 107–108.

Madan, Francis F. "Milton, Salmasius and Dugard," *The Library,* 4th ser., IV (1923).

——. "A New Bibliography of the Eikon Basilike," *Oxford Bibliographical Society Publications,* new ser., III (1949).

Madelin, Louis. *La Fronde.* Paris, 1931.

Malo, Henri. *Les corsaires dunkerquois et Jean Bart.* Vol. I. Paris, 1913.

Malvezin, Théophile. *Histoire du commerce de Bordeaux.* Vol. II. Bordeaux, 1892.

Mandrou, Robert. "Les soulèvements populaires et la société française du XVIIᵉ siècle," *Annales: économies, sociétés, civilisations,* XIV (1959), 756–765.

Merriman, Roger Bigelow. *Six Contemporaneous Revolutions.* Oxford, 1938.

Moote, A. Lloyd. "The French Crown Versus Its Judicial and Financial Officials, 1615–1683," *Journal of Modern History,* XXXIV (1962), 146–160.

——. "The Parlementary Fronde and the Seventeenth Century Robe Solidarity," *French Historical Studies,* II (1962), 330–355.

Moreau, Célestin. *Bibliographie des Mazarinades.* 3 vols. Paris, 1850–1851.

Morize, André. "Samuel Sorbière principal à Orange: sa conversion (1650–1653)," *Bulletin—Société de l'histoire du Protestantisme français,* LVI (1907), 503–525.

——. "Thomas Hobbes et Samuel Sorbière," *Revue germanique,* IV (1908), 195–204.

Mousnier, Roland. "Quelques raisons de la Fronde: les causes des journées révolutionnaires parisiennes de 1648," *Dix-septième siècle,* Nos. 2–3 (1949), 33–78.

———. "Trevor-Roper's 'General Crisis' Symposium," in *Crisis in Europe, 1560–1660,* pp. 97–104.

———. "Recherches sur les soulèvements populaires en France avant la Fronde," *Revue d'histoire moderne et contemporaine,* V (1958), 81–113.

Parker, William Riley. *Milton's Contemporary Reputation.* Columbus, 1940.

Picavet, Camille-Georges. "Le français et les langues étrangères dans la diplomatie au temps de Louis XIV," *Revue des sciences politiques,* LI (1928), 578–592.

Porshnev, Boris F. "Angliiskaia revoliutsiia i sovremennaia ei frantsiia," in *Angliiskaia burzhuaznaia revoliutsiia XVII veka.* Ed. E. A. Kosminskii and IA. A. Levitskii. Moscow, 1954. Vol. II, 71–89.

———. "Angliiskaia respublika, frantsuzskaia fronda i vestfalskii mir," *Srednie veka,* III (1951), 180–216.

———. "Otkliki frantsuzskogo obshchestvennogo mneniia na angliiskuiu burzhuaznuiu revoliutsiiu," *Srednie veka,* VIII (1956), 319–347.

———. *Les soulèvements populaires en France de 1623 à 1648.* Ed. Robert Mandrou, Ecole Pratique des Hautes Etudes, VIᵉ Section, Centre de Recherches Historiques. Oeuvres Etrangères, Vol. IV. Paris, 1963.

Prestwich, Manna. "Diplomacy and Trade in the Protectorate," *The Journal of Modern History,* XXII (1950), 103–121.

Puaux, Frank. "L'évolution des théories politiques du Protestantisme français," *Bulletin—Société de l'histoire du Protestantisme français,* LXII (1913), 386–413.

Rathery, J. B. "Des relations sociales et intellectuelles entre la France et l'Angleterre," *Revue contemporaine,* XXII (1855), 159–178.

Rostenberg, Leona. *Literary, Political, Scientific, Religious and Legal Publishing . . . in England, 1551–1700.* 2 vols. New York, 1965.

Rothkrug, Lionel. *Opposition to Louis XIV: The Political and Social Origins of the French Enlightenment.* Princeton, 1965.

Bibliography of Materials Cited in the Text

Routledge, F. J. *England and the Treaty of the Pyrenees*. Liverpool, 1953.

Sainte-Aulaire, Louis-Clair de Beaupoil de. *Histoire de la Fronde*. 3 vols. Paris, 1827.

Schilfert, Gerhard. "Zur Geschichte der Auswirkungen der englischen bürgerlichen Revolution auf Nordwestdeutschland," in *Beiträge zum neuen Geschichtsbild, zum 60 Geburtstag von Alfred Meusel*. Ed. Fritz Klein and Joachim Streisand. Berlin, 1956.

Scott, Eva. *The King in Exile*. London, 1905.

Scoville, Warren C. *The Persecution of Huguenots and French Economic Development, 1680–1720*. Berkeley, 1960.

Serpell, David R. *The Condition of Protestantism in France and Its Influence on the Relations of France and England, 1650–1654*. Toulouse, 1934.

"Seventeenth-Century Revolution," *Past and Present*, No. 13 (1958), 63–72.

Simon, André L. *The History of the Wine Trade in England*. Vol. II. London, 1909.

Stankiewicz, W. J. *Politics and Religion in Seventeenth-Century France*. Berkeley, 1960.

Trevor-Roper, H. R. "The General Crisis of the 17th Century," *Past and Present*, No. 16 (1959), 32–64.

Wedgwood, C. V. *The Trial of Charles I*. London, 1964.

Wolf, John B. "The Formation of a King," *French Historical Studies*, I (1958), 40–72.

Index

Index

Battifol, Louis, 4n., 41n., 43n.
Bavaria, 114
Bayle, Pierre, 61
Bayonne, 148
Beaufort, François de Vendôme, Duc de, 14, 44, 84, 90, 97, 180, 235, 237, 238, 240
Bellièvre, Pierre de, *see* Grignon, Pierre de Bellièvre, Comte de
Bellièvre, Pompone de, 22n., 26n., 30n., 31n., 116n.
Bellings, secretary to Lord Rochester, 247n.
Bergerac, 143
Bernard, Leon, 274n.
Bernhard, Israel (pseud. for Joachim Hane?), 251n.
Berthod, Père François, 43n.
Bertrand, Louis, 144n.
Bigby, Dorothy A., 29n., 117n., 118n.
Biscay, 252
Bischoffshausen, Sigismund von, 185n., 268n.
Blake, Robert, 128, 175–177, 179–180, 183, 185, 187, 192, 241, 261
Blancmesnil, Président of Parlement of Paris, 38
Blarut, deputy from Bordeaux, 203, 214
Blaye, 197, 201
Bléneau, battle of, 230
Blet, Pierre, 172n., 265n.
Blois, 42n., 68, 120n.
Bochart, Samuel, 67, 74, 107, 109
Boileau-Despréaux, Nicolas, 257n.
Bordeaux (father of Antoine), 252n., 271
Bordeaux, Antoine de:
negotiations with England during the Fronde, 185–191, 196, 205–206, 208, 210, 211n., 212, 241–243, 245
negotiations with England after the Fronde, 252–254, 255n., 259, 264n., 266n., 268–272
Bordeaux, Archbishop of (Henry de Béthune), 144n.

Bordeaux (city), 149, 154, 159, 164, 165–166, 167, 174–175, 183, 192–195, 197, 244, 246, 262, **264**
England, relationship with, 136–139, 142–143, 145, 147, 160–162, 164–168, 196, 201–214, 242, 245, 247, 254, 261, 267–270, 273–274
Bordeaux, deputies from, 200, 202–209, 268–270
Bordeaux, Hôtel de Ville, 181–182, 202–203, 207
Bordeaux, Parlement of, 12, 140, 143–144, 181–182, 201, 203
Bossuet, Jacques-Bénigne, Bishop of Meaux, 262n.
Bouillon, Frédéric-Maurice, Duc de, 57, 144
Boulogne, 118
Bourelly, Jules, 256n.
Bourg, 203, 211, 213
Bourgogne, Lewis de, 161
Bourlemont, Henry d'Anglure de, 129n.
Bowman, Jacob N., 253n.–254n.
Brailsford, H. N., 181n.
Brasset, Monsieur, 116n., 222n.
Brégy, Monsieur, 234, 235n.
Brest, 155, 174, 178, 251
Brest, Governor of, 155, 191
Brienne, Henri-Auguste de Loménie, Comte de, 18, 20–22, 26, 34, 118, 131, 138, 141, 154, 173, 238
cited in correspondence, 27n., 35n., 117n., 119n., 120n., 121n., 133n., 135n., 185n., 186n., 187n., 188n., 189n., 190n., 191n., 196n., 205n., 208n., 209n., 210n., 211n., 212n., 243n., 245n., 253n., 255n., 266n., 268n., 269n., 270n., 271n., 272n.
Brouage, 164, 175, 195, 196
Broussel, Pierre, 38
Browne, Richard, 23, 39, 144n., 149n., 224n.
Brussels, 203, 204, 225

Index

Buckingham, George Villiers, 1st Duke of, 50
Burgundy, 16
Byron, John, 1st Baron Byron, 216n., 217

Cabale des Importants, 11, 36
Caesar, Julius, 163
Cailloué, Denis, 67
Calais, 135, 171, 174, 175, 177, 190, 251, 270
Candale, Louis-Charles, Duc de, 207, 211n., 214n.
Capel, Arthur, 1st Baron Capel of Hadham, 100
Caracène, Marquis de, 263n.
Cardeñas, Don Alonso de, 121, 133, 171n., 175, 204, 206, 210
Carteret, George, 155, 177
Castelnau, Marquis de, 267n.
Castres, 143
Catalonia, 1, 54, 101, 246, 270
Catholics, 21, 24, 31, 51, 57, 64, 65, 67, 71, 72–73, 89, 96, 99, 107, 113n., 139, 144, 152, 181, 200, 202, 205, 208, 229, 253, 258, 259, 265, 273, 275
Censorship, 63, 82, 263
Champagne, 233
Chancellor of the Exchequer, see Hyde, Edward, 1st Earl of Clarendon
Chapman, Hester W., 229n.
Charenton, synod at, 108
Charles I, King of England, 5, 6, 19, 21, 22–23, 24, 26, 28, 34–35, 41, 49, 50, 57, 127, 138, 215, 216, 233, 260, 261
  French policy toward, 20, 27, 29, 112–113, 115–118, 120, 129
  press accounts of, 51, 53–54, 56, 58–59, 60, 63–66, 68–71, 74–77, 80–82, 86, 87n., 90, 93–101, 104–106, 107–111, 240
  tactics in Civil War, 28, 30–33, 45–47, 240

Charles II, King of England, 56, 63, 70, 72, 73, 86, 90–91, 96, 102, 215–218, 221, 224, 226, 227, 239–242, 274n., 275
  Eikon Basilike, concern with, 65–66, 68
  French policy toward, 119–121, 122, 153, 216, 222–223, 249–250, 252, 254, 258, 272
  Fronde, mediation attempts, 230–239
  Irish troops, 242–247
  marriage plans, 227–229
  press accounts of, 239–241
  ships of, 129–131, 139, 155–156, 178, 191, 251–252, 254
  Spain, relationship with, 134, 152, 218–221, 256, 257, 259
Charon, Président, Parlement of Bordeaux, 143–144
Châtillon, Isabelle-Angélique de Montmorency, Duchesse de, 229
Chéruel, Pierre-Adolphe, 3, 32n., 36n., 39n., 40n., 44n., 46n., 208n.
Chevreuse, Marie de Rohan-Montbazon, Duchesse de, 97, 234
China, King of, 54
Chouppes, Aymar, Marquis de, 193n.
Christine de Bourbon, Duchesse de Savoie, 41
Clanricarde, Ulick de Burgh, 5th Earl of, 216n.
Clarendon, Earl of, see Hyde, Edward, 1st Earl of Clarendon
Cleyrac, Bordeaux agent in Spain, 214
Coadjutor of Paris, see Retz, Jean François Paul de Gondi, Cardinal de
Cochin, Augustin, 265n.
Colbert, Jean Baptiste, 43, 222n., 267n., 275n.
Colletet, Guillaume, 86
Cologne, 252
Commons, House of, see England, Parliament of

Index

Index

Du Plessis-Praslin, Caesar de Choiseul, Comte, 140n.
Durand-Lapie, Paul, 53n.
Duretête, leader of Ormée, 202–203, 214

Eikon Basilike, 58, 65–69, 76
Elizabeth I, Queen of England, 6
Emeri, Michel-Particelli d', 46
Emperor, 114, 115
Empire, 10, 19–20, 115–116
England:
  Army, 35, 117, 135
  Church of, 7, 30, 31, 65, 99
  Council of State, 57, 62, 149, 161, 164, 165n., 176, 183n., 190, 192, 195, 208, 210n., 268
  embargo against France, 124–126, 127, 137, 147, 148, 157, 158, 254
  exiles from, 19, 23–25, 38–39, 41–42, 50, 58, 63–68, 71, 107, 120, 191, 213, 215–247, 250–252
  Parliament of, 5–7, 21, 23–24, 26–28, 32–39, 43–44, 55–59, 63, 69, 80, 83–85, 88, 90–93, 96, 99–100, 110, 117, 120, 124, 126–127, 129, 131–132, 135, 142, 157, 164–167, 177, 182, 186–190, 192, 203–205, 220, 253, 275
Eon, Jean, 126n.
Epernon, Bernard de Nogaret, Duc d', 96, 136–137, 140–141, 143, 193n.
Estrades, Godefroy, Comte d', 168–169, 172, 174–176, 222n., 253, 270n., 271
Estrées, Maréchal d', 38
Etampes, 235
Europe, 135
Evelyn, John, 24
Exeter, 23

Fairfax, Thomas, 44, 71, 84–85, 88n., 90, 96, 97, 100, 105, 118

Farnell, J. E., 157n.
Feillet, Alphonse, 264n.
Firth, Charles H., 21n., 161n., 256n.
Fitzjames, Colonel John, 169, 172
Flanders, 46, 124, 134, 210
Fontainebleau, 243
Foss, John, 120n.
Fouquet, Nicolas, 263n.
France:
  embargo against England, 122–127, 165, 254, 261
  Estates-General, 39, 91
Frank, Joseph, 62n.
Franklin, Alfred, 25n.
French, J. Milton, 57n., 59n., 60n.
French Academy, 68
French Revolution of 1789, 1, 249
Frost, Walter, 150n.

Galland, A., 67n., 75n., 107n., 202n.
Gardiner, Samuel R., 4n., 168n., 169, 170n., 171n., 172n., 206n.
Garonne, 209
Gassendi, Pierre, 72–73
Gazette de France, 51–53, 55–56, 61, 63, 76, 80–82, 87, 128, 190, 248, 262
Geneva, 266
Genoa, 124, 157
Gentillot, Sieur de, 154–155, 169–170, 172–174, 177, 179–180, 185, 209
Gerard, Charles, 223n.
Germany, 61, 159, 244
Gilles de la Tourette, G., 52n.
Gironde, 142, 193–194
Goulas, Nicolas, Sieur de La Mothe, 40–41
Gravelines, 170, 172–173, 257
Graymond, P. de, 140n., 222n.
Greek waters, 157
Grève, Place de la, 60
Grignon, Pierre de Bellièvre, Comte de, 22n., 25n., 26n., 27n., 34n., 35, 116n., 117–120, 121n., 122, 133, 135, 138, 260

Index

Grose, Clyde L., 169n.
Guémenée, Princess, 229, 234
Guernsey, Island of, 139, 155, 159, 190
Guizot, François P. G., 4n., 134n., 135n., 175n., 251n., 256n.
Guyenne, 16, 136, 137n., 140–142, 148, 161, 164–165, 167, 182–183, 196, 199, 201–203, 206, 211–212, 230, 242, 244–247, 253, 259, 270, 271

Hague, The, 62, 218, 222
Hallelby, Charles, 42n.
Hamilton, James, 1st Duke of, 100
Hampton Court Conference, 6
Hane, Joachim, 265
Harcourt, Comte d', 263
Hardacre, Paul H., 23n.
Haro, Don Luis de, 219–220
Hatin, Louis E., 52n., 53n.
Hatton, Christopher, 66n., 67n., 68n., 222n., 224n., 225n., 227n.
Henri IV, King of France, 24, 58
Henriette-Anne, sister of Charles II of England, 23
Henriette-Marie, Queen of England, 23–24, 50, 58–59, 65, 113n., 117, 119, 217, 219, 223–224, 242, 254, 258, 275
England, comparisons with France, 38–39, 41–42
England, source of information about, 24–26, 29, 31n.
Fronde, involvement in, 225–226, 230–231, 232, 235–236, 238, 240, 244
marriage plans for sons, 227–229
press accounts of, 70–71, 91, 99, 102, 105, 221
Héraut, Louis, pastor of Alençon, 109
Hill, Christopher, 2n., 7n.
Hobbes, Thomas, 71–73
Elementorum philosophiae sectio tertia de cive, 72–73
Leviathan, 73

Hobsbawm, E. J., 3n.
Hocquincourt, Charles de Monchy, Maréchal d', 263–264
Holland, Henry Rich, 1st Earl of, 100
Holland, 1, 75, 93, 109, 134, 136, 193n., 210
Charles II resident in, 70, 119, 121, 223, 227
foreign policy of, 113n., 114, 118, 168, 173, 184, 210, 217, 250
publishing in, 61, 67, 72, 258
shipping and commerce, 123–124, 126–127, 146, 148, 157–159, 176, 193–195
war with England, 158, 250
Honfleur, 177
Honfleur, Governor of, 177
Horne, Peter, 251n.
Hoskins, S. Elliot, 128n.
Hospital, François, Maréchal de l', 36n.
Huguenots, 16, 50, 57, 99, 139, 144, 154, 164, 181
English interest in, 137, 159, 162, 167, 170–171, 197–202, 203, 208–209, 250, 259, 266, 268–269, 272, 273–274
English royalists, attitude toward, 64–65, 66–68, 71, 73–75, 106–111
French government attitude toward, 11, 36, 45, 138, 140, 141–143, 159, 172, 253, 265, 268–269
Hyde, Edward, 1st Earl of Clarendon, 42, 61, 63n., 73, 75, 177n., 191n., 215, 216n., 217n., 218–221, 223–224, 228n., 230n., 231n., 232n., 234n., 236n., 241n., 242, 246–247

Inchiquin, Murrough O'Brien, 1st Earl of, 224
Infanta, 275

Index

Index

Index

Palais Royal, 85
Palatine, Anne de Gonzague, Princess, 262n.
Papal States, 54
Paris, 5, 14, 15, 16, 18, 21, 22, 23, 24, 26, 29, 35, 36, 38, 39, 40, 41, 42n., 43, 47, 52, 60, 61, 63, 64, 65, 66, 67, 70, 72, 74, 75, 81, 90, 93, 95, 97, 98, 115, 117, 119, 120, 123, 129, 130, 135, 136, 137, 148, 149, 150, 152, 154, 155, 159, 161, 162, 179, 180, 183, 184, 185, 186, 187, 188, 191, 192, 201n., 218, 219, 223, 226, 230, 231, 232, 233, 235, 237, 238, 240, 241, 242, 250, 251, 253, 257, 258, 263, 266, 267
    Civil Lieutenant of, 60
    Hôtel de Ville, 238
    Parlement of, 8, 11–14, 25n., 36–40, 43–47, 60, 67, 74, 80, 82–85, 88–93, 97, 99, 102–103, 110, 115, 122–123, 130, 135–136, 158, 162, 201n., 223, 230–232, 262, 264, 266–267
    Sovereign Courts of, 12, 40
    University of, 60
Parker, William Riley, 61n.
Parliament, see England, Parliament of
Partisans, 13
Past and Present, 3
Patin, Guy, 136n.
Paulucci, Lorenzo, 167n., 186n., 205n., 210n.
Penn, William, 157
Périgueux, 213, 264
Petit, Monsieur, 266n.
Philip IV, King of Spain, 133–134, 171n., 218–220, 255
Picardy, 185, 188, 270
Picavet, Camille-Georges, 55n.
Poitiers, 161, 264
Poitou, 137n., 252
Poland, 1
Pompey, 163
Pontac, Sieur de, 192n., 269n.

Popham, Edward, 132
Porrée, Baptiste, 66–68
Porshnev, Boris F., 2n.–3n., 5, 16n., 53n., 87n., 112–113, 123n.
Portugal, 1, 54, 156
Presbyterians, 31, 33, 71, 74–75, 106–107
Preston, Colonel Thomas, 242–243
Prestwich, Manna, 274n.
Prevveray, François, 64
Provence, 16
Puaux, Frank, 202n.
Puckering, Henry, 157n.
Pyrenees, 220
Pyrenees, Treaty of, 257, 274

Queen Regent, see Anne of Austria, Queen of France
Querini, Giacomo, 247n.

Radcliffe, George, 255n.
Rathery, J. B., 4n., 55n.
Ré, Island of, 183, 193
Renaudot, Théophraste, 52, 55–56, 76, 81–82
Rennes, Parlement of, 130, 179
Retz, Jean François Paul de Gondi (the Coadjutor), later Cardinal de, 14, 43, 44, 60, 81, 83–87, 110n., 149, 154n., 162, 223, 226, 258–259, 263, 266, 267, 270, 274–275
Rhineland, 114
Richelieu, Armand-Jean du Plessis, Cardinal de, 8–10, 12, 18, 29, 46, 48, 96, 233
Rivet, André, 68n., 69n., 74n., 87n.
Rochefort, 137n.
Roman Republic, 93
Rome, 124, 258, 263
Rostenberg, Leona, 62n.
Rothkrug, Lionel, 123n.
Rouen, 66–67, 69–70, 123, 157n., 159, 192, 193
    Parlement of, 12, 130, 160, 264
Routledge, F. J., 275n.
Royal Society, 55

Index

Royan, 203
Rueil, Peace of, 14, 43, 81, 136–137
Rupert, Count Palatine of Rhine, Prince, 56, 128, 190, 247
Russia, 1

Sabran, Melchior de, 22, 27n., 29, 34
Sagredo, Giovanni, 184n., 186n., 188n., 205n., 210n., 213n., 241n., 245n., 249n.
Saint-Agoulin, Sieur de, 244n.
Saint-Amant, Marc-Antoine Gérard de, 53n.
St. Germain, 41, 81, 136, 240
St. Malo, 155, 177–179, 190, 193
St. Martin, 193
Sainte-Aulaire, Louis-Clair de Beaupoil de, 3
Sainte-Croix, Monsieur, 210n., 211n.
Saintonge, 137n., 144, 202, 264, 270
Saint-Simon, Claude de Rouvroy, Duc de, 197, 270n.
Saint-Thomas, Sieur de, 164, 183, 196
Salomon de Virelade, François-Henri, 123n., 149–150
San Sebastian, 270
Sarrau, Claude, 74, 76n.
Sassier, Guillaume, 64
Saumaise, Claude de, 59–60, 73–76, 109
  Defensio regia pro Carolo I, 59, 74, 76
Savoie, Duc de, 253
Schilfert, Gerhard, 2n.
Scot, Thomas, 161
Scotland, 20, 24, 55, 56, 133, 134, 139, 145, 153, 217, 222, 224, 227, 245
Scots, 21, 33, 51, 66, 86, 113, 119, 142, 145, 146, 216
Scoville, Warren C., 137n.
Scudéry, Madeleine de, 88n.
Séguier, Pierre, 8, 123n., 126n., 127n., 130, 140n., 193n.

Serpell, David R., 4n.
Servien, Abel, 36n., 40n., 114, 115n., 117n., 153–154, 177n., 180n., 187n., 196n., 270n., 271n.
Sévestre, Pierre, 221
Sexby, Colonel Edward, 161, 167, 198, 200–201, 205, 208, 213, 268–269, 274
Seymour, Henry, 228n.
Sicily, 1
Simon, André L., 190n.
Skippon, Philip, 139
Sorbière, Samuel, 72
Spain, 9–10, 14, 52, 94, 114–115, 124, 142, 150, 168, 182, 202, 270, 273, 275
  Condé, assistance for, 15, 164, 180, 192, 195, 203, 210–214, 242, 244, 246, 257, 263–264
  England, relations with, 19–20, 113n., 116, 121, 133–135, 152–153, 167, 171–176, 184–186, 206, 210–213, 242, 256–257, 259, 260, 261, 274
  English royalists, relations with, 218–221, 224, 246–247, 256–257
Spanish West Indies, 254
Spon, Charles, 136n.
Stankiewicz, W. J., 107n.
States-General, see Holland
Stouppe, Jean Baptiste, 253, 266, 269
Strafford, Thomas Wentworth, 1st Earl of, 32, 47–48, 80, 104–105
Streisand, Joachim, 2n.
Sussex, 189
Sweden, 1
Switzerland, 1, 93, 172

Talon, Omer, 43, 158
Targa, Pierre, 64
Taylor, Mr., 61n., 242n.
Testard, Paul, 68
Théobon, Sieur de, 197

311

Index